Principles of
Administrative Law

Principles of Administrative Law

Second edition

D C M Yardley LLD (BIRM), MA, D Phil (OXON)
of Gray's Inn, Barrister,
Chairman of the Commission for Local Administration in England; sometime Barber Professor of Law, University of Birmingham, and Rank Foundation Professor of Law, University of Buckingham

London
Butterworths
1986

United Kingdom	Butterworth & Co (Publishers) Ltd, 88 Kingsway, London WC2B 6AB and 61A North Castle Street, Edinburgh EH2 3LJ
Australia	Butterworths Pty Ltd, Sydney, Melbourne, Brisbane, Adelaide, Perth, Canberra and Hobart
Canada	Butterworth & Co (Canada) Ltd, Toronto and Vancouver
New Zealand	Butterworths of New Zealand Ltd, Wellington and Auckland
Singapore	Butterworth & Co (Asia) Pte Ltd, Singapore
South Africa	Butterworth Publishers (Pty) Ltd, Durban and Pretoria
USA	Butterworth Legal Publishers, St Paul, Minnesota, Seattle, Washington, Boston, Massachusetts, Austin, Texas and D & S Publishers, Clearwater, Florida

© Butterworth & Co (Publishers) Ltd 1986

All rights reserved. No part of this publication may be reproduced or transmitted in any form or by any means, including photocopying and recording, without the written permission of the copyright holder, application for which should be addressed to the publisher. Such written permission must also be obtained before any part of this publication is stored in a retrieval system of any nature.

This book is sold subject to the Standard Conditions of Sale of Net Books and may not be re-sold in the UK below the net price fixed by Butterworths for the book in our current catalogue.

British Library Cataloguing in Publication Data

Yardley, D.C.M.
   Principles of administrative law.
   ——— 2nd ed.
   1. Administrative law ——— England
   I. Title
   344.202′6   KD4897

ISBN Hardcover 0 406 68992 X
      Softcover 0 406 68993 8

Typeset by Sprint, Beckenham, Kent
Printed by Biddles Ltd, Guildford

To our dear cats, who performed a service once similarly memorialised by P G Wodehouse. Their constant assistance at the typewriter when I was drafting the chapters of this book was always welcome, though it did not necessarily advance the date of completing the work.

Preface

The purpose of this book remains the same as when it was first published in 1981, namely to provide an overall view of administrative law. I have made no attempt to rival any of the major textbooks or monographs on the subject, but instead to write essays that stress the main function of administrative law, which is the control of power and the maintenance of a fair balance between the competing interests of the administration and the citizen. Students often find it difficult to grasp the subject as an entity for three main reasons. First, most of the law on the central topic of judicial review is judge-made (though often including statutory interpretation) and the record of the judges in this area has not been good on the score of consistency; the result is that the law often appears untidy and unclear. Secondly, because textbooks on constitutional law must for the sake of completeness include a section on administrative law, readers are sometimes confused as to whether the subject is an elementary part of a first-year course or is a more advanced subject in its own right. Thirdly, the subject is circular in the sense that it is impossible to introduce it by clear and separate stages – one cannot, for instance, deal with delegated legislation without also dealing in part with the ultra vires principle; it is in turn impossible to deal with ultra vires without mentioning the remedies available, as well as the power of judicial review over inferior tribunals or inquiries. There are countless other examples which might be given of the essentially interwoven character of administrative law; the need to present the whole picture from an early stage can result in some confusion for students.

In trying to draw the strands of the law together in these essays I have hoped in particular to highlight the work of the more progressive courts and judges, so that the reader is able to cut through the tangle of confused case law and discern the true path of coherent doctrine. Some of this century's judges have been adept at leaving on one side the precedents which hinder development, and boldly striking out afresh in the interest of justice, and it is hoped that this book emulates their example. In the result these essays do not cover all aspects of administrative law (and certainly not all available precedents) but rather concentrate upon those topics and principles which appear to me to be of doctrinal importance. It is intended that the book should be read at the end of an administrative law course, and that the exposition should be sufficiently clear and uncompromising to enable the principles of the subject, and the context of each part of it, to come to the surface of the student's mind, so that he may be the better equipped to face a searching examination.

For this edition I have rewritten several parts of the book, expanded others, and generally endeavoured to take account of the major developments of the past five years. These include the recent reshaping of local government by the Local Government Act 1985, the onward march of 'privatisation', the reorganisation of administrative tribunals in the social security field, and rapid developments concerning ombudsmen. I am not alone in having hoped that the findings of the JUSTICE/All Souls Review Committee, which was set up in 1979, would by now have been published, but it seems that its deliberations have been unexpectedly prolonged, and there is still no sign of the eventual Report. Accordingly I have had to content myself with making some modest predictions about the likely content of the Report on the basis of my own beliefs about the way it will go. There has been a wealth of judicial decisions in this field since 1982, and I have tried to give an account of the most significant of these cases, especially those which have clarified the exact place in our law of the modern application for judicial review, and those which have stressed both the power and some of the limitations of the principles upon which the possibility of judicial review rests. All in all it is hoped that this edition remains true to the intentions of the book as it first appeared, and continues to point to the essential principles of the law without unnecessary embellishment. English administrative law is certainly not yet perfect, but it does work, and on the whole carries out its intended functions in a manner which is far from discreditable; if that assessment is clearly indicated by these essays the book will not have been in vain. I remain, as ever, grateful to Butterworths for the consideration and assistance they have given me while I have been working to produce this edition.

D C M Y
Oxford
November 1985

Contents

Preface vii
Table of statutes xi
List of cases xv

1 The purposes of administrative law 1
Administrative agencies: the Crown 4
Local government authorities 6
The police 7
Public corporations 9
What is administrative law? 15
A circular subject 18

2 Delegated legislation 21
Formal Parliamentary safeguards 23
Political safeguards 29
Judicial control 30
The disquiet about Ministers' powers is allayed 36

3 Ultra vires, unreasonableness and error of law 42
Ultra vires as the basis for review 42
The practical application of the ultra vires principle 44
Is the French law of judicial review superior to that of England? 46
Power exercised unreasonably is void 48
The *Padfield* case 55
Television licences, Skytrain, and the schools cases 62
Error of law 77
The *Anisminic* case 81
Are all acts in error of law void? 86
The no evidence rule 89

4 Natural justice 92
Judicial, quasi-judicial and administrative powers and duties 92
The central position of natural justice 101
Student cases 110
The development of a modern rule of fair procedure 111

5 **Remedies** 117
The old remedies 118
The modern 'application for judicial review' 126
The *McWhirter* and *Gouriet* cases 134
Should there be a specialist administrative court, or a wholesale reform of judicial review? 143
Crown proceedings 148
Public interest immunity 156

6 **Tribunals and inquiries** 170
Administrative tribunals 173
Inquiries 194
The Franks Committee and after 199
The Council on Tribunals 202
Appeals under the Tribunals and Inquiries Act 1971 204
Other reforms 207
Developments in Australia 210

7 **Ombudsmen** 213
The Parliamentary Commissioner for Administration 217
Similar developments in other countries 223
Other United Kingdom ombudsmen 225
The work of ombudsmen in practice 230
Conclusions 238

Index 243

Table of statutes

	PAGE
Act of Settlement (1700)	6
Administration of Justice Act 1960	120, 133
s 16	120
Administration of Justice (Miscellaneous Provisions) Act 1938	
s 7	119
9	130
Administrative Appeals Tribunal Act 1975 (Australia)	211, 212
Administrative Decisions (Judicial Review) Act 1977 (Australia)	136, 138, 143, 146, 202, 210
s 5 (1)	144, 145
(a)-(j)	144
(2) (a)-(g)	144
(h), (j)	145
(3)	145
(a), (b)	145
Administrative Procedure Act 1946 (USA)	200
s 10 (e)	75
Agricultural Marketing Act 1958	55
s 19	55, 57, 58
(6)	58
20	57, 58
Air Force Act 1955	219
Arbitration Act 1950	186
Army Act 1955	219
Bill of Rights (1688)	3, 17, 64
Caravan Sites and Control of Development Act 1960	49
Chronically Sick and Disabled Persons Act 1970	234
Cinematograph Act 1909	44
Civil Aviation Act 1971	66
s 22	65
Commissioner for Complaints Act (Northern Ireland) 1969	226
Common Law Procedure Act 1852	129
Companies Act 1948	166
s 165, 167	108

	PAGE
Criminal Law Act 1967	8
Crown Proceedings Act 1947	17, 121, 149
s 1	149, 153, 154
2	149, 154, 156
(1)	154
(5)	154
(6)	156
10	155, 156
11	121, 155
28	156
28 (1)	156
38, 40	155
Declaration of Abdication Act 1936	3
Defence (Transfer of Functions) Act 1964	155
Education Act 1902	50
s 7	50
Education Act 1944	76
s 8	76, 77
13	69
68	70, 72, 73
99 (1)	77
Education Act 1976	73
Education Act 1979	73
Evidence (Amendment) Act 1979 (New South Wales)	169
Extradition Act 1870	219
Finance (No 2) Act 1940	32
s 33	32
Fire Services (Emergency Provisions) Act 1941	27
Foreign Compensation Act 1950	82
s 4 (4)	82, 84
Foreign Compensation Act 1969	82
s 3	83
Freedom of Information Act 1982 (Australia)	168
Fugitive Offenders Act 1967	219
Furnished Houses (Rent Control) Act 1946	18, 174, 176

xii *Table of statutes*

	PAGE
Health and Social Services and Social Security Adjudications Act 1983	191
Housing Act 1925	31
s 40	31
Housing Act 1957	89, 102, 103
Sch 4	90
Housing Act 1974	87
Housing Act 1980	18, 174, 176, 177, 178, 190
s 72	176, 178
(3)	176
141, 142	177
Increase of Rent and Mortgage Interest (War Restrictions) Act 1915	174
Industrial Relations Act 1971	153
Industry Act 1975	10
Judicature Amendment Act 1972 (New Zealand)	129
Judicature (Northern Ireland) Act 1978	130
Judicial Review Procedure Act 1971 (Ontario)	129
Land Compensation Act 1973	232
Lands Tribunal Act 1949	184
Law Reform (Husband and Wife) Act 1962	
s 1	155
Leasehold Reform Act 1967	
s 1 (4A)	86
Local Government Act 1972	5, 6, 8, 68, 227
s 112	54
161	52
Local Government Act 1974	227
Local Government Act 1985	6
Local Government (Scotland) Act 1975	227
London Government Act 1963	6, 50, 53
Mental Health Act 1959	171
s 3	187
Mental Health Act 1983	187
Mental Health (Amendment) Act 1982	209
Metropolis Local Management Act 1855	
s 76	96
Metropolitan Public Carriage Act 1869	95
Mutiny Act 1717	38

	PAGE
National Assistance Act 1948	189
National Fire Service Regulations (Indemnity) Act 1944	
s 1	27
Schedule	27
National Health Service Act 1946	78
National Health Service Reorganisation Act 1973	226
National Health Service (Scotland) Act 1972	226
National Insurance Act 1946	189
National Insurance Act 1965	
s 75 (1)	88
National Insurance (Industrial Injuries) Act 1946	189
Naval Discipline Act 1957	219
New Towns Act 1946	10
Northern Ireland Act 1974	
Sch 1	227
Ombudsman Act 1954 (Denmark)	216
Ombudsman Act 1976 (Australia)	224
Parks Regulation Act 1872	27
Parliamentary Commissioner Act 1967	217, 226, 238
s 5 (1)	221
(2)	64
12 (3)	221, 229
Sch 2	219, 225
Sch 3	219, 220, 225
Parliamentary Commissioner Act (Northern Ireland) 1969	226
Parliamentary Commissioner (Consular Complaints) Act 1981	220
Parliamentary Commissioner (Ombudsman) Act 1962 (New Zealand)	216, 223
Patent, Designs and Trade Marks Act 1888	
s 1 (2)	30
Police Act 1964	9
s 48	9
Police Act 1976	229
Police and Criminal Evidence Act 1984	29
Post Office Act 1953	
s 58	136
Prison Act 1952	105
Prosecution of Offences Act 1985	7
Public Health (London) Act 1891	35
Rent Act 1957	53
Rent Act 1965	17, 106, 175, 177
Rent Act 1968	17, 174, 175

	PAGE
Rent Act 1974	17, 174, 175
Rent Act 1977	17, 106, 174, 176, 177, 178
s 17, 18	177
19, 20	178
70	179
Rules Publication Act 1893	30
Social Security Act 1975	189
Social Security Act 1979	190
Social Security Act 1980	190
Solicitors Act 1974	229
Statutory Instruments Act 1946	23, 29
s 1	22
12	29
Statutory Orders (Special Procedure) Act 1945	26
Summary Jurisdiction Act 1848	78
Sunday Entertainments Act 1932	
s 1 (1)	45
Supplementary Benefit Act 1966	155
Supreme Court Act 1981	141
s 31	132
Telecommunications Act 1984	14
Telegraph Act 1863	
s 45	136
Theft Act 1968	8
Town and Country Planning Act 1947	
s 16	195
Town and Country Planning Act 1959	195

	PAGE
Town and Country Planning Act 1971	
s 245	111
Trade Union and Labour Relations Act 1974	153
s 14	136
Transport Act 1947	11
Transport (London) Act 1969	
s 1	74
Tribunals and Inquiries Act 1958	79, 106, 201, 202
s 9	121, 126, 184, 195, 204
11	82, 84
12	121, 188, 199
Sch 1	184
Tribunals and Inquiries Act 1966	173, 195, 202
Tribunals and Inquiries Act 1971	173, 183, 202
s 11	195
12	121, 184, 188, 199, 202, 205, 211
13	121, 126, 184, 186, 204
14	82
Sch 1	184, 204
Water Charges Act 1976	62
Wireless Telegraphy Act 1949	
s 1 (2), (4)	63

List of cases

	PAGE
Adams v War Office (1955)	156
Air Canada v Secretary of State for Trade (No 2) (1893)	167
Anisminic Ltd v Foreign Compensation Commission (1969)	81, 84, 85, 87
Arlidge v Islington Corpn (1909)	35
Armah v Government of Ghana (1968)	85
Ashbridge Investments Ltd v Minister of Housing and Local Government (1965)	89, 90, 91
Associated Provincial Picture Houses Ltd v Wednesbury Corpn (1948)	44, 45, 48, 51, 54, 55, 71
A-G v Cockermouth Local Board (1874)	139
A-G v Wilts United Dairies (1922)	64, 65
A-G ex rel McWhirter v Independent Broadcasting Authority (1973)	124, 125, 134, 139, 141
Bailey v Williamson (1873)	27, 28
Barnard v National Dock Labour Board (1953)	49, 122
Board of Education v Rice (1911)	49, 96, 121
Breen v Amalgamated Engineering Union (1971)	61
British Oxygen Co Ltd v Board of Trade (1969)	61
British Oxygen Co Ltd v Board of Trade (1971)	61
Bromley London Borough Council v Greater London Council (1983)	74

	PAGE
Bruce v Waldron (1963)	158
Burmah Oil Co Ltd v Bank of England (1980)	166
Buxton v Minister of Housing and Local Government (1961)	196
Calvin v Carr (1980)	110
Campbell v Tameside Metropolitan Borough Council (1982)	167
Central London Property Trust Ltd v High Trees House Ltd (1947)	224
Chapman v Earl (1968)	126
Chertsey UDC v Mixnam's Properties Ltd (1965)	49
Chief Constable of North Wales Police v Evans (1982)	111
Churchward v R (1865)	152
Cocks v Thanet District Council (1983)	132
Coleen Properties Ltd v Minister of Housing and Local Government (1971)	90
Combe v Combe (1951)	224
Congreve v Home Office (1976)	63, 64, 65, 231
Conway v Rimmer (1967); affd. (1968)	158, 161, 163, 165, 168, 169, 218
Cooper v Wandsworth Board of Works (1863)	95, 96, 98
Corbett v Social Security Commission (1962)	158
Council of Civil Service Unions v Minister for the Civil Service (1985)	115
Crompton (Alfred) Amusement Machines Ltd v Customs and Excise Comrs (No. 2) (1974)	167

xv

xvi *List of cases*

	PAGE
Crown Lands Comrs v Page (1960)	151
Customs and Excise Comrs v Cure and Deeley Ltd (1962)	32, 33, 34
D v National Society for the Prevention of Cruelty to Children (1978)	166
Davy v Spelthorne Borough Council (1984)	132
Daymond v South West Water Authority (1976)	62
De Falco v Crawley Borough Council (1980)	131
Defiant Cycle Co Ltd v Newell (1953)	36
Duncan v Cammell Laird & Co Ltd (1942)	157, 159, 160, 161, 163, 164, 169
Dunkley v Evans (1981)	31
Dyson v A-G (1911)	123
Ellis v Home Office (1953)	159
Enever v R (1906)	8
Errington v Minister of Health (1935)	94
Estate and Trust Agencies (1927) Ltd v Singapore Improvement Trust (1937)	71
Fairmount Investments Ltd v Secretary of State for the Environment (1976)	103
Falmouth Boat Construction Co Ltd v Howell (1950)	151
Fisher v Oldham Corpn (1930)	7
Flast v Cohen 392 US 83 (1968)	140
Fletcher's Application, Re (1970)	239
Franklin v Minister of Town and Country Planning (1948)	94
Fry, ex p (1954)	105
Givaudan & Co Ltd v Minister of Housing and Local Government (1966)	198

	PAGE
Glasgow Corpn v Central Land Board (1956)	158
Glynn v Keele University (1971)	110
Gouriet v Union of Post Office Workers (1978)	125, 126, 134, 135, 138, 139, 140, 141, 146
Gregory v London Borough of Camden (or Camden London Borough Council) (1966)	125
Grosvenor Hotel, London (No 2), Re (1965)	160
HK (Infant), Re (1967)	114
Hall & Co Ltd v Shoreham-by-Sea UDC (1964)	54
Heywood v Hull Prison Board of Visitors (1980)	131
Howard v Secretary of State for the Environment (1975)	29
Imperial Tobacco Ltd v A-G (1979)	141
Institute of Patent Agents v Lockwood (1894)	31
Iveagh (Earl) v Minister of Housing and Local Government (1964)	199
James v Minister of Housing and Local Government (1965)	86
Johnson v Sargant & Sons (1918)	35
Jones v Robson (1901)	35
Kent County Council v Batchelor (1978)	141
Kruse v Johnson (1898)	34
Kulamma v Manadan (1968)	60
Laker Airways Ltd v Department of Trade (1977)	65, 67, 71
Lavender (H) & Son Ltd v Minister of Housing and Local Government (1970)	61

List of cases xvii

	PAGE
Law v National Greyhound Racing Club Ltd (1983)	132
Lewis v Heffer (1978)	109
Liversidge v Anderson (1942)	67
Lonrho Ltd v Shell Petroleum Co Ltd (1980)	166
McEldowney v Forde (1971)	34
McInnes v Onslow Fane (1978)	112, 113, 114
Malloch v Aberdeen Corpn (1971)	99
Meade v London Borough of Haringey (1979)	76, 77
Merricks v Nott-Bower (1965)	160
Metropolitan Properties Co (FGC) Ltd v Lannon (1969)	106, 107, 126, 177
Michaelides v O'Neill (1974)	126
Miller v Minister of Health (1946)	94
Minister of Health v R, ex p Yaffe (1931)	31, 32
Minister of National Revenue v Wrights' Canadian Ropes Ltd (1947)	71
Ministry of Housing and Local Government v Sharp (1970)	2
Nakkuda Ali v M F De S Jayaratne (1951)	94, 95, 96, 98, 103
Nash v Finlay (1901)	34
New South Wales v Bardolph (1934)	152
Norwest Holst Ltd v Secretary of State for Trade (1978)	108
Norwich Pharmacal Co v Customs and Excise Comrs (1974)	167
O'Reilly v Mackman (1983)	132, 140
Ostreicher v Secretary of State for the Environment (1978)	102

	PAGE
Padfield v Minister of Agriculture, Fisheries and Food (1968)	15, 55, 56, 57, 59, 61, 62, 71, 98, 121
Pearlman v Keepers and Governors of Harrow School (1979)	86, 87
Pickwell v Camden London Borough Council (1983)	54, 71, 76
Prescott v Birmingham Corpn (1955)	52, 53, 75
Priddle v Fisher & Sons (1968)	126
Punton v Ministry of Pensions and National Insurance (1963)	80
Punton v Ministry of Pensions and National Insurance (No 2) (1963); affd. (1964)	79, 80, 123, 134
R v BBC, ex p Lavelle (1983)	132
R v Barnsley Licensing Justices, ex p Barnsley and District Licensed Victuallers' Association (1960)	107
R v Barnsley Metropolitan Borough Council, ex p Hook (1976)	103
R v Blundeston Prison Board of Visitors, ex p Fox-Taylor (1982)	105
R v Board of Visitors of Hull Prison, ex p St Germain (1979)	105
R v Cheltenham Justices, ex p Secretary of State for Trade (1977)	166
R v Criminal Injuries Compensation Board, ex p Lain (1967)	100
R v Deputy Industrial Injuries Comr, ex p Moore (1965)	102
R v Electricity Comrs, ex p London Electricity Joint Committee Co (1920) Ltd (1924)	99, 104, 119
R v Gaming Board for Great Britain, ex p Benaim and Khaida (1970)	114

xviii   List of cases

	PAGE
R v Greater London Council, ex p Blackburn (1976)	124, 125, 135, 139
R v Hanson (1821)	120
R v Hereford Corpn, ex p Harrower (1970)	125
R v Hillingdon London Borough Council, ex p Royco Homes Ltd (1974)	55, 99
R v Hull Prison Board of Visitors, ex p St Germain (No 2) (1979)	105
R v Huntingdon District Council, ex p Cowan (1984)	111, 132, 140
R v Immigration Officer, ex p Shah (1982)	132
R v IRC, ex p National Federation of Self-Employed and Small Businesses Ltd (1980); affd. (1982)	142
R v IRC, ex p Rossminster Ltd (1980)	131
R v Kensington and Chelsea (Royal) London Borough Council, ex p Birdwood (1976)	122
R v Knightsbridge Crown Court, ex p International Sporting Club (London) Ltd (1982)	88
R v Leyland Justices, ex p Hawthorn (1979)	111
R v Local Comr for Administration for the North and East Area of England, ex p Bradford Metropolitan City Council (1979)	234
R v London Transport Executive, ex p Greater London Council (1983)	75
R v Ludlow, ex p Barnsley Corpn (1947)	80
R v Mahoney (1910)	43
R v Merseyside County Council, ex p Great Universal Stores Ltd (1982)	75
R v Metropolitan Police Comr, ex p Blackburn (1968)	124
R v Metropolitan Police Comr, ex p Parker (1953)	103
R v Minister of Health, ex p Davis (1929)	119

	PAGE
R v Nat Bell Liquors Ltd (1922)	85
R v Northumberland Compensation Appeal Tribunal, ex p Shaw (1952)	78, 79, 119
R v Paddington Valuation Officer, ex p Peachey Property Corpn Ltd (1966)	86, 125
R v Preston Supplementary Benefits Appeal Tribunal, ex p Moore (1975)	87
R v Secretary of State for Home Dept, ex p Hosenball (1977)	107
R v Secretary of State for the Environment, ex p Brent London Borough Council (1982)	97
R v Secretary of State for the Environment, ex p Norwich City Council (1982)	68
R v Secretary of State for the Environment, ex p Ostler (1977)	86
R v Secretary of State for the Environment, ex p Powis (1981)	91
R v Secretary of State for the Home Department, ex p Benwell (1985)	97
R v Sheer Metalcraft Ltd (1954)	35
R v Sussex Justices, ex p McCarthy (1924)	115
R v Thames Magistrates' Court, ex p Greenbaum (1957)	125
Racecourse Betting Control Board v Secretary for Air (1944)	79
Re Racal Communications Ltd (1981)	87
Rederiaktiebolaget Amphitrite v R (1921)	150, 151
Reynolds v United States 192 F 2d 987 (3d Cir 1951)	160
Ridge v Baldwin (1964)	2, 97, 98, 99, 101, 104, 115, 129
Ripon (Highfield) Housing Order 1938, Re, White and Collins v Minister of Health (1939)	49
Roberts v Hopwood (1925)	51, 53

List of cases xix

	PAGE
Robertson v Minister of Pensions (1949)	151
Rogers v Home Secretary (1973)	165
Roncarelli v Duplessis (1959)	67
Rooke's Case (1598)	61
Sabey (H) & Co Ltd v Secretary of State for the Environment (1978)	111, 113
Sankey v Whitlam (1978)	168, 169
Secretary of State for Education and Science v Tameside Metropolitan Borough Council (1977)	14, 68, 71, 72, 73, 74, 75, 77, 89, 116
Shore v Wilson (1842)	139
Short v Poole Corpn (1926)	46
Smith v Moss (1940)	155
South East Asia Fire Bricks Sdn Bhd v Non-Metallic Mineral Products Manufacturing Employees Union (1981)	87, 88
Springer v Doorly (1950)	26
Stevenson v United Road Transport Union (1977)	105
Tamlin v Hannaford (1950)	11, 13

	PAGE
Taylor v Munrow (1960)	53
Thorson v A-G of Canada (No 2) (1974)	140
Tunstall, Re, ex p Brown (1966)	158
Universal Camera Corpn v National Labor Relations Board 340 US 474 (1951)	75
Uppal v Home Office (1978)	131, 134, 148
Van der Linde v Calitz (1967)	158
Wandsworth London Borough Council v Winder (1984)	132
Waterfalls Town Management Board v Minister of Housing (S Rhodesia) (1956)	151
Watt v Lord Advocate (1979)	87
Webb v Minister of Housing and Local Government (1965)	55
Wednesbury Corpn v Ministry of Housing and Local Government (1965)	160
Whitehall v Whitehall (1957)	158
Williams v Home Office (1981)	167

1 The purposes of administrative law

> For forms of government let fools contest;
> Whate'er is best administered is best.
>
> Alexander Pope, *An Essay on Man*

Many have been the jurists, and even judges, who have denied that there is in England any body of law which may properly be called administrative law. The old fallacy propagated, probably partly unwittingly, by Dicey in his celebrated lectures, first published in 1885,[1] that there is no such thing as administrative law in England has died hard. Dicey was in fact at pains to draw a distinction between England, where all aspects of human behaviour are subject to control and review in the ordinary courts of the land, and France, where a separate body of courts existed for the purpose of determining disputes between citizens and any part of the executive arm of government. This distinction was, and still is, perfectly valid. But it was unfortunate that Dicey went on to draw the conclusion that administrative courts in France must necessarily favour the administration against any individual wherever a dispute exists between them, and that therefore the French *droit administratif* offends against the desirable principle of equality before the law. Dicey's view was drawn upon time and again as a basis for national pride, and especially for the making of satisfactory comparisons between our own fair system of law and what has been alleged to be an unfair system across the Channel in France. This type of bigotry has perhaps been aped in recent years by the tendency of divers people on this side of the Channel to blame a large number of economic and other setbacks upon the iniquities of the European Economic Community or Common Market. Neither of these practices has been securely rooted in fact, but each has brought with it the small comfort of attacking our ancient enemy, France.

One of the intentions in these essays is to draw attention to the considerable progress made in recent years by the work of some of the outstanding judges, and in the forefront will be the work of Lord

---

1 *The Law of the Constitution* ch IV.

Reid and Lord Denning. But even these great men have not been immune from the contagion first started by Dicey. Thus Lord Denning in 1970 opined:[2]

> Our English law does not allow a public officer to shelter behind a *droit administratif*.

And Lord Reid six years earlier said:[3]

> We do not have a developed system of administrative law – perhaps because until fairly recently we did not need it . . .

though it is clear from the context of the latter pronouncement that he was mainly concerned to stress that all types of administrative action in England are subject to review by the ordinary, rather than special, courts, which after all was the same perfectly valid premise from which Dicey started. A little thought will inevitably point to the conclusion that a body of law in England must always have existed to regulate relations between the citizens and the state, whatever the nature of that law may have been, and any suggestion that governmental power has only arisen in recent decades is insupportable. Sir William Wade, in his important textbook *Administrative Law*,[4] has shown how the steady march of governmental power to cover almost all aspects of the citizen's life was not just a product of the First World War and the profound changes wrought upon society as its result. There were many signs even in the nineteenth century of state intervention and the gradual growth of government control. Maitland in 1888 wrote:[5] 'We are becoming a much governed nation, governed by all manner of councils and boards and officers, central and local, high and low, excercising the powers which have been committed to them by modern statutes.' But the rate of progress towards such control has gained momentum most markedly in the period starting with the Second World War, and it is no exaggeration to say that the power of governmental intervention today bears very little resemblance to its modest predecessor of a century ago.

It is well enough known that in the reign of Elizabeth I Parliament normally met for only about a month or two each year, during which time it would grant money to the Queen in return for certain royal concessions of power, in the form of the Royal Assent to bills passed through the two Houses of Parliament. These concessions led in course of time to a considerable accretion both of the area of power

2 *Ministry of Housing and Local Government v Sharp* [1970] 2 QB 223 at 226.
3 *Ridge v Baldwin* [1964] AC 40 at 72.
4 5th edn, ch 1.
5 *Constitutional History of England* (1955 reprint) p 501.

of Parliament and of its substance; and the process was hastened by the assertion in the Bill of Rights 1688 of the legislative supremacy of Parliament over the Crown. A by-product of the 1689 Revolution, however, was the basis of the present partnership between Parliament and government. Once the legislative sovereignty of Parliament had been established it would always have been legally possible for Parliament, by statute, to reduce or even to sweep away the powers of the Crown. No Monarch could effectively resist such legislation, for the refusal of the Royal Assent could have been overcome either by another revolution or else by Parliament's insistence upon the Sovereign's abdication – a process carried out in the case of King Edward VIII by His Majesty's Declaration of Abdication Act 1936. So, in order to safeguard the retention of their powers, including all areas of the Royal Prerogative, it became essential for successive governments to work out a *modus vivendi* with Parliament. The solution reached in the course of the eighteenth century was undoubtedly assisted by the disinterest of the early Hanoverian Kings in affairs of state in England, a circumstance which enabled the government as a whole to take over from the Monarch the exercise of almost all real executive power. It was then a fairly natural result of the need for ministers to work harmoniously with Parliament that in a fairly short space of time the government came to be formed from among the leaders of the party or group which commanded a majority in the more important House of Parliament, the Commons. From this device we get not only the doctrine of ministerial responsibility to Parliament, but also, by the latter part of the twentieth century, the virtual control of Parliament by the government once it has been formed. The post-Revolution partnership between Parliament and government was not always clear-cut or fully appreciated until much nearer our own time, but today it is so well recognised that we know that the power of the executive arm of government may be legally extended by the instrument of statute to whatever length that may be chosen by the government of the day.

Readers of the political novels of Anthony Trollope will recall that he describes Parliament in the mid-nineteenth century as meeting each year in February, and ending the session about the beginning of August. He also draws a picture of a markedly more leisurely legislature, with a working day shorter than it normally is today, and with most Ministers bearing a distinctly lighter workload than their present-day successors. Although Trollope's characters and plots were fictional, the essence of his description of public life was not too exaggerated. Parliament, which in the late sixteenth century had met for usually no more that eight weeks a year, was three centuries later meeting on most normal working days throughout about half of each year. With its new-found identity of interest with the Crown its area of legislative power was unlimited in scope, and it could easily be persuaded by its leaders to confer vast executive powers upon them. Yet even then most of the great areas of executive incursion upon individual rights had scarcely been thought of. State intervention in the regulation of factories and provision for public health had begun, and a number of inspectorates had been created. Compulsory acquisition of property had already arisen in connection with the enclosure of land and the building of railways. The Civil Service was being reformed (a matter which was the heart of the plot of Trollope's *The Three Clerks*), and the Victorian age was also to produce statutes creating new local government authorities, the germ of town and country planning law, and public provision for education. But whole areas of regulation which concern us all so closely today were to be virtually untouched and probably unthought of by Parliament or government until the present century, and it is mostly from the past forty years that we derive the vast controls covering such matters as the National Health Service, compulsory state insurance and all the many facets of the welfare state, controls over prices and the level of wages, industrial relations, comprehensive education, and an ever more complex system of taxation. So now, in the reign of Queen Elizabeth II, Parliament must meet for most of the year, and works during almost impossibly long hours on each week-day when it is in session. It is spurred by the government to pass legislation deemed by the Crown to be desirable or necessary, and inevitably this legislation frequently confers further executive powers upon the government or upon specified Ministers or government agencies. Accordingly the balance of power has shifted decisively from the individual to the state, and it is in monitoring this shift that administrative law is relevant.

Administrative agencies: the Crown

It is of course clear to all lawyers that the primary agency through which administration is carried out is the Crown. The term 'Crown' is perfectly logical, given the monarchical character of our Constitution. But unfortunately many students find difficulty, at least at the outset of their legal studies, in distinguishing satisfactorily between the Monarch and the Crown. One small criticism which may diffidently be levelled at the otherwise admirable and graphic volume of *Essays in Constitutional Law*, by Professor R F V Heuston, is that the essay on the Royal Prerogative[6] concentrates perhaps unduly upon the prerogative powers of the Monarch, and somewhat underplays the part taken in this area of law by the Crown as a whole. For most practical purposes it is the Crown, not the Monarch, which is of relevance to administrative lawyers. Indeed a key feature of our modern Constitution is the virtual removal of the Monarch from the practice of political power. The Crown embraces the whole of the central government (of which the Monarch is not more than titular head), from the Prime Minister down through the Cabinet and other more junior Ministers, and includes the Civil Service and the armed forces. Primary administrative powers may be exercised, either by prerogative or under the authority of statute, by any individuals from this numerous group acting within the course of their Crown service. Thus, for the purposes of administrative law, executive power may be wielded just as much by the lowliest inland revenue clerk or private soldier as by the Prime Minister, the Home Secretary or the Minister of Agriculture. Authority is of course exercised by superior officers in the hierarchy of the Crown over more junior officials, but, subject to the limits set by prerogative or statute, all such persons may at different times represent the power of the state over other citizens.

But there are other administrative authorities which do not form part of the Crown. In theory there is no limit to the variety of different types of authority which may have executive power conferred upon them by statute, for this is implicit in the legislative sovereignty of Parliament. Executive powers (and, as we shall see in the next chapter, legislative powers) certainly have been conferred upon such diverse authorities as railways, water authorities, the Post Office, and universities, all to be exercised within the limits set by the primary statutes. But it is unlikely that Parliament would seek to confer such powers upon named individuals unless there should be good reason to do so. In recent years the Crown, through Parliament, has been able to confer all the special executive powers it considers necessary upon different quasi-governmental organisations by the device of expanding the concept of the public corporation. Administrative authorities other than the Crown, therefore, fall for the most part under the headings of local government authorities, the police, and public corporations. It may be desirable to dwell for a moment on these.

6   2nd edn, 1964, ch 3.

6   *The purposes of administrative law*

Local government authorities

The organisation of local government in England and Wales is principally governed by the London Government Act 1963 and the Local Government Acts 1972 and 1985. In rural areas there is a hierarchy of geographical units by counties, districts and parishes, while in urban areas the parish has no local government significance, and only the two upper tiers of authority may exist. A complication is introduced by the fact that the six most urbanised parts of the country outside London are designated metropolitan counties, and thus are intended in many ways to resemble the organisation of the metropolis of London. Within Greater London and the metropolitan counties most local government powers are vested in all-purpose district or borough councils (the ancient City of London Corporation counts in this respect as one of the London Boroughs). Certain matters, however, and notably fire and civil defence, are the responsibility of joint boards composed of members of the various district or borough councils within the county. The twenty 'Outer London Boroughs' are education authorities. But a curiosity of the local government arrangements for London is that for the area covered by the twelve 'Inner London Boroughs', including the City of London, there is a specially constituted, directly elected, body called the Inner London Education Authority which administers the education service within this area. A number of minor local government functions in the centre of London are still exercised by the benchers of the two Inns of Court called the Inner and Middle Temples. There are also several separate authorities specially created to administer a number of highly important public services which often stretch their bounds beyond the confines of the area governed by the London Boroughs. These bodies include the Metropolitan Water Board, the Thames Water Authority, the Port of London Authority and the London Regional Transport Board, which controls the underground railways. But these latter bodies are not constituted by direct election and are better considered as public corporations, rather than local authorities. They will be referred to again as such presently.

Outside London and the metropolitan counties all county councils have exclusive powers over such matters as structure plans for the county, highways, traffic, consumer protection, refuse disposal, education, youth employment, personal social services and libraries. They also exercise a number of powers concurrently with district councils, including the control of museums and art galleries, swimming baths, parks and open spaces, tree preservation, and many aspects of town development. Non-metropolitan district councils have exclusive powers over such matters as housing, planning development control, building regulations, markets and fairs, local licensing, refuse collection, clean air and home safety.

The lowest tier of local government authority is the parish council which may exist in rural areas, or, for some very sparsely populated areas, the parish meeting. The powers of these bodies are comparatively minor, and their exercise only rarely gives rise to serious controversy, though the Law Reports from time to time do contain accounts of litigation stemming from the activities of these humble bodies. Their powers cover such matters as the maintenance and signposting of footpaths and bridleways, allotments, bus shelters, village greens and burial grounds.

The police

It is commonly thought by laymen that the police are servants either of the Crown or of local authorities. But neither belief is well-founded. Police officers have a duty to enforce the criminal law, they possess certain powers of entry and inspection, and wide powers of arrest, and they are frequently closely involved in the preparation of prosecutions.[7] But they are not under any direct duty to the Crown or to the local authorities within whose areas they operate as to the manner in which they carry out their functions. The police are organised in local forces, and maintained by local authorities, with the exception of the Metropolitan Police Force and the City of London Police Force, for both of which there are rather more special arrangements. For the Metropolitan Police Force in particular the Home Secretary carries out many of the functions exercised in relation to the police elsewhere by local authorities. For all the police forces the central government has considerable financial control and regulatory powers, which are used to ensure that conditions of service, dress, pay and allowances are uniform throughout the country. But the essential fact remains that, with the partial exception of the Metropolitan Police Force, there is no central or local government control over the day-to-day work of the police.

At common law a police officer is himself solely and individually responsible for the exercise or purported exercise of his various powers. The case of *Fisher v Oldham Corpn*[8] illustrates this point. In early April 1929 a warrant was issued by an Oldham magistrate for the arrest of one Russell, who was said to be well known to the Oldham police, on a charge of obtaining money by false pretences (a crime the

---

7   The conduct of prosecutions, however, is the responsibility of the independent Crown Prosecution Service set up by the Prosecution of Offences Act 1985.
8   [1930] 2 KB 364.

substance of which was later somewhat altered by the Theft Act 1968). The Oldham police suspected that Russell had fled to London, so they called upon the assistance of the London police in apprehending him. Mr Fisher, who was a timber merchant at Plaistow, but who in former years had become well known to the police in his own locality, had been sentenced several times for the offence of obtaining money by false pretences. The London police believed that he was the wanted man, and so he was arrested by a London police officer on 25 April, and spent the night in a cell. The following day he was handed over to Inspector Sharples of the Oldham police, and was taken in custody to Oldham, where he was detained for several hours before the mistake was discovered and he was released. Thereupon Fisher brought an action against the corporation of the borough of Oldham claiming damages for false imprisonment. The defendants denied that they were liable for the action of the Oldham police in causing the arrest and detention of the plaintiff, and they succeeded in their defence. McCardie J, after an illuminating review of the history of the police, and their position at common law, posed the following illustration to make his point:[9]

> Suppose that a police officer arrested a man for a serious felony? Suppose, too, that the watch committee of the borough at once passed a resolution directing that the felon should be released? Of what value would such a resolution be? Not only would it be the plain duty of the police officer to disregard the resolution, but it would also be the duty of the chief constable to consider whether an information should not at once be laid against the members of the watch committee for a conspiracy to obstruct the course of criminal justice.

McCardie J was using terms some of which have been superseded by subsequent reforms. Thus, the ancient borough corporations were replaced by district councils under the Local Government Act 1972; watch committees have been replaced by the present police authorities consisting as to two-thirds of members of local councils within the area of the police force concerned, and as to one-third of magistrates for the constituent areas; and the distinction in criminal law between felonies and misdemeanours was abolished by the Criminal Law Act 1967. But the substance of what he said remains as valid today as it was in 1930. As Griffith CJ put it in an earlier Australian case:[10]

> The powers of a constable qua peace officers, whether conferred by common or statute law, are exercised by him by virtue of his office and cannot be exercised on the responsibility of any person but himself.

9 [1930] 2 KB 364 at 372.
10 *Enever v R* (1906) 3 CLR 969

The Report of the Royal Commission on the Police, which was published in 1962,[11] specifically approved the maintenance of the local basis for police forces, and the independence of the police from either central or local control as to the way in which they perform their duties, though subject to some overriding powers of the Home Secretary as to general efficiency. Accordingly the Police Act 1964, which was based upon various detailed recommendations in the Royal Commission Report, does not dilute this essential independence of the police, despite the powerful dissenting argument in the Report by Professor A L Goodhart QC, urging the creation of a single unified police force. It may therefore be said that although police officers are subject to certain powers exercised by local authorities, including those of appointment and dismissal, and may be termed servants of the Crown in a general though not specific sense, the details of the discharge of their service are owed to none other than that stern mistress, the law. In only one respect has the individual police officer's independence been modified by the 1964 Act. It is now provided by section 48 of that Act that a Chief Constable is vicariously liable for torts committed by officers under his direction and control in the performance or purported performance of their functions, and that any award of damages made against a Chief Constable under this provision shall be paid from the police funds provided partly by the local police authority, and partly by central government grant. But this modification does not affect the essential independence of all police officers from any executive power outside the force.

Public corporations

Mention has already been made of the Metropolitan Water Board, the Thames Water Authority, the Port of London Authority and the London Regional Transport Board, all of which are authorities specially designed to control and run the undertakings under their care. All have their base in London, but all possess powers extending beyond the area of Greater London. They are examples of a type of public corporation, a generic heading under which it is now possible to place a large and disparate band of public authorities, all of which may have powers which must be considered in any survey of the boundaries and practice of administrative law. Professor J F Garner[12] defines a public corporation as

 a legal entity established normally by Parliament and always by legal

11 Cmnd 1728.
12 'Public Corporations in the United Kingdom', ch 1 in *Government Enterprise* p 4.

authority (usually in the form of a special statute) charged with the duty of carrying out specified Governmental functions (more or less precisely defined) in the national interest, those functions being confined to a comparatively restricted field, and subjected to some degree of control by the executive, while the corporation remains judicially an independent entity not directly responsible to Parliament. It is a 'person' in law, possessing but rarely any of the privileges of the Crown, and subject to the ordinary rules of the law in such matters as contractual and tortious liability, and being liable to state or local taxation.

It is clear enough from such a wide definition that the natures and character of public corporations may differ greatly, and that they may come into being for countless purposes. It is a common general impression that public corporations are the product of nationalisation, and that they have been set up to exercise monopolistic powers in areas of industry effectively barred by Parliament to private enterprise. But this is only a part of the story. Many public corporations certainly are the result of the acquisition of ownership and monopoly by the state, and as examples we might mention the National Coal Board, the British Railways Board, London Regional Transport, the Post Office, and the various area Gas Boards and Electricity Boards. But others, though properly described as commercial, may not necessarily possess monopoly powers. An example of this latter type of undertaking was the British Airways Corporation, which was the modern successor of a civil aviation industry nationalised at an early stage in its development. But this nationalisation was not intended to preclude all private civil flying. Since the Second World War the nationalised airlines therefore had to compete not only with international airline companies based abroad, but also with such flourishing non-public corporations as British Caledonian Airways. In 1986 British Airways was itself 'privatised'. Two public corporations, the British Broadcasting Corporation and the Independent Broadcasting Authority, are given monopoly powers between then in the field of public broadcasting, but they are deliberately set in competition with each other.

Some public corporations are regulatory rather than commercial. Of these the Bank of England and the Trinity House Corporation, with its control over lighthouses and pilotage in United Kingdom waters, are long-standing examples. More recent examples are the development corporations for new towns first provided for by the New Towns Act 1946, and the National Enterprise Board, established by the Industry Act 1975. The various area Tourist Boards share with the National Enterprise Board not only the possession of certain powers of enforcement, but also powers which may best come under the heading of encouragement or incentive for private persons and non-government organisations.

More variations upon the original theme are provided by bodies sometimes called Quangos (quasi-autonomous non-governmental organisations).[13] The word 'Quango' is used mainly by those who deplore their existence, and as a term of abuse. This type of variation can cover any corporate body with government connections, though not subject to direct government control, on which the members are paid, though most of them may often be giving their services on a part-time basis. It is often suspected that loyal government or political party supporters are rewarded for their staunchness by appointment to one or more places as members of Quangos, for which part-time and not always very arduous service they will be paid an annual fee of perhaps £1,000 or so. Quangos may be considered to include several of the bodies already mentioned, as well as such institutions as Regional Health Authorities. But the Conservative Government which came to power in 1979 has tried to implement a policy of reducing the number of Quangos.

All the public corporations so far mentioned are governed by statutes which usually provide that reports and accounts are to be submitted to Parliament every year, and under the relevant statutes the government very often retains the power to nominate or appoint a proportion of the directors, managers or members of the board, including the chairman.[14] But there is no offer of investment facilities for the general public. Subject to specific statutory provisions to the contrary, the corporation remains fully liable civilly and criminally, though they are not normally servants or agents of the Crown. This point was expressly clarified in 1950 as regards the British Transport Commission (a predecessor of the British Railways Board) by the Court of Appeal in *Tamlin v Hannaford*.[15] Denning LJ, as he then was, gave a particularly clear description of the position of the Commission:

> The Transport Act 1947 brings into being the British Transport Commission, which is a statutory corporation of a kind comparatively new to English law. It has many of the qualities which belong to corporations of

---

13   In some usages 'Quango' is said to stand for 'quasi-autonomous national governmental organisations'.
14   The exact title may vary. For example, the chairman of the Bank of England is called the Governor.
15   [1950] 1 KB 18 at 22.

other kinds to which we have been accustomed. It has, for instance, defined powers which it cannot exceed; and it is directed by a group of men whose duty it is to see that those powers are properly used. It may own property, carry on business, borrow and lend money, just as any other corporation may do, so long as it keeps within the bounds which Parliament has set. But the significant difference in this corporation is that there are no shareholders to subscribe the capital or to have any voice in its affairs. The money which the corporation needs is not raised by the issue of shares but but borrowing; and its borrowing is not secured by debentures, but is guaranteed by the Treasury. If it cannot repay, the loss falls on the Consolidated Fund of the United Kingdom; that is to say, on the taxpayer. There are no shareholders to elect directors or to fix their remuneration. There are no profits to be made or distributed. The duty of the corporation is to make revenue and expenditure balance one another, taking, of course, one year with another, but not to make profits. If it should make losses and be unable to pay its debts, its property is liable to execution, but it is not liable to be wound up at the suit of any creditor. The taxpayer would, no doubt, be expected to come to its rescue before the creditors stepped in. Indeed, the taxpayer is the universal guarantor of the corporation. But for him it could not have acquired its business at all, nor could it now continue it for a single day. It is his guarantee that has rendered shares, debentures and such like all unnecessary. He is clearly entitled to have his interest protected against extravagance or mismangement.

But there are other persons who have also a vital interest in its affairs. All those who use the services which it provides – and who does not? – and all whose supplies depend on it, in short everyone in the land, is concerned in seeing that it is properly run. The protection of the interests of all these – taxpayer, user and beneficiary – is entrusted by Parliament to the Minister of Transport. He is given powers over this corporation which are as great as those possessed by a man who holds all the shares in a private company, subject, however, as such a man is not, to a duty to account to Parliament for his stewardship. It is the Minister who appoints the directors – the members of the Commission – and fixes their remuneration. They must give him any information he wants; and, lest they should not prove amenable to his suggestions as to the policy they should adopt, he is given power to give them directions of a general nature, in matters which appear to him to affect the public interest, as to which he is the sole judge, and they are then bound to obey. These are great powers but still he cannot regard the corporation as being his agent, any more than the company is the agent of the shareholders, or even of a sole shareholder. In the eye of the law, the corporation is its own master and is answerable as fully as any other person or corporation. It is not the Crown and has none of the immunities or privileges of the Crown. Its servants are not Crown servants, and its property is not Crown property. It is, of course, a public authority and its purposes, no doubt, are public purposes, but it is not a government department nor do its powers fall within the province of government.

It is small wonder that the average citizen may find it hard to grasp the fact that these corporations, which have been set up at the instigation of the government, usually to carry out aspects of government policy, and which are reliant upon an allocation of Treasury funds by Parliament, and subject to elements of ministerial direction, are not a part of the identity of the central government itself. It is small wonder also that even the House of Commons in 1958 found considerable difficulty in determining whether or not a Minister was sufficiently responsible for the day-to-day running of a public corporation, so that he could be asked questions in the House on such matters. Mr George Strauss MP had written a letter to the Paymaster General, who represented the Minister of Power (a peer) in the Commons. In it he alleged that the London Electricity Board had behaved in scandalous manner in the way in which it invited tenders for the purchase of its scrap metal. The Paymaster-General disclosed the contents of the letter to the Board, which, after some exchange of correspondence, informed Mr Strauss that it intended to sue him for libel. Mr Strauss claimed that this amounted to a breach of one of the privileges of the House, freedom of speech in debate, which has come to include the freedom of members to correspond, without fear of legal proceedings, with Ministers upon matters for which such Ministers are responsible. Mr Strauss's claim was supported by the subsequent Report upon the matter to the House by the Committee of Privileges, but on a free vote in the House itself the claim was ultimately rejected. This vote was in line with the decision in *Tamlin v Hannaford*, for it recognised that the Minister was not responsible for the public corporation concerned.[16] A Commons Select Committee on Parliamentary Privilege has since recommended (in 1967) that *all* communications between MPs and Ministers should be covered by absolute privilege. Surprisingly the House has not yet acted on this recommendation, but even if it should do so this would only extend the privileges of Parliament, and would not affect the now well-established distinction between the Crown and public corporations.

One further complication must be mentioned. Not all corporations in which the government has its stake are wholly public. A number

---

16 See 591 HoC Official Report (5th series) col 208; and Yardley 'The House of Commons and its Privileges since the Strauss Affair' (1962) XV Parliamentary Affairs 500.

14　*The purposes of administrative law*

have been acquired by gradual stages, and some have remained only partially acquired by the state. The variations by which the Crown has encouraged, ameliorated, supported or rationalised the private sector of industry in the United Kingdom are too complex for consideration in this book.[17] But Professor T C Daintith[18] has defined a mixed enterprise as one

> a substantial part of whose capital is privately subscribed, which is constituted as a company subject to the Companies Act or is otherwise endowed with corporate status, in which the Government itself, a public corporation, or a local authority has a substantial financial interest of a permanent character, coupled with the ability to exercise a measure of internal control by way of voting power conferred by the ownership of shares or by the possession of a right to nominate directors or both.

There are in fact many businesses and organisations in which the government has some substantial financial interest in terms of the above definitions, even though the element of private participation remains, and in recent years has often been increased by the selling off of government holdings ('privatisation'). All such corporations may to some extent possess legal powers conferred by Parliament which impinge upon the rights of others. Among the most important examples from the world of commerce are British Petroleum Ltd, in which until 1979 the Crown had a 51 per cent stake in the shares issued (some of these shares having since been sold, the government now owning less that 40 per cent of its shares), Short Brothers and Harland Ltd, the aircraft builders, and British Telecom, in which the Crown's shareholding is just under 50 per cent.[19]

It is a matter of little concern to the citizen which type of administrative authority is concerned in any dispute which may affect him. Indeed it is not uncommon these days for disputes even to arise between an agency of the Crown and some other type of administrative authority, as in the celebrated case of *Secretary of State for Education and Science v Tameside Metropolitan Borough Council*,[20] which will be discussed in chapter 3 of this book. What is of concern, however, is that power exercised by any administrative authority should be restricted within the boundaries properly set for it by law.

17　See generally *Government Enterprise*, edited by W. Friedmann and J F Garner.
18　'The Mixed Enterprise in the United Kingdom', ch 3 in *Government Enterprise* p 56.
19　The Telecommunications Act 1984 inter alia abolished British Telecom's exclusive coverage in the field of telecommunications.
20　[1977] AC 1014.

What is administrative law?

The kernel of the whole subject of administrative law is this control of power within its lawful compass. Provided this essential umpiring function of the law is kept in mind, it is of much less consequence to attempt to formulate an acceptable definition of administrative law. Indeed no generally agreed definition has ever been put forward, and this is partly because the law operates positively as well as negatively. The law is employed not just to disqualify unlawful exercise of power, but also to compel the performance of legal duties which have been neglected. The case of *Padfield v Minister of Agriculture, Fisheries and Food*,[1] a highly important modern case in which the courts compelled a Minister to carry out his legal duty, is an example of the positive action of administrative law, and it will be at the centre of the discussion in chapter 3 of this book.

Apart from a small, though significant, reservoir of power left by the 1689 Revolution settlement to the prerogative of the Crown (and always subject at any time to removal or restriction by statute), administrative power is invariably to be traced to statutory authorisation. In a sense, therefore, the function of the courts is little more than one of statutory interpretation. But such a conclusion would overlook many of the subtleties of the English legal system. Judges have not infrequently denied that they make law, but commentators have learned to take such modest assertions with a pinch of salt. Although courts are bound by statute, and thus must apply any rule established either by or under the authority of Act of Parliament, this has not deterred them from applying such important common law presumptions as the rules of natural justice (which will be discussed in chapter 4 of this book), and by so doing interpreting the relevant legislation in such a way as to surprise Parliament. Dicey, as part of the formulation of his theory of the Rule of Law, said:[2]

> the general principles of the constitution (as for example the right to personal liberty or the right of public meeting) are with us the result of judicial decisions determining the rights of private persons in particular cases brought before the Courts; whereas under many foreign constitutions the security (such as it is) given to the rights of individuals results, or appears to result, from the general principles of the constitution . . . Our constitution, in short, is a judge-making constitution . . .

This passage betrays once more Dicey's deep distrust of 'foreign constitutions', and we would do well to put on one side this somewhat unreasoning prejudice. But again he was basically right in his

1 [1968] AC 997.
2 *The Law of the Constitution* pp 195, 196.

assessment of the position and power of the courts in England. He meant that, although the courts are bound by Parliament, the practical application of Parliamentary sovereignty always depends upon the interpretation placed by the courts upon the rules laid down by Parliament. The judges invariably affirm that they are applying Parliament's enactments, but their application of such enactments may at times appear to conflict with Parliament's intentions. Again, although statute law is ever more pervasive, there remain areas of common law left untouched by it. Here the law is constantly being developed by the courts, and the function of the judges as law-makers can scarcely be denied.

Later in this book it is proposed to examine the part in our law played by special tribunals and procedures. They are an important part of our modern administrative and legal system. But they, as well as all other inferior institutions in the state, always remain subject to the overall power of judicial review in the ordinary superior courts.

The 'superior' character of the courts of the level of High Court and above is important, for whichever way one turns this judicial supervisory power, inherent in the superior courts, is inescapable. Some may deplore it, and politicians not infrequently chafe under it, but is is probable that there is no acceptable substitute which could be found for it in a democratic country. To allow politicians, elected to office through the vagaries of the electorate's majority wishes at any one time, to be judges of their own ambit of authority for a period of up to five years before the next General Election could spell tyranny, at least in the short term. Where so much power in the modern state reposes in the administration, an impartial umpire between the conflicting interests of the administration and the citizen is essential, and such an umpire must be immune from the threat of dismissal as a result of deciding any issue in a manner which may be unpopular with the government. Only the judges of our superior courts, with their security of tenure established by the Act of Settlement 1700 meet these requirements. No one has yet suggested any more suitable person or body to act as umpire, and it is suggested therefore that it is an essential part of our administrative law to recognise and support the power of review that resides in the judges.

This is not to say, however, that the purpose of administrative law is to stifle administration. By the proper exercise of the courts' supervisory power illegal power is excised, but this leaves the legal use of power untouched. Thus the practice of administrative law should lead to the assistance of good administration, and positively encourage administrative powers only to be validly exercised. Thus Pope's couplet, which heads this chapter, could scarcely be taken as the motto of our modern courts. Pope's early eighteenth-century views were tinctured by anti-democratic, part-authoritarian attitudes to be found at that time. Our courts today would only consider administration to be good if it is not merely efficient, but also legal.

Dicey, in drawing attention to the absence of special administrative courts in England, was stressing the place of the ordinary courts in asserting control over the exercise of power by all other inferior bodies. The meaning of 'superior courts', as already mentioned, implies that the word 'inferior' may be indiscriminately applied to tribunals, inquiries, administrative officers, and indeed since the Bill of Rights 1688 to the Crown in all its manifestations. Even certain older prerogative rules which made it technically impossible to sue the Crown directly in tort or for breach of contract, and which drove prospective plaintiffs to legal fictions in order to prosecute their suits, were for the most part abrogated by the Crown Proceedings Act 1947, as will be seen in chapter 5. The fact that all inferior authorities are subject to the power of judicial review exemplifies still further the judge-made character of our Constitution.

Though much of the detailed work of the courts is in essence statutory interpretation, in carrying out this task the courts rely heavily on such common law presumptions, built up over the centuries, as the rules of natural justice. The constant efforts of the courts to maintain a fair balance in the exercise of power by administrative authorities over the individual have not infrequently caused surprise in administrative quarters. New statute law may always invade, curtail, alter or wholly supersede older common law rules, but when statute law tends to infringe common law liberties the courts habitually interpret it as restrictively as possible. This after all is in one sense merely to apply the doctrine of Parliamentary sovereignty to the letter. But in another, and more practical, sense it is discharging the stewardship entrusted by the balance of our Constitution to the courts to ensure that the requirements of governing the modern state do not ride roughshod over normally accepted liberties.

In the absence of special administrative courts, or a written Constitution, the growth of administrative agencies and their powers in England has been untidy and largely unplanned. New tribunals, agencies, and even ministries and departments of state have been created at the whim of Parliament and government as the need may appear to them to have arisen. Some have later been abolished, but most have remained as part of a patchwork system. Clear relationships between old and new agencies have often not been worked out, even within closely linked fields. A classic example of this untidiness was the creation by the Rent Act 1965 of rent officers to determine fair rents for private unfurnished lettings, and of rent assessment committees to hear appeals from such determinations. The Act left largely untouched the older rent tribunals which had existed since they were set up by the Furnished Houses (Rent Control) Act 1946, and which were responsible for fixing reasonable (not fair) rents for private furnished lettings, as well as for determining within certain time limits any question of security of tenure which may arise. For years the two systems existed side by side, sharing offices, staff and, to some extent, even membership. Some rationalisation was achieved by later Rent Acts in 1968, 1974 and 1977. But the dual schemes for private rent regulation still remained, albeit with a different dividing line between their respective jurisdictions since the Rent Act 1974 came into force. This was contrary to most rhyme and reason, and was a fault in the system which was not eliminated till the Housing Act 1980 came into force, as we shall see in chapter 6 of this book.

A circular object

The only clear link between all aspects of administrative law is the overall power of judicial review. But it is difficult to appreciate the full force of this until all parts of the subject have been examined. And it is here that further problems are encountered, for the pattern of the subject is different from most other legal core subjects. In studying the law of contract, it is sensible to proceed by way of an examination of the methods of creating contracts, through the difficulties encountered in the law where mistakes are made or misrepresentations have occurred, to the different manners whereby contracts may be discharged, and the remedies which may be sought by those who suffer through breach of contract. A logical course can also be adopted by the student of the law of torts, in that he can be guided through each of the separate torts one by one, and also examine quite separately the problems of joint tortfeasors and the defences which may be available where an action in brought. Again, in criminal law it is perfectly straightforward to study the subject by taking such matters as the requisite mental element which must be proved in order to obtain a conviction for crime, then considering the various defences open to an accused, and finally by examining each individual crime or group of crimes one by one. In these and many other legal subjects studied the component parts can be clearly mapped out by the textbook writer or lecturer. However intrinsically different the subjects the logical path for the student can be isolated and dealt with in turn. Even in constitutional law the path to be traced by the student is clearly laid out, from general principles, through the legislative, executive and judicial arms of government, the Rule of Law, constitutional conventions, police powers and civil liberties.

But in administrative law, which is in a sense applied constitutional law, no such clear course can be followed. The subject is circular, for no one part of it can be studied satisfactorily in isolation before proceeding to the next. In examining the legislative powers conferred upon administrative authorities it is impossible to avoid referring also to subordinate legislation, and to various different types of administrative authority. Subordinate legislation cannot be studied without considering also the safeguards upon it, including judicial review. The principles of judicial review are difficult to isolate from judicial remedies; and judicial remedies can scarcely be discussed without reference at the same time to tribunal procedures and to extra-judicial remedies. And so it goes on.

Professor Heuston, in his *Essays in Constitutional Law*,[3] writes:

> Nothing is more saddening for the ordinary teacher of law than to examine in constitutional law, for he reads scores of scripts, the authors of which seem to believe one or more of the following fallacies. First, that the government of the country is carried on almost entirely by administrative tribunals; secondly, that these tribunals are governed by, or issue, rules known as 'delegated legislation'; and thirdly, that the task of the Executive is simply to carry out or execute the rules which Parliament has laid down for the government of the country.

These fallacies still persist, and have indeed been added to by, inter alia, the belief that delegated legislation will be void if it is in breach of natural justice, and the conviction that such defective delegated legislation can be quashed by an order of certiorari.

This book does not set out to be an exhaustive treatise of administrative law, nor is it intended to cover even in part all its various topics, or to review all the important case law. It is, however, hoped that by discussing several of administrative law's more important or contentious areas it will be possible to illuminate for the student some of its darker places. The logical development of the subject has been hampered by the endemic lack of consistent doctrine emanating from the courts. Yet it is hoped to be able to show that the inconsistencies have been greatly mitigated in recent years by the work of some judges, and that there is now a clearer path through the law which may be followed. Lord Reid and Lord Denning in particular have been prepared to cut straight through previously equivocal precedents, and to declare in forthright terms what the law should be. They are the most notable of the judges who have shown us the path to be taken for the future, but several others have played

3 At p 164.

important parts in the process. The intention in this book is to signpost this path. Once it is generally recognised by all who must study administrative law it may be that the further development of the law can be smoother and more coherent.

2 Delegated legislation

> But the privilege and pleasure
> That we treasure beyond measure
> Is to run on little errands for the Ministers of State.
>
> Sir W S Gilbert *The Gondoliers*

We have already noted that Parliament is the supreme legislative authority in the United Kingdom, and that for many practical purposes Parliament is controlled by the Government of the day. It is well enough understood, however, that Parliament has insufficient time or expertise to be able to shoulder the direct responsibility for all legislation, and that therefore it delegates legislative authority to other lesser bodies or persons. The fact that the Crown is so much in control of the policy behind most primary legislation means that the repositories of this delegation of legislative power are usually those chosen by the Government and that most important subordinate legislative powers are conferred upon Ministers. Accordingly most of the concern of administrative lawyers about delegated legislation centres round this area of ministerial power, though local authorities and public corporations in particular also possess significant portions of legislative authority.

It is of course open to Parliament, as the sovereign legislature, to confer legislative powers upon anyone it cares. There is no reason in theory to prevent Parliament from granting such powers to the captain of an England cricket team, or to the author of a book on administrative law, though it rarely acts with such eccentricity. Yet as a single example of rarely thought of repositories of delegated legislative power we might take the universities. Under the appropriate Acts of Parliament universities are empowered to make regulations concerning minimum qualifications for candidates who seek admission, syllabuses, examinations, residence, and a whole host of other matters which impinge upon the ultimate objective of the acquirement of an academic degree which is recognised in the world at large as an important qualification for later life. In the case of the University of Oxford these powers have even been exercised so as to regulate the dress to be worn by both senior and junior members of the university for lectures, attendance at examinations and so on. Often the actual regulations made by universities are subject to approval by the Privy Council or some other body, and the actual nature of the powers of each individual university will depend to some extent upon terms of the Royal Charter under which it came into being or was recognised. But the principle remains clear, that the university may, within limits of its own well-recognised area of authority, make rules which will have the force of law, and which cannot be circumvented by those who would prefer to gain a university degree without conforming to the requirements laid down by that university.

But the main types of delegated legislation are local authority byelaws, public corporation byelaws, Rules of the Supreme Court and of such other courts as County Courts, regulations made by the European Commission or the Council of Ministers, and ministerial or department regulations. In practice the most important and most common form of delegated legislation is this latter type, for subordinate laws affecting the whole country will be made by Ministers or their departments, rather than by local authorities or public corporations. Most ministerial regulations are made and designated as such, but some of the most important rules of all are made in the form of Orders in Council, which are intended to be laws of the greatest significance short of actual Acts of Parliament. A number of the regulations made by the institutions of the European Community are also made within the United Kingdom in the form of Orders in Council. As regards the effect in law of delegated legislation no significance attaches to the particular variety of subordinate legislation involved, but there is more importance attaching to the classification when it comes to the safeguards attaching to the m ethod of law-making. Thus local authority byelaws cannot be made by local authorities alone, for they always require in addition the approval of the relevant Minister, normally these days the Secretary of State for the Environment so far as England is concerned. Just as ministerial regulations are the most important form of delegated legislation, so they attract the most solemn form of safeguard in their making, that of the attention of Parliament itself.

Ministerial regulations are designated as 'statutory instruments' by the Statutory Instruments Act 1946, section 1. The Act then goes on to make provision that each such instrument shall be numbered, printed and published and for the laying of statutory instruments before Parliament. A Minister may sometimes certify that certain schedules to an instrument, or other documents referred to in it, need not be printed, usually for reasons of bulk.[1] These provisions apply only to statutory instruments, and not to other possibly lesser forms of delegated legislation; and it is in the provision for 'laying' that the special attention of Parliament is fixed upon each statutory instrument. Yet the 1946 Act does not make the laying process obligatory in relation to all statutory instruments. It is a process which is available for them all, but it will only be required where the enabling Act under which an instrument has been made itself so provides. But today it would be rare for an Act to fail to require an instrument to be laid before Parliament.

Formal Parliamentary safeguards

The Statutory Instruments Act 1946 provides for the process which is to be followed where by any Act a statutory instrument is required to be laid before Parliament. Because the initial qualification for beginning the process of laying before Parliament is thus a matter of what any individual Act of Parliament has itself provided, the possible variations in the actual types of laying before are legion. In particular some Acts provide than an instrument shall be laid in draft before it comes into effect, while others provide that it shall already be complete before laying. Again, although most instruments are to be laid before both Houses of Parliament, a few, notably those concerned with Parliamentary elections, must only be laid before the Commons. There is no reason in theory why an Act should not provide for laying before the Lords only, though no instance of such a provision exists as yet. A particular difference in procedure is brought about by the two main variations in laying before Parliament envisaged by the 1946 Act, namely instruments or drafts of instruments which require an affirmative resolution of either House to permit them to continue in force or to come into force, and instruments which are subject to annulment by either House. Where either this affirmative procedure or the negative procedure is required, there is a period of time, normally forty Parliamentary days, during which the procedure must be completed. If an affirmative resolution has not been passed within the required period, then the instrument either falls or fails to come into being; whereas if a negative resolution has not been passed within that period, the instrument simply continues in force.

There is little point here in going further into the details of the laying procedure itself. But perhaps its most important practical effect

---

1 Statutory Instruments Regulations 1947, SI 1947/1, reg 7.

is to trigger off the now well-organised procedure for Parliamentary scrutiny of statutory instruments. The first committee for the purpose of scrutiny of what were then known as statutory rules and orders, before they gained their modern name by virtue of the 1946 Act, was set up by the House of Lords in 1925, and was called the Special Orders Committee. Its task was to scrutinise and report on instruments requiring an affirmative resolution in the Lords before coming into effect or continuing in force. It was not until 1944 that the Commons set up a committee for the same type of purpose. This was at first called the Select Committee on Delegated Legislation, and later the Select Committee on Delegated Legislation, and later the Select Committee on Statutory Instruments. This was a delayed implementation of one of the recommendations of the Report of the Donoughmore-Scott Committee on Ministers' Powers,[2] which will shortly be discussed. The Select Committee was charged with the duty of scrutinising a wider range of instruments than those subject to the work of the Special Orders Committee, including those which were subject to the procedure of annulment. These two committees were for all practical purposes replaced in 1973 by a new Joint Committee on Statutory Instruments with members drawn from both Houses of Parliament. The new committee has totally replaced the old Lords Committee, but the Commons' Select Committee still remains to deal with those few instruments which require laying before the Commons only.

The function of the new Joint Committee, as laid down by the two Houses, is to consider every instrument laid or laid in draft before either House, in order to determine whether the attention of the Houses should be specially drawn to any instrument for any of the following reasons:

(a) that it imposes a tax on the public;
(b) that it is made in pursuance of an enactment containing specific provisions excluding it from challenge in the courts;
(c) that it purports to have retrospective effect where there is no express authority in the enabling statute;
(d) that it has been unduly delayed in publication or laying before Parliament;
(e) that it has come into operation before being laid before Parliament, and there has been unjustifiable delay in informing the Speaker of the delay;
(f) that it is of doubtful vires or makes some unusual or unexpected use of the powers conferred by the enabling statute;

2 Cmd 4060 (1932), pp 67–69.

(g) that for any special reason its form or purport requires elucidation; or
(h) that its drafting appears to be defective.

It can be seen that the Joint Committee is not concerned with policy, but only with matters of form, though the introduction for the first time in 1973 of the power to consider whether an instrument may perhaps be ultra vires has given this new committee more teeth than its predecessors possessed. Governments and their departments are fully entitled to incorporate their policies in subordinate legislation without fear of crossing the new committee, but the work of the committee is effective in seeing that formal defects are not overlooked. It is, however, a tribute to the work of draftsmen that very few defects are actually discovered by the committee.

Yet, although the Joint Committee is not concerned with policy, the House of Commons, again in 1973, set up a Standing Committee to consider the merits of any statutory instruments and draft statutory instruments which may be referred to it. In recent years this new committee has done more and more work, serving a valuable function in debating issues of policy which have always been outside the purview of the various scrutiny committees. Yet this does not conflict with the requirement that the Government should govern, for the composition of the committee, like that of all Commons committees, ensures that the Government maintains a majority of members. What is achieved is that merits as well as form are ventilated in a committee of the Commons, thus guarding against unforeseen errors and blunders.

In 1974 the Commons set up another committee to deal with related matters, the Select Committee on European Secondary Legislation. At much the same time the Lords created their Select Committee on the European Communities. Both these committees have the task of singling out and bringing to the attention of Parliament the more important legislative proposals within the European Community. The Commons Committee must in any event make a report on Community business to the House at least every six months. The intention is that the two committees should make their views on Community proposals known in sufficient time to enable debates in Parliament to take place before the Council of Ministers makes a final decision on any matter. It does not always work out quite this way, but as time goes on it is likely that the objective will be achieved on most occasions.

At all stages of the study of delegated legislation it is important to keep clearly distinct the enabling Act and the subordinate instrument made under it. But some confusion is apt to arise from the existence of orders which are in a sense hybrid – provisional orders and special procedure orders. Both are forms of subordinate legislation in that they are made by authorities acting under statutory powers, but they are also peculiar in that they can only come into effect after special procedures involving the consent of Parliament. The older form is that of the provisional order which must be confirmed. An Act grants to a statutory authority (such as a local council) the power to make a provisional order after holding an inquiry and considering objections, but this order will not take effect until confirmed by a later Act of Parliament. Confirmation is usually obtained by a Provisional Orders Confirmation Act, designed to confirm several different orders by the one Act. This form of procedure is still used in some instances, but more usually it has been succeeded by the special procedure order, introduced by the Statutory Orders (Special Procedure) Act 1945. This provides a rather more expeditious procedure, dispensing with confirmation by an Act of Parliament. Instead the order takes effect automatically in the absence of opposition, though it is annullable by either House, and any petitions in opposition to it are examined by a joint committee of the two Houses. The essence of both these procedures depends more upon the holding of local inquiries before the orders concerned may take effect than upon the exact nature of the Parliamentary seal of approval. Inquiries will be considered in their own right in chapter 6 of this book.

The processes of laying before and scrutiny by the Joint Committee on Statutory Instruments and other Parliamentary committees, including those concerned with European Community regulations, make up what may be termed the *formal* Parliamentary safeguards in the making of delegated legislation. They are formal both because the actual procedures for bringing these safeguards to bear are laid down, and also because the procedures are intended to be obligatory. Yet one problem which has never yet been squarely faced either by Parliament or by the courts is whether a provision in an enabling Act for Parliamentary supervision in the making of delegated legislation is mandatory or directory. The balance of academic opinion, as can be seen from all the various textbooks on the subject, has always been that such a provision is only directory, and that therefore a failure to lay an instrument before Parliament will not involve the Minister responsible in any penalty or invalidate the instrument concerned. This was directly held to be the position in law by the West Indian Court of Appeal in 1950,[3] but the nearest to a clear decision on the

---

3 *Springer v Doorly* (1950) LRB G 10.

subject in England came with the decision in 1873 by the Court of Queen's Bench in *Bailey v Williamson*.[4]

By the Parks Regulation Act 1872 it was provided that any person who acted in contravention of any regulation made under the Act would be liable to a criminal penalty. It was also provided that any regulation made under the Act was forthwith to be laid before the Houses of Parliament if sitting, or, if Parliament was not sitting, within three weeks after the beginning of the next session, and to be subject to annulment by Parliament. The Act had received the Royal Assent on 27 June 1872, and rules for Hyde Park were made and published on 30 September, Parliament being then not sitting. The appellant was convicted in November of delivering an address in Hyde Park in a manner contrary to the rules. Parliament was still in recess at the time, and the rules had still not been laid before Parliament. Although the judges who heard the appeal thought that it would have been more satisfactory if the Act had distinctly stated whether the rules, if they were made when Parliament was not sitting, were to be operative in the interval from the time they were made to the time when Parliament should next meet, they nevertheless held that the conviction had to be upheld.

On the other hand can be cited an instance of 1944, when the Home Secretary, Mr Herbert Morrison, made some National Fire Service Regulations under the Fire Services (Emergency Provisions) Act 1941, and it was realised that he had not on previous occasions followed the terms of the Act, which had provided that such regulations were to be laid before Parliament 'as soon as may be' after they were made, subject to annulment within twenty-eight days. In fact the Home Secretary had overlooked this provision when making no less than twenty-three different sets of regulations under the Act during the period 1941–44. The National Fire Service Regulations (Indemnity) Act 1944 was forthwith passed by Parliament. Section 1 of this Act, which is in effect the only provision in it, makes interesting reading:

> **1 Indemnity**—The Secretary of State is hereby freed, discharged and indemnified from and against all consequences whatsoever, if any, incurred or to be incurred by him by reason of the said failure to lay before Parliament the regulations specified in the Schedule to this Act as soon as may be after they were made, and those regulations shall be deemed to have been duly laid before Parliament in accordance with the requirements of the statute under which they were made.

This section might possibly be taken to imply that the provision the

---

4 (1873) LR 8 QB 118.

Home Secretary overlooked had been mandatory, but we must bear in mind that the indemnification is only expressed to cover 'all consequences whatsoever, if any'. The most logical argument for the view that a requirement to lay regulations before Parliament is merely directory is that each Act containing such a requirement is specifying internal Parliamentary procedure, and that where this procedure is overlooked it is a matter for Parliament itself to put right, and not for the courts. Perhaps this is one reason why the matter has given rise to no more clear-cut decision in the century since *Bailey v Williamson*. Or perhaps on the other hand it is a tribute to the efficiency of modern Parliamentary safeguards in the making of delegated legislation that the courts have not been called upon to settle any crucial dispute based upon this issue.[5]

It was as a direct result of the Morrison affair that the House of Commons first set up its Select Committee on Delegated Legislation, shortly afterwards renamed the Select Committee on Statutory Instruments. Apparently the Commons in 1944 thought that the creation of such a committee would ensure that similar oversights would be avoided thereafter. Yet the irony is that it could do no such thing. The Scrutiny Committee, as it is so often called, only becomes seised of statutory instruments or draft instruments once they have been laid before Parliament, and it is not its function to draw the attention of Ministers to the necessity to lay such instruments or drafts before the House. It may well be that some Minister in the future may fail to realise his obligation to lay an instrument or its draft before Parliament, and there might then be an opportunity for the English courts to decide whether the statutory instruction involved is mandatory or only directory. But in the meanwhile it is at least curious to reflect that the substance of a recommendation of the Committee on Ministers' Powers concerning the scrutiny of delegated legislation was brought into effect as a direct result of an error on the part of a Minister which concerned a different area of Parliamentary supervision.

The scope of subordinate legislative powers is of course limited by the terms of each enabling statute, but in additional these powers may be further limited by conditions which must be observed if they

---

5 The term 'imperative' is in some decisions used alongside 'mandatory' and 'directory'. Thus, in *Howard v Secretary of State for the Environment* [1975] QB 235, a planning case not directly relevant to our present argument, the Court of Appeal considered that an imperative requirement is one the breach of which is a nullity, a mandatory requirement is one the breach of which is voidable, though such breach may be cured, and a directory requirement is one the breach of which has no adverse effect provided that equally efficacious steps are taken to meet the spirit of the requirement.

are to be validly exercised. Such conditions may be either procedural or substantive. Examples of procedural conditions would be the form in which a compulsory acquisition order must be made and the procedures, including inquiries, which may have to precede the final making of such an order. Although a compulsory purchase order is not such an obvious piece of delegated legislation as is a statutory instrument, the fact remains that the effect of such an order is to bring about a legal result. The compulsory purchase only takes effect after a preliminary procedure designed to safeguard the rights of all parties affected, but once in force the result is to convey the land concerned from one to another; and for the former owner to remain on the land affected or to continue to use it would be a trespass. Thus law has been made.

Political safeguards

In addition to the formal Parliamentary safeguards upon the making of the more important forms of delegated legislation there are other possible Parliamentary safeguards which are inherent in the power of members of either House to ask questions on any subject relevant to the work of a Minister or his department, to call for a debate, and even to move the censure of a Minister or of the Government. It can be appreciated that all these possible aspects of the procedure of Parliament might be used in respect of a wider range of subordinate legislation than just statutory instruments. If sufficient pressure is brought to bear upon a Minister by any of these methods it may bring about a change of policy, and thus in the end be even more drastic in its effect than any of the more formal Parliamentary processes. But here we are on the border of what may be more properly described as political, rather than Parliamentary, safeguards, for after all *any* form of pressure, if sufficiently sustained and influential may cause a change of ministerial or Government policy. Some of the most effective political campaigns on specific issues, such as the siting of an airport or the construction of a relief road, have been waged in the press, on television and by public meetings and petitions, rather than just within the walls of the Palace of Westminster.

Sometimes an enabling Act may require prior consultation to take place before certain delegated legislative powers are carried out. And the accent in the Statutory Instruments Act 1946 upon publication of instruments also gives rise to some publicity, though it may be questioned whether sufficient publicity is achieved under the present law. Before the Statutory Instruments Act 1946, section 12, repealed it, the Rules Publication Act 1893 made it obligatory for prior notice of certain types of subordinate legislation to be given in the *London, Edinburgh* or *Belfast Gazettes,* though perhaps these journals only achieved a limited general circulation. It would probably be difficult to devise a satisfactory system of prior publicity for delegated legislation which would not be either largely ignored (as for example a rule requiring draft instruments to be displayed on notice boards outside town or county halls) or unwarrantably expensive in relation to the result achieved (as by some form of mass circularisation). With the present form of systematic Parliamentary control or supervision of the most important delegated legislation it may be argued that at least the representatives of the people are kept informed of changes in the area of delegated law. It may also be added that trade journals and professional associations are likely to be apprised as soon as possible of developments affecting the trades or professions concerned in any change. Department consultation with affected interests has in any case become the normal practice, regardless of whether it is required by the enabling Act, and this also must achieve a measure of publicity.

Judicial control

Judicial control of subordinate legislation may arise in various ways, but probably it is most usually invoked where a person defends himself against a charge, whether criminal or civil, that he has infringed a rule laid down by delegated legislation. Here the court will be called upon to express its opinion upon the legal validity or otherwise of a particular instrument or regulation. But sometimes the initiative will be in the hands of a party who challenges the legislation, as where he brings an action for damages against someone who has acted in reliance upon the purported subordinate rule. In such a case the plaintiff, in order to succeed in his action, must prove the invalidity of the subordinate legislation. Again, the plaintiff may seek an injunction on the basis of the invalidity of the instrument, or he may seek an order of certiorari against the Minister which, if granted, would have the effect of quashing any order made by the Minister under apparent subordinate legislative powers. The intricacies of the various remedies which may be sought, together with recent reforms in the procedure surrounding these remedies, will be explored in chapter 5 of this book.

In a sense judicial control of delegated legislation will prove to be either wholly successful or a total failure. The basis of judicial control is the doctrine of ultra vires, which is a subject for more detailed discussion in the next chapter, but it is enough for present purposes to state that anyone who challenges the validity of delegated legislation in the courts will only succeed if he can prove that it is ultra vires the enabling Act, and thus void. If the challenged instrument is found by the court not to be ultra vires, then it is intra vires and entirely valid.[6] The point was made in a House of Lords case towards the end of the nineteenth century, *Institute of Patent Agents v Lockwood*.[7] This was a Scottish appeal to the Lords, and was concerned with the interpretation of the Patent, Designs and Trade Marks Act 1888, under section 1(2) of which the Board of Trade was empowered to make rules dealing with the registration of patent agents, such rules to be 'of the same effect as if they were contained in the Act'. The Lords held that a certain set of rules which had been made was intra vires the enabling Act, but certain dicta in the speeches, and particularly in the speech of Lord Herschell LC, seemed to suggest that a provision of the kind in the 1888 Act would preclude all judicial review. Probably the Lords had not intended to go so far, and had only meant to stress the complete validity of the subordinate legislation once it was found to be intra vires.

The *Lockwood* decision was placed in its true context by a later Lords decision in 1930, *Minister of Health v R, exp Yaffe*.[8] There the Housing Act 1925 had conferred powers on the Minister of Health to make orders confirming local authority improvement schemes, with or without modification, and, in section 40, had provided that 'The Order of the Minister when made shall have effect as if enacted in this Act'. Liverpool Corporation purported to make an improvement scheme under the Act, and the Minister made an order approving it with modifications. Mr Yaffe, who was the owner of two houses which were to be compulsorily acquired under the scheme, applied for a certiorari to quash the Minister's confirmation order because at the local inquiry held by the Minister the necessary provisions for the furnishing of plans had not been complied with. The Court of Appeal, reversing the Divisional Court at first instance, unanimously held that as the statutory provisions had not been complied with the purported order by the Minister was not an order at all, and that therefore there was nothing to take effect under section 40 of the Act. The House of Lords disagreed with the finding of the Court of Appeal on compliance with the statutory provisions, and thus reversed their decision and disallowed the certiorari. But they entirely approved

---

6 In certain rare cases, however, the court may sever that part of a statutory instrument which is invalid, leaving the remainder of it as validly in force: see eg *Dunkley v Evans* [1981] 3 All ER 285.
7 [1894] AC 347.
8 [1931] AC 494.

the principle as stated in the Court of Appeal concerning the effect of judicial control of delegated legislation. The Donoughmore-Scott Committee on Ministers' Powers endorsed the view of the Lords in *Yaffe*, and put the effect of the decision as follows:[9]

> The House laid it down that while the provision makes the order speak as if it were contained in the Act, the Act in which it is contained is the Act which empowers the making of the order, and that therefore, if the order as made conflicts with the Act, it will have to give way to the Act. In other words, if in the opinion of the Court the order is inconsistent with the provisions of the Act which authorises it, the order will be bad.

Thus the application of the ultra vires doctrine is really a two-part process. First the purported delegated instrument will be examined by the court to see whether or not it is properly made within the powers conferred by the enabling Act. Then, depending upon the outcome of this examination, the second stage in the process will involve a finding either that the purported instrument is wholly good or that it is wholly bad. If it is found in the first part of the procedure to be intra vires, then it must be accepted by the court as fully valid, and of an effect which is as binding as it would have been had its contents been stated in the enabling Act of Parliament itself. But if in the first stage it is found to be ultra vires, then it will not be worth the paper it is written on, and will be wholly without legal effect.

It is perhaps not surprising that there are few reported cases of delegated legislation being challenged on the ground of ultra vires, for the most important and far-reaching delegated legislation so far as the ordinary citizen is concerned is to be found in the vast body of statutory instruments, and these for over a third of a century have been subjected to fairly stringent Parliamentary supervision when being made. Indeed, as has been seen above, the Joint Committee on Statutory Instruments is now expressly empowered to report upon any possibility that an instrument or draft instrument may be ultra vires. Very few statutory instruments, therefore, are likely to get through the Parliamentary net and still to give rise to any serious doubt as to vires. But the power of the courts to impose their judicial scrutiny always remains, and occasional cases on this subject are reported. One notable such case was *Customs and Excise Comrs v Cure and Deeley Ltd*,[10] a decision at first instance in 1962.

The Finance (No 2) Act 1940 had, inter alia, introduced purchase tax, a predecessor of the modern value added tax, and under section 33 it gave power to the Commissioners of Customs and Excise to make regulations providing for 'any matters for which provision

9 Cmd 4060, p 40.
10 [1962] 1 QB 340.

appears to them to be necessary' for the collection and enforcement of the new tax. This appeared to be very subjective in its terms, and the Commissioners proceeded to exercise their power very widely. In particular, in a set of regulations made in 1945, regulation 12 specified that if any person fails to furnish a return as required by the regulations or furnishes an incomplete return, the Commissioners may determine the amount of the tax appearing to them to be due and demand payment thereof, and the amount so determined shall be deemed to be the proper tax due from that person. The defendant company, which manufactured various metal articles subject to purchase tax, had not submitted complete returns, and the Commissioners determined that a sum of something over £2,600 was due in tax. The company claimed that only about £600 was due, and, in being sued for the balance of the alleged £2,600, raised the main defence that regulation 12 was ultra vires. This was treated as a preliminary point, and the trial proceeded on the basis that if the regulation were held to be valid the courts would be precluded from questioning the actual amount of the tax which the Commissioners alleged to be due. Sachs J decided that the court should approach the problem in two stages. First, it should look at the enabling Act to decide the limits of the powers granted; and secondly, it should then consider such further matters as the reasonableness of the regulations in the light of whether Parliament has conferred subordinate powers in objective or subjective terms, and of all other relevant circumstances. Thus, even though the power to make regulations was granted to the Commissioners in terms which appeared to be very wide, even subjective, the court still retained the jurisdiction to determine the limits of this power. In the event the judge decided that regulation 12 was ultra vires, and that therefore the assessment of tax due in this case was wholly invalid. Accordingly judgment was given for the defendants. Sachs J found no less than three grounds upon which the regulation was ultra vires:[11]

> First, it is no part of the functions assigned to the commissioners to take upon themselves the powers of a High Court Judge and decide issues of fact and law as between the Crown and the subject. Secondly, it renders the subject liable to pay such tax as the commissioners believe to be due, whereas the charging sections impose a liability to pay such tax as in law is due. Thirdly, it is capable of excluding the subject from access to the courts and of defeating pending proceedings. This is a distinct ground that needs to be stated separately not least because there is nothing in the regulation to preclude the commissioners from making a determination

11 [1962] 1 QB 340 at 369.

on a transaction whilst proceedings are pending in the High Court either for a declaration or for the determination of a case stated.

It is clear from *Cure and Deeley Ltd,* and from several other cases, that the courts will adopt a broad approach in considering whether or not delegated legislation is ultra vires. Sachs J specifically referred to considerations of reasonableness, and these will form an important part of our discussion in the next chapter of this book. For the moment it is enough to note that the exercise of delegated legislative power unreasonably, for an improper purpose, or in a way which gives rise to uncertainty will be enough to invalidate it. An instance may be taken from a case dealing with emergency regulation in Northern Ireland, *McEldowney v Forde.*[12] Under statutory authority the then Government of Northern Ireland possessed a wide power to make regulations 'for preserving the peace and maintaining public order', though there was a proviso that the ordinary avocations of life were to be interfered with as little as possible. One of the regulations made under this power made it a criminal offence to be a member of an organisation describing itself as a 'republican club' or of 'any like organisation howsoever described'. The appellant had been convicted of membership of such a club, though no evidence had been adduced that there was any threat to public order involved. He challenged the regulation as being ultra vires. Had he succeeded his conviction would inevitably have been quashed as groundless in law. In the event, however, by a bare majority of three to two the House of Lords decided that the regulation was intra vires, and that therefore the conviction must be upheld. But it was a close thing, for the two Law Lords in the minority, agreeing with the Lord Chief Justice of Northern Ireland below, found that the regulation was too wide in its terms and too vague in its meaning to fall within the enabling power.

Most challenges to the vires of delegated legislation on grounds of unreasonableness, improper purpose or uncertainty probably fail, as where, in *Kruse v Johnson* in 1898,[13] a byelaw making it an offence to sing within 50 yards of a dwelling was held to be valid. But there are a number of challenges which are successful, mostly against delegated legislation which has not had to go through the hoop of Parliamentary safeguards in its making. In *Nash v Finlay* in 1901[14] a local authority byelaw which provided that 'no person shall wilfully annoy passengers in the streets' was held to be void for uncertainty.

12 [1971] AC 632.
13 [1898] 2 QB 91.
14 (1901) 85 LT 682.

And eight years later, in *Arlidge v Islington Corpn*,[15] a byelaw made by the corporation under the Public Health (London) Act 1891 was also held to be void. The byelaw required the landlord of a lodging-house to cause every part of the premises to be cleansed in the month of April, May or June every year. This was in itself a laudable object, but the definitions in the byelaw made it clear that it applied not just to those houses in which landlords were themselves resident, but also to those where they were not, and where they might have no right of entry at all. The Divisional Court held that it would be quite unreasonable to require a landlord to commit an act of trespass in order to comply with the byelaw, and thus the byelaw was bad.

So far the rules whereby the courts enforce the ultra vires principle in respect of delegated legislation are similar to its broader application which will be considered in the next chapter. But there is one special rule which applies to the courts' control of delegated legislation only, and which has no place in the discussion we shall embark upon in chapter 3. This is the rule that a statutory instrument, though otherwise perfectly valid, may be held to be inapplicable in an individual instance where it has not yet been published and has not been adequately brought to the attention of the public or to the notice of the individual concerned in the case. This is perhaps a very rare instance of ignorance of the law proving to be a good defence, and it is certainly exceptional so far as the general run of English law is concerned. The courts take great care to be sure that members of the public are not taken by surprise by statutory instruments,[16] a tenderness not to be found where primary legislation is an issue! Yet the judges will enforce the law contained in a statutory instrument providing suitable steps have been taken to bring the purport of the instrument to the notice of the public, or of the defendant in a criminal case, or of any affected party in a civil suit. Such a case was *R v Sheer Metalcraft Ltd* in 1954,[17] where the accused company and its managing director were charged on indictment with fourteen infringements of the Iron and Steel Prices Order 1951,[18] which laid down the maximum price for various products. This statutory instrument had been printed and published, but the schedules to the Order which specified the actual price limits for the products had not been included in the published Order. As has been mentioned earlier in this chapter, it is acceptable, under the Statutory Instruments Regulations, for a Minister making an instrument to

15 [1909] 2 KB 127.
16 See eg *Jones v Robson* [1901] 1 KB 673, and *Johnson v Sargant & Sons* [1918] 1 KB 101.
17 [1954] 1 QB 586.
18 SI 1951/252

certify that the printing of schedules is unnecessary. But in this case he had failed so to certify. At the trial Streatfeild J directed the jury that (contrary to defence arguments) this failure was not fatal to the prosecution, but that it placed a burden upon the Crown to prove that at the date of the alleged contraventions reasonable steps had been taken for bringing the instrument to the notice of the public or of persons likely to be affected by it. As the jury was apparently satisfied that the steps taken were satisfactory, the accused were found guilty on all counts.

But a case going the other way was *Defiant Cycle Co Ltd v Newell*, decided in the Divisional Court the previous year.[19] There again the problem before the court concerned breaches of regulations laying down the maximum price for articles in the iron and steel industry, though on this occasion the breaches were less serious and amounted to summary offences. The Solicitor-General admitted that the steps taken to bring the unprinted schedules to the attention of the public and of interested parties were less adequate, as copies of the schedules had merely been distributed to the offices of the Ministry of Supply. The appellants had been convicted at first instance by magistrates, but the Divisional Court quashed the convictions. Again the court had no difficulty in disposing of the appellants' argument that the statutory instruments concerned were invalid, but this time the court held that the Minister had not proved that he had taken reasonable steps to bring the purport of the regulations to the notice of the appellants. Accordingly the magistrates had overlooked the fact that the appellants had a good defence to the charges, and the convictions were quashed.

The disquiet about Ministers' powers is allayed

The enormous growth of the use of subordinate legislative powers in the twentieth century has sometimes given rise to a fear that the liberties of the individual are being swamped by the arbitrary use of great and unnecessary powers by Ministers and Government departments. In the 1920s there was something of a general outcry against the broad powers to legislate which Parliament, under the guidance or pressure of the Government, had become accustomed to confer upon Ministers. Even the Lord Chief Justice of the day, Lord Hewart, in 1929 published a book, entitled *The New Despotism*, which was deeply critical of delegated legislative powers and of the pretensions and encroachments of bureaucracy. This book was

19 [1953] 2 All ER 38.

perhaps a trifle rough-hewn and crude in its attack, but it was certainly influential upon the Lord Chancellor, Lord Sankey, who in October of the same year appointed the Committee on Ministers' Powers 'to consider the powers exercised by or under the direction of (or by persons or bodies appointed specially by) Ministers of the Crown by way of (a) delegated legislation and (b) judicial or quasi-judicial decision, and to report what safeguards are desirable or necessary to secure the constitutional principles of the sovereignty of Parliament and the supremacy of the law'. This Committee sat under the chairmanship first of the Earl of Donoughmore, and later of Sir Leslie Scott KC, who went on to become Lord Justice Scott, and it issued its Report in April 1932.[20] We are concerned here only with the effect of the Report upon delegated legislation, and shall consider in later chapters its impact upon judicial or quasi-judicial powers. But the Report is generally regarded as providing a classic account of the history of and reasons for the existence of delegated legislation, as well as suggesting various ways in which the safeguards against abuse of ministerial powers could be strengthened.

The reception of the Report was in a sense rather perverse, for it was generally applauded, and yet only a small number of its positive recommendations for reform were ever directly implemented. It may be that the explanation for this lies in the whole tone and style of the Report. Several distinguished lawyers sat on the Committee, and the Report itself, which was rumoured to have been largely drafted by the great legal historian Sir William Holdsworth, was distinctly legalistic. Accordingly lay Parliamentarians found it heavy going, and it was easier for them to shelve it for the time being: and Reports once shelved are rarely later implemented. The legislative fate of the Donoughmore-Scott Report was notably different from that of the later Franks Committee on Administrative Tribunals and Enquiries,[1] published in 1957, which we shall be considering in chapter 6. The Franks Committee contained a preponderance of non-lawyers, and its Report was non-legalistic in style and tone. Furthermore the Franks Report was published little over a year after the Committee had been set up, while the same Parliament was sitting. The main impetus for the setting up of the Franks Committee had come from the backbenchers in the House of Commons on the (Conservative) Government side, and the same MPs were present to greet the product of their pressure. The Franks Report was thus published on a tide of Parliamentary opinion favourable to reform in the area of its inquiry, and it was small wonder that most of its main recommen-

20   Cmd 4060.
1   Cmnd 218.

dations had been brought into effect either by direct legislation or by changes in administrative practice within a year of its appearance. No such swift legislative endorsement was to follow the publication of the Report of the Committee on Ministers' Powers – and yet criticism of delegated legislative powers and their exercise gradually but surely died down in the wake of its appearance. In retrospect it is easy to see that the appearance of the Report in 1932 was the turning point, and that the history of our delegated legislation contains the paradox of a Report which was largely ignored by the legislators, but which had a profound and lasting effect upon general thought about its subject matter.

The key feature of the Donoughmore-Scott Report was perhaps that it brought to the public notice the fact that there was nothing startlingly new about the exercise of subordinate legislative powers. Examples of statutes containing enabling powers are quoted in the Report going as far back as the fourteenth century, and increasing in frequency until there was an appreciable number of such powers created in the eighteenth century. One instance was the Mutiny Act 1717, which enabled the Crown under sign manual to set up court-martials for the trial of military offenders. The Report also went on to point out that there are important social reasons why subordinate legislative powers should be more numerous in the modern age than ever before. It will be recalled that at the beginning of this book we stressed the vastly increased area of work of modern Governments and Parliaments. The Committee on Ministers' Powers was making a similar point in a different way, and the force of the Committee's argument has been even strengthened in the half century since it was made, for government powers over many aspects of everyday life have been further markedly increased. It is now generally recognised and accepted that subordinate legislative powers are necessary in order to ease the pressure of time in Parliament, and to enable the Government adequately to carry out its duties with sufficient speed and flexibility.

As was again stated in the last chapter, wherever there is a concentration of power it is the business of the law to ensure that there are adequate safeguards against its undue exercise, and the 1932 Report made a number of constructive suggestions for the strengthening of existing safeguards. But the thinking public was far more directly influenced by the reminders from the Committee of the various safeguards which already existed – the ultra vires rule giving rise to judicial control, the provisions in enabling Acts that certain rules or orders should be laid before the Houses of Parliament, and the divers ways in which political action can cause a reappraisal of policy. Although virtually nothing was done immediately after the publication of the Report to implement its positive suggestions for reform, in the course of the succeeding half-century several of these recommendations have eventually come into their own. Thus, as we have seen, the Report's recommendations for the more effective scrutiny of what came to be known as statutory instruments were gradually implemented, first in 1944 largely as a result of an accident, and then in 1973 as a result of possibly more constructive thought. The Committee on Ministers' Powers had built its recommendations upon its discovery of the House of Lords' Special Orders Committee, and had suggested that both Houses should have Standing Committees with wider powers of scrutiny, rather akin to those of the Commons' Select Committee set up in 1944. It is a measure of the failure of Parliament to attempt to implement the actual suggestions of the 1932 Report that no effort was made by the Lords in or about 1944 to widen the powers of the Special Orders Committee to enable it to scrutinise all statutory instruments or draft instruments. Further reform in the Lords had to wait till 1973.

A more glaring failure to heed the detailed views of the Donoughmore-Scott Committee is provided by the total absence to this day of any effort to take up the suggestion that there should be a process of scrutiny, not just of the exercise of delegated legislative powers by Ministers, but also of the creation of these powers. The Committee on Ministers' Powers recognised the essential partnership between Parliament and the Government of the day, and that under the Westminster-type Constitution it is almost always possible for the Government to force its policies through Parliament in legislative form by the use of its Commons majority. This carries with it the danger not just of oppressive direct legislation, but also that Ministers may give themselves virtually autocratic powers, including the powers of legislation. We shall see in succeeding chapters that the courts have felt themselves far from hamstrung when faced with apparently sweeping ministerial powers created by Parliament, but the Donoughmore-Scott Committee considered that a greater effort should be made within Parliament itself to prevent unduly oppressive ministerial powers being created. Accordingly the Report recommended that the Standing Committee to be set up in each House should consider and report not only upon statutory instruments and draft instruments, but also upon Bills which contain any proposals for conferring law-making powers on Ministers. This latter suggestion fell on deaf ears, and has never been picked up since 1932.

It is paradoxical to suggest that a Report has been effective when so few of its actual recommendations were heeded. But it does appear that what was really needed fifty years ago was reassurance that delegated legislation is essential for the proper carrying on of legitimate government, and a reminder and delineation of the safeguards already provided within the law. This was, it seems, enough to allay the fears which were rampant earlier in the century, and there are few now who would feel that the problem areas of English administrative law include delegated legislation, other than incidentally. It is instructive to compare the tone adopted by the late Sir Carleton Allen in the three editions of his well-known book, *Law and Orders*. This book first appeared in 1945, and to some extent it echoed the fears of Lord Hewart's *The New Despotism*, though the criticisms of delegated legislative powers posited by Allen were more measured and reasoned than those of Lord Hewart. Yet by the time Sir Carleton Allen published his second edition in 1956 (and, a fortiori, his third edition in 1965) his fears had been largely assuaged. More remarkable still is the tone adopted by Professor J A G Griffith, a noted critic of many aspects of English law, in his chapter on Constitutional and Administrative Law in *Law Reform NOW*, a book edited by Gerald Gardiner QC (later to become Lord Gardiner LC in the Labour Government which came to power in 1964) and Professor Andrew Martin, and published in 1963.[2] The purpose of the book was to provide a collection of essays by lawyers, all members of the Labour Party, upon different areas of English law, pointing out the reforms which a future Labour Government would be called upon to effect. One might have expected Professor Griffith to produce some radical views, but his section on delegated legislation is only about one-and-a-half pages long, and ends with the following two short sentences:

> Given the assumption that Ministers, in order to carry out their present-day duties, need the power to make subordinate regulations, the only remaining question is whether the safeguards against the abuse of this power are adequate. It is suggested that they are.

It is a bold lawyer who asserts that the state of any one part of English law is perfectly satisfactory, and Professor Griffith should not be taken as suggesting that the system is incapable of improvement. But his reaction is symptomatic of the state of informed opinion as it has progressed since 1932. The Review Committee set up in 1979 by the JUSTICE Educational and Research Trust and All Souls College, Oxford, which will be referred to more particularly in chapter 5 of this book, has included within its terms of reference an examination of whether the procedures for the scrutiny and review of subordinate legislation and administrative rule-making are adequate. Though we still await the Committee's report, it will be of considerable interest

---

2 Page 34.

to find whether this new committee will produce further constructive suggestions in this context. But perhaps it is at least fair to conclude that in this one field of administrative law most of the battles may now be over.

3 Ultra vires, unreasonableness and error of law

> Reason is the life of the law, nay the common law itself is nothing else but reason.
>
> Sir Edward Coke *First Institute*

The primary ground upon which judicial review of administrative action may be based is that the jurisdiction of the authority concerned is defective. Once more, therefore, the issue in administrative law often boils down to one of statutory interpretation. This is at the heart of the doctrine of ultra vires, but the ways in which the doctrine may be invoked are almost unlimited. If a validly created power is exercised by the wrong authority, the latter will have acted ultra vires. Again, if the right authority exercises the power excessively or against the wrong person or in some other unlawful way, then a court may similarly condemn the illegality. And there are countless possible variations. Even though a power is apparently exercised by the right authority, that authority may not have been properly appointed or constituted, or some fact which is a condition precedent to the possession of power may have been absent, or power may have been exercised in bad faith, unreasonably, for an improper purpose, or after taking irrelevant considerations into account. Where an act is shown to be ultra vires the effect is that it is void. Judicial control of administrative action is not only the part of administrative law which most interests lawyers. It is also, and more importantly, the ultimate safeguard for the ordinary citizen against unlawful action by what would otherwise appear to be the more powerful administration.

Ultra vires as the basis for review

It is not yet our present purpose to consider the remedies whereby judicial control may be enforced. But it is desirable at this stage to distinguish between appeal and review. An appeal consists of a re-hearing of all or part of an issue which has already been dealt with at first instance, and results in the substitution for the original decision of a new decision, again upon all or part of the merits. Review, however, is far more basic, and involves the consideration by a court of some aspect of the original proceeding which may rob it of any validity or existence in law at all. The court must examine the fundamental point at issue, rather than any aspect of the merits of the case, and if satisfied that the complaint of the applicant is substantiated it will make an order which carries with it, either directly or by implication, acceptance of the argument that the whole proceeding below was void. It is in this context that the doctrine of ultra vires must be seen, for the assertion that an act is ultra vires is one of fundamental illegality.

Various attempts have been made from time to time to distinguish between different aspects of ultra vires. In an early Irish case,[1] Gibson J distinguished between 'want or excess of jurisdiction when the inquiry begins or during its progress' and 'abuse of jurisdiction (as by misstating the complaint, etc., or disregard of the essentials of justice and the conditions regulating the functions and duty of the tribunal;'. Some portion of Gibson J's second category would seem to come more properly within the rules of natural justice, discussed in the next chapter of this book, and the same may be said of several other classifications used by writers on administrative law. Most textbook writers on the subject have tried their hands at providing at least a description of the alleged boundaries and kinds of ultra vires activity. In the earlier editions of Sir William Wade's *Administrative Law* examples of ultra vires acts were classified according to the nature of the fault. Thus the learned author drew a distinciton between doing the wrong thing, acting in the wrong manner, defects connected with motives, reasonableness and good faith, and defects concerned with jurisdiction over fact and law. But it is noteworthy that in Professor Wade's much-expanded fourth and fifth editions, published in 1977 and 1982, the effort to classify ultra vires activities has been largely abandoned in favour of a rather wider approach. Chapters 8 to 12 of his book now embrace two major parts of the work, and cover Part III on Powers and Jurisdiction and Part IV on Discretionary Power. In these sections of his book Professor Wade provides a comprehensive account of the legal nature of powers, the problems of jurisdiction over fact and law, the problems of invalidity, and then the use and abuse of discretion.

It seems clear that the leading textbook writer in English administrative law has now recognised that there is little to be gained by attempting to classify the ultra vires principle in any rigid way.[2]

1 *R v Mahoney* [1910] 2 IR 695 at 731.
2 The present writer urged this viewpoint in *A Source Book of English Administrative Law* (2nd edn) p 93.

44 *Ultra vires, unreasonableness and error of law*

Whether the fault against which a complaint is levelled is an excessive use of a legal power (thus going beyond the bounds of that power), or whether there never was any such legal power anyway, or whether the power itself was defective, or whatever the reason for holding an activity to be ultra vires may be, the fact remains that what at first sight, or in the eyes of the administrator, may have seemed to be legal is not legal at all, and that it can be set aside accordingly. In many of the cases it is at first sight difficult to determine whether the authority concerned had no power to act or had merely acted in excess of lawful power. If there really was a lawful power at the outset, the effect of a decision that an act is now ultra vires is to say that the authority has stepped beyond that power. It can therefore make very little difference, if any, whether the act be considered as an excess of jurisdiction or as having been taken without any jurisdiction at all.

It is suggested here that it is highly probable that the subtlety with which many writers have tried to analyse the different types of ultra vires activity, or of abuse of discretionary power, has little practical use. The late Professor S A de Smith, in his admirable treatise, *Judicial Review of Administrative Action*,[3] indulged in such analysis to clear and painstaking effect. Yet the judges have rarely followed suit, and customarily they have simply been prepared to treat as a nullity any executive act which, for whatever reason, is lacking in a sound jurisdictional basis. No attempt, therefore, will be made in these pages to distinguish between different aspects of the ultra vires rule, and indeed it may even be suggested that efforts at such distinctions are always a waste of time which is better spent in analysing the particular powers and discretions that have been granted by different statutes and then are called in issue in the leading cases on the subject.[4]

The practical application of the ultra vires principle

A case of seminal importance on this subject is *Associated Provincial Picture Houses Ltd v Wednesbury Corpn*.[5] The plaintiff company were owners and licensees of the Gaumont Cinema in Wednesbury, Staffordshire, and the defendant corporation was the licensing authority for that borough under the Cinematograph Act 1909. The plaintiffs had been granted by the defendants a licence to give performances on Sundays under section 1(1) of the Sunday

---

3 3rd edn, ch 6. A 4th edn of the book was published in 1980.
4 For a different viewpoint see P P Craig *Administrative Law* chs 9 to 11.
5 [1948] 1 KB 223.

Entertainments Act 1932. But the licence was granted subject to a condition that 'no children under the age of 15 years shall be admitted to any entertainment whether accompanied by an adult or not'. Section 1(1) of the 1932 Act provided that the authority may attach to a licence 'such conditions as the authority think fit to impose'. The plaintiffs brought an action for a declaration that the condition was ultra vires and unreasonable, but in the event they were unsuccessful. In the Court of Appeal the judgment of Lord Greene MR, with which Somervell LJ and Singleton J agreed, was remarkable for passages of great clarity:[6]

> What then are those principles? They are well understood. They are principles which the court looks to in considering any question of discretion of this kind. The exercise of such a discretion must be a real exercise of the discretion. If, in the statute conferring the discretion, there is to be found expressly or by implication matters which the authority exercising the discretion ought to have regard to, then in exercising the discretion it must have regard to those matters. Conversely, if the nature of the subject-matter and the general interpretation of the Act make it clear that certain matters would not be germane to the matter in question, the authority must disregard those irrelevant collateral matters. There have been in the cases expressions used relating to the sort of things that authorities must not do, not merely in cases under the Cinematograph Act but, generally speaking, under other cases where the powers of local authorities came to be considered. I am not sure myself whether the permissible grounds of attack cannot be defined under a single head. It has been perhaps a little bit confusing to find a series of grounds set out. Bad faith, dishonesty – those, of course, stand by themselves – unreasonableness, attention given to extraneous circumstances, disregard of public policy and things like that have all been referred to, according to the facts of individual cases, as being matters which are relevant to the question. If they cannot all be confined under one head, they at any rate, I think, overlap to a very great extent. For instance, we have heard in this case a great deal about the meaning of the word 'unreasonable'.
>
> It is true that the discretion must be exercised reasonably. Now what does that mean? Lawyers familiar with the phraseology commonly used in relation to exercise of statutory discretions often use the word 'unreasonable' in a rather comprehensive sense. It has frequently been used and is frequently used as a general description of the things that must not be done. For instance, a person entrusted with a discretion must, so to speak, direct himself properly in law. He must call his own attention to the matters which he is bound to consider. He must exclude from his consideration matters which are irrelevant to what he has to consider. If he does not obey those rules, he may truly be said, and often is said, to be acting 'unreasonably'. Similarly, there may be something so absurd that no sensible person could ever dream that it lay within the powers of

6 [1948] 1 KB 223 at 228.

the authority. Warrington LJ in *Short v Poole Corpn*[7] gave the example of the red-haired teacher, dismissed because she had red hair. That is unreasonable in one sense. In another sense it is taking into consideration extraneous matters. It is so unreasonable that it might almost be described as being done in bad faith; and, in fact, all these things run into one another . . .

In the result, this appeal must be dismissed. I do not wish to repeat myself but I will summarize once again the principle applicable. The court is entitled to investigate the action of the local authority with a view to seeing whether they have taken into account matters which they ought not to have taken into account, or, conversely, have refused to take into account or neglected to take into account matters which they ought to take into account. Once that question is answered in favour of the local authority, it may be still possible to say that, although the local authority have kept within the four corners of the matters which they ought to consider, they have nevertheless come to a conclusion so unreasonable that no reasonable authority could ever have come to it. In such a case, again, I think the court can interfere. The power of the court to interfere in each case is not as an appellate authority to override a decision of the local authority, but as a judicial authority which is concerned, and concerned only, to see whether the local authority have contravened the law by acting in excess of the powers which Parliament has confided in them.

This decision set the pattern for English law which has continued unbroken in principle to the present day. There is no sound basis for a belief that the courts cannot question the way in which a lawfully conferred discretion may be exercised by an administrative authority, and it would today be a fruitless argument in court to assert that there is any doubt about the court's right to set aside an administrative action or decision which amounts to an abuse of otherwise valid power. Yet an attitude of undue respect accorded to the letter of statute law, bred by habitual acceptance of the doctrine of Parliamentary sovereignty, has taken a long time to erase, and the flexible rules for judicial review of administrative action in France have sometimes been compared favourably with what has been thought to be a more rigid English position.

Is the French law of judicial review superior to that of England?

In their admirable book *French Administrative Law*[8] Professors L Neville Brown and J F Garner contrast French administrative law rules

---

7 [1926] Ch 66 at 90, 91.
8 3rd edn, ch 9.

concerned with *détournement de pouvoir* (abuse of power) with the English rule dependent on an application of the ultra vires doctrine. Under the *détournement de pouvoir* rules the French administrative courts may inquire directly into the motives which inspired administrative action. This, the distinguished authors suggest, is essentially subjective and direct, though they conclude that the English courts 'often arrive, by an elaborate process of statutory construction, at a result similar to that which would have been reached in the *droit administratif* by a simpler route'.[9]

Professors Brown and Garner quote many cases in suport of their accurate description of French law. For present purposes one must suffice, the famous case of *Barel*,[10] decided in 1954. The Minister responsible had refused four young men permission to sit the examination for entry to the École Nationale d'Administration, which carries out a training role somewhat akin to the British Civil Service College, though perhaps on a more concentrated and highly organised basis. It had been suggested in a national newspaper that the Government had decided to refuse entry to the examination to any candidates who were Communists, but a short time later the Minister denied this categorically in a statement made in the National Assembly. The young men concerned then referred the matter to the highest administrative court, the Conseil d'Etat, who quashed the Minister's refusal to allow them to sit the examination because he would give no reasons justifying his decision, and it was therefore presumed by the Conseil d'Etat that there were in fact no reasons which would justify such a use of his discretion. If in fact it had been the case, and the Minister had admitted it, that the candidates were refused entry because they were Communists, then the Conseil could have interfered with the exercise of the Minister's discretion as a mistake of law, because he would have violated one of the general principles of French administrative law of freedom of opinion and equal access to the Civil Service. But as it was, the Conseil d'Etat's decision was a clear case of control of the abuse of power, or perhaps, in English terms, review for unreasonableness.

It is of course true and well-known that the French *droit administratif* is a comprehensive body of rules and doctrine, worked out in their own separate system of administrative law courts, whereas in England the ordinary courts have had to do the work of fashioning and enforcing administrative law, and have had to use the same writs, orders and remedies as are employed in the general field of our civil law. Nevertheless English law has been able to respond to the

9 Page 150.
10 CE, 28 May 1954.

challenging prospect of such direct rules providing suitable redress for *détournement de pouvoir* across the Channel. Nor has this been achieved merely by pointing to minor defects of the French system. All legal systems have their defects, and the French *droit administratif* is not immune from this general rule. Dr Carol Harlow[11] has roundly criticised the French system for its delays, amounting to up to three-and-a-half years in the hearing of first instance cases, and up to another two-and-a-half years in appeals to the Conseil d'Etat. She also considers the French remedies to be unduly rigid, and she condemns the Conseil d'Etat's reluctance to order administrative decisions to be suspended pending the hearing of an appeal. But there is little point here in pursuing such criticisms, and in any case the totality of evidence from France suggests that, despite some faults, the system of review of administrative action works generally well. The question at issue is whether the English rules also generally work well for England, despite minor faults. In answer we can put on one side the unfortunate influence of Dicey, already described in chapter 1 of this book; and we can also take with a pinch of salt Lord Reid's assertion, similarly quoted, that 'we do not have a developed system of administrative law', for this same Law Lord has been in the van of those judges who have been developing administrative law principles with great rapidity in the second half of the twentieth century. The prime distinction between France and England in this field lies not in the substantive rules which can be enforced to control the abuse of powers, but in the machinery, the adjective law, whereby these rules may be brought into play. The substance of the English rules revolves round the concept of unreasonableness.

Power exercised unreasonably is void

Lord Greene's judgment in *Associated Provincial Picture Houses v Wednesbury Corpn*, already quoted, asserts that all the various shades of ultra vires activity merge together, and that no clear distinction in principle can be made between them. If an act is obviously outside the letter of the power conferred by Parliament no problem of classification arises. But it would be rare, and anyway fruitless, for an administrative authority to attempt to act in such a way. There are occasional examples. Thus a local authority which had power under a Housing Act to acquire land compulsorily for housing, provided that it was not part of any 'park, garden or pleasure ground', was held to have acted ultra vires where it did in fact

---

11 'Remedies in French Administrative Law' [1977] PL 227.

compulsorily acquire parkland.[12] Similarly, the suspensions and dismissals of workers by a port manager were held to be invalid where it was shown that the London Dock Labour Board, which had the power to suspend and dismiss, had wrongly delegated this power to the port manager.[13]

Much more likely, however, is the inadvertent overstepping of the legal limits laid down by Parliament. Such an instance was *Chertsey UDC v Mixnam's Properties Ltd*.[14] The Caravan Sites and Control of Development Act 1960 gave power to local authorities to grant licences for caravan sites 'subject to such conditions as the authority may think necessary or desirable to impose . . . in the interests of persons dwelling thereon in caravans, or of any other class of persons, or of the public at large'. The Chertsey Council had issued a licence subject to conditions, inter alia, that individual site rents should be agreed with the Council and that no premiums should be charged on incoming dwellers, that the dwellers should be granted security of tenure similar to that under the Rent Acts for controlled tenancies, that the dwellers should be free to choose where they do their shopping, and should not be restricted as to the callers they receive, or in the formation of tenants' or political associations. The site-owner company challenged these conditions as going beyond the powers conferred by the Act, and the House of Lords agreed that this was the case. The Lords held that although the Act conferred apparently very wide powers to impose conditions on site-owners, the conditions must nevertheless relate to the use of any site. Here the conditions actually imposed extended to the contents of the agreements for letting caravans made with individual dwellers, and thus they strayed outside the powers conferred, and were void.

The distinction drawn in *Mixnam* between what is ultra vires and what would be intra vires is fairly fine, and the authority in cases of this type has usually acted in all good faith. But the courts go further when they question the activities of administrative authorities on the basis that they have been unreasonable. Let us examine a few of the leading cases in this century. The 1911 case of *Board of Education v Rice*[15] has a background of complicated religious controversy, and it is representative of the old sectarian strife which has now been eradicated from Great Britain, though, unhappily, not yet from Northern Ireland. Indeed it was the last of the great religious struggles to reach the English courts.

12 *Re Ripon (Highfield) Housing Confirmation Order*, 1938, *White and Collins v Minister of Health* [1939] 2 KB 838.
13 *Barnard v National Dock Labour Board* [1953] 2 QB 18.
14 [1965] AC 735.
15 [1911] AC 179.

Ultra vires, unreasonableness and error of law

The Education Act 1902, now long since repealed and replaced, was an attempt to place provided schools (ie non-church schools provided by local authorities) and non-provided schools (ie independent schools set up and run by religious bodies, usually the Church of England) in the same position as regards standards, maintenance, efficiency and rates of pay of teachers; and the local education authorities under the Act (at that time county and county borough councils, and some borough and urban district councils) were bound by the Act to provide certain funds for the upkeep of non-provided schools and for supplementing the salaries of their teachers. some local education authorities objected so strongly to what they considered an attempt to make them subsidise Church of England schools that they took the extreme step of refusing to obey the Act, though most of them later acquiesced in its observance. The strong non-conformist elements of the Swansea Borough Council, however, persisted in their refusal to obey the Act, and the Council refused to pay salaries to teachers in non-provided schools at the same rate as it paid to teachers in provided schools. Under section 7 of the 1902 Act, the duty of maintaining and keeping efficient a non-provided school was a matter which could be a 'question' between the local education authority concerned and the school managers, and such a question would then be refered to the Board (later the Ministry, and more recently the Department) of Education for decision. The managers of some non-provided schools complained about the Swansea Borough Council's action, and the Board of Education directed that there should be a public inquiry into the complaint. Mr Hamilton KC, later Lord Sumner, was appointed to conduct the inquiry, and he found in favour of the managers, reporting that the local education authority had failed to maintain the schools and keep them efficient. This report was, however, only advisory to the Board of Education, and the Board, despite the report, gave its decision in a document which failed to deal with the matters in issue, which were whether the authority had determined reasonable salary rates for the teachers, and had discharged its statutory duties under the Act. Indeed the eventual decision did not even adopt the findings of the public inquiry which had been favourable to the managers.

The school managers obtained from the Divisional Court a writ of certiorari to remove the Board's decision into the court, and to quash it, and also a writ of mandamus directing the Board to hear and determine the questions which had arisen between the managers and the education authority according to law. This decision was affirmed both by the Court of Appeal and by the House of Lords. All the judgments in the three courts go the same way, though different shades of opinion appear as to why the Board of Education had failed to determine the question put before it. Although all the judges involved took the view that the Board was wrong in ignoring the findings of Mr Hamilton's inquiry, only the Earl of Halsbury in the House of Lords went so far as to say bluntly that the Board had been guilty of acting improperly. Yet it is clear from the context and from a full reading of the case that the decision of the Board was flagrantly wrong, and was known by everyone to be so. The judges were feeling their way cautiously towards implementation of a principle of unreasonableness, but full recognition of it was to await the decision of the Lords in *Roberts v Hopwood* in 1925,[16] and the elegant statement of the principle by Lord Greene in the *Wednesbury Corpn* case, already discussed above.

Roberts v Hopwood is perhaps the most famous of all this line of cases, and it is also an important illustration of the fact that many decisions of the courts concerning possible unreasonable actions of administrative authorities impinge to some extent upon party politics. This is not surprising when one remembers that the Crown in the shape of the government of the day is formed by party politicians most of whom have been elected on a party ticket to the House of Commons, and that increasingly throughout the twentieth century the members of local authorities have also been elected to their positions on party tickets. Accordingly those who object to the activities of central or local government are often at odds with the particular political slant of the authority concerned. Certainly the *Poplar* case, as *Roberts v Hopwood* is generally known, was the creature of party political controversy.

The Poplar Borough Council just after the First World War was dominated by the Labour Party. It was one of the boroughs within the area then covered by the London County Council, though today it forms only a portion of a much larger London Borough created by the London Government Act 1963. In 1920 the Poplar Borough Council, wishing to set an example as model socialist employers, introduced a minimum weekly wage for all their employees of £4 for men and women alike. The previous minimum wage had been a little over £3 a week for men and about £2. 10. 0 for women. The introduction of equal pay for men and women in any sphere of employment was unusual in the early twentieth century, but apparently no issue was taken on this point at the beginning. But in 1921 and 1922 there was a marked fall in the cost of living and of wages generally, something which has not been seen since the Second World War, when unemployment has often gone hand in hand with

16 [1925] AC 578.

inflation of prices and wages. With the fall in the cost of living and wages it was quite normal in many walks of life in the early 1920s for employees to accept a reduction in wages with little demur. But the Poplar Borough Council was determined to stick to its principles as a model employer, and accordingly it continued to maintain its own £4 minimum wage. Now the Council's statutory power was to pay their servants 'such salaries and wages as [they] may think fit', which would appear on its face to be a very wide power indeed. But the district auditor, who must make an annual inspection of local government accounts, disallowed a proportion of the wages actually paid to the employees, amounting to some £5,000 in all, as being an 'item of account contrary to law', and he surcharged it upon the councillors responsible, thus making them personally liable to repay the sum.[17] The House of Lords unanimously upheld the district auditor's order, for they held that Parliament must have intended that in fixing wages the Council should have regard to the labour market. By acting without regard to it, and for extraneous reasons which Lord Atkinson colourfully described as 'eccentric prinicples of socialist philanthropy' and 'feminist ambition', the Council had abused their powers and fixed wage rates which were excessive.

It is unlikely in these politically sensitive times that a Law Lord would today go so far as Lord Atkinson did in his assessment of the motives of the Poplar Council. But even discounting his rather strong language the legal message is clear. The Council had acted with improper motives and unreasonably. The test of these motives was determined by the legislation which was being interpreted. Even though the Act concerned appeared to confer a subjective power to pay such wages as the Council 'may think fit', the Lords were taking the view that a Council could not think fit unless it actually *thought* fit – that is, considered all relevant factors before coming to a considered decision on the basis of all such evidence. before it. It was not enough for a local authority to be high-minded and hope to set a general example for others; it must only act in reasonable accordance with the evidence before it, and by purposely ignoring such a relevant factor as the general level of wages it was stepping outside the boundaries of the discretion granted by Parliament and thus acting ultra vires.

Since the Second World War the stream of case law has been constant, and indeed in recent years it has become more like a flood. In *Prescott v Birmingham Corpn*[18], a scheme for allowing free travel on

17 District auditors no longer have the power to surcharge those responsible for unlawful expenditure: a court order is necessary (Local Government Act 1972, s 161).
18 [1955] Ch 210.

the Corporation buses to old-age pensioners came under fire. The Birmingham Council at that time ran their own buses under Acts of Parliament which empowered the Council to charge 'such fares and charges as they may think fit'. In 1952 the Council resolved to allow free travel on their transport services to all men aged seventy and over, and to all women aged sixty-five and over, who were resident in the city. The estimated annual cost of the concession was £90,000, a loss which would fall on the ratepayers. One of these ratepayers brought an action for a declaration that the scheme was ultra vires and illegal, and the Court of Appeal held that the declaration should be granted. The court held that a local authority owned a fiduciary duty to their ratepayers, and that their statutory authority to run the transport services was authority to run them on commercial lines, even if at a loss, but that it did not entitle them to give subsidies to one class of the community at the expense of another merely for the sake of benevolence or philanthropy. The grant of the concession was not a proper exercise of their discretionary power. The court did suggest that free or cheap travel for children might be perfectly legal, as there would probably be valid commercial reasons for such concessions, but the Council were not at liberty to use the ratepayers' money to inaugurate a new form of social subsidy under the cloak of their transport service. One may speculate upon the generosity of heart of the applicant in *Prescott*, and also perhaps wonder whether the court drew the line in the right place. But, even with these possible doubts, the principle of the decision remains the same as those already discussed. It required the passage of a later Act of Parliament specifically to authorise the granting of the kind of concession attempted so abortively by the Birmingham City Council.

A case very reminiscent of *Roberts v Hopwood* is *Taylor v Munrow* in 1960.[19] The local authority were under a statutory duty to review from time to time the rents charged by landlords of premises which had formerly been held under requisition by the authority, and to subsidise tenants out of the general rate fund where it was considered that the increased rents which the landlords were allowed to charge by law would cause hardship to the tenants. The Rent Act 1957 permitted a general increase in rents, and the Council concerned in this case, the St Pancras Borough Council (another authority which was absorbed by a new and larger borough after the London Government Act 1963), decided as a matter of policy, and without looking at individual cases, to pay higher subsidies to the owners, thus causing all the increased rents brought about by the 1957 Act to be paid from the rates. The reason for the Council's decision was

19 [1960] 1 All ER 455.

a dislike of the Government policy underlying the 1957 Act, and it bore no direct relationship to possible hardship upon tenants. The district auditor disallowed the additional subsidies, and the court upheld his decision to surcharge the councillors responsible with the amount of the increased rents so arbitrarily paid by the Council. The Council had a duty both to the tenants and to the general body of ratepayers. Their statutory discretion to determine rents was not absolute, but one which could only be discharged after due consideration of relevant factors.

On the other hand, in *Pickwell v Camden London Borough Council*,[20] the district auditor failed in his attempt to obtain a declaration that the Council had acted unreasonably, and thus unlawfully, in agreeing to pay its manual workers at a rate considerably in excess of a nationally agreed figure so as to end a strike. Section 112 of the Local Government Act 1972 provided, inter alia, that 'an officer [appointed by a local authority] shall hold office on such reasonable terms and conditions, including conditions as to remuneration, as the authority appointing him thinks fit . . .' The Divisional Court held that a payment would be unlawful if it is one which cannot be justified by reference to the objects for which a statutory power was granted. The court was entitled to make a declaration of illegality only if it was shown that the authority ignored relevant material, was motivated by philanthropic enthusiasm (as in the *Poplar* case), was wholly unreasonable (as in the *Wednesbury Corpn* case), or failed to hold the balance between the conflicting interests of ratepayers, inhabitants of the area and employees. There was evidence that the industrial dispute affected Camden more than other boroughs. The court therefore decided that in the circumstances it had not been shown that the council had ignored the interest of its ratepayers: it had taken into account the matters relevant to the decision and had reached a conclusion on them properly in accordance with the discretion given by statute. Accordingly the declaration was refused.

In the field of planning law, vital in a country so densely populated and so physically small as England, the courts have several times in recent years set aside conditions imposed by local planning authorities when granting planning permission on the ground that they were unreasonable. Of necessity in this account it is possible to give no more than a glimpse of the problem, which was at the heart of the *Mixnam* case, already discussed. But in *Hall & Co Ltd v Shoreham-by-Sea UDC*,[1] a requirement upon landowners that they should construct a strip of roadway along their entire frontage, and give the public a

20 [1983] QB 962.
1 [1964] 1 All ER 1.

right of passage over it, was held to be an invalid planning condition. Again, in *R v Hillingdon London Borough Council, ex p Royco Homes Ltd*,[2] a condition imposed upon a builder that he should let his house to persons on the local authority's housing waiting list was quashed by the Divisional Court as being unreasonable and ultra vires, for it was purporting to make the builder undertake part of the council's own duties as a housing authority. And in *Webb v Minister of Housing and Local Government*,[3] where an urban district council, acting under statutory powers as a coast protection authority, had made a scheme for the building of a sea wall, which included the construction of a promenade behind the wall, and for which land was to be compulsorily acquired, the scheme was held to be invalid by the court because the land to be acquired was not genuinely required for coast protection. Thus the compulsory purchase order was quashed.

The *Padfield* case

A modern case of the very first importance in this field is *Padfield v Minister of Agriculture, Fisheries and Food*, reported in 1968.[4] It did not in fact provide any marked variation from the earlier pattern of case law, nor did it add substantially to the position as already firmly stated by Lord Greene in the *Wednesbury Corpn* case. But it does provide an absolutely clear statement of the court's powers at the highest judicial level, and is totally uncompromising on the nature of these powers of review.

The case concerned the milk marketing scheme for England and Wales. The Agricultural Marketing Act 1958 makes various provisions concerning agricultural marketing schemes, and the scheme involved in the *Padfield* case was only one of a number in existence at the time. Under the milk marketing scheme producers had to sell their milk to the Milk Marketing Board, which fixed the different prices for it in each of the eleven regions into which England and Wales were divided. The Board consisted largely of members elected by the producers in the individual regions, so that each region had equal representation on the Board. Section 19 of the Act made provision for the establishment of a committee of investigation, to be charged with the duty, *if the Minister in any case so directs*, of considering, and reporting to the Minister on . . . any . . . complaint made to the Minister as to the operation of any scheme which, in the opinion of the Minister, could not be considered by a consumers' committee.

2 [1974] QB 720.
3 [1965] 2 All ER 193.
4 [1968] AC 997.

The section then went on to provide:

> If a committee of investigation report to the Minister that any provision of a scheme or any act or omission of a board administering a scheme is contrary to the interests of consumers of the regulated products, or is contrary to the interests of any persons affected by the scheme and is not in the public interest, the Minister, *if he thinks fit to do so* after considering the report (a) may by order make such amendments in the scheme as he considers necessary or expedient for the purpose of rectifying the matter; (b) may by order revoke the scheme; (c) in the event of the matter being one which is within the power of the board to rectify, may by order direct the board to take such steps to rectify the matter as may be specified in the order.

The two phrases which we have italicised above in the statutory provisions are important. At first sight they would seem to give as wide subjective discretionary powers as one could possibly find in an Act of Parliament, and this was certainly the view taken in *Padfield* itself by the Minister. The differentials in the prices paid to the milk producers reflected the varying costs of transporting milk from the producers to the consumers, but the differentials at the time in question had been fixed several years before, since when transport costs had altered. The South-Eastern Region producers contended that the differential between that region and the Far-Western Region should have been altered in a way which would incidentally have affected other regions. But the constitution of the Milk Marketing Board made it impossible for the South-Eastern producers to obtain a majority for their proposals. So they asked the Minister of Agriculture to appoint a committee of investigation under the terms of the Act. Of course had the Minister agreed to do so, and if the committee were to report in their favour, the Minister would have had power under the Act 'if he thinks fit' to give mandatory directions to the Board; and the South-Eastern producers hoped that this chain of results would have followed from their complaint and request.

The Minister, however, declined to refer the matter to a committee appointed under the terms of the Act. The letters from the Ministry which explained his decision not to accede to the request contained references to the wide issues affecting other regions, suggested that the matter should be left to 'the normal democratic machinery', stated that the Minister owed no duty to any particular region, that he has to bear in mind that he would be expected to give effect to the committee's report, and that in any case he had an unfettered discretion whether or not to refer the complaint. Thereupon the producers applied to the court for a mandamus, and the House of Lords, by a majority of four to one, held that the order should be made, directing the Minister to consider the complaint according to law. The Lords expressly held that Parliament had conferred a discretion upon the Minister so that it could be used to promote the policy and objects of the Act which were to be determined by the construction of the Act, and that this was a matter of law for the court. Although there might be reasons which would justify the Minister in refusing to refer a complaint, his discretion was not unlimited. It must be exercised properly and, if it appeared that the effect of his refusal to appoint a committee of investigation was to frustrate the policy of the Act, the court was entitled to interfere.

Lord Reid, who led the Lords in many of their most forward-looking decisions during a period of some fifteen years or so up to his retirement as a Law Lord in January 1975,[5] provided a very clear statement of the problem and of its proper judicial solution.[6]

> It is implicit in the argument for the Minister that there are only two possible interpretations of this provision – either he must refer every complaint or he has an unfettered discretion to refuse to refer in any case. I do not think that is right. Parliament must have conferred the discretion with the intention that it should be used to promote the policy and objects of the Act; the policy and objects of the Act must be determined by construing the Act as a whole and construction is always a matter of law for the court. In a matter of this kind it is not possible to draw a hard and fast line, but if the Minister, by reason of his having misconstrued the Act or for any other reason, so uses his discretion as to thwart or run counter to the policy and objects of the Act, then our law would be very defective if persons aggrieved were not entitled to the protection of the court. So it is necessary first to construe the Act.
>
> When these provisions were first enacted in 1931 it was unusual for Parliament to compel people to sell their commodities in a way to which they objected and it was easily foreseeable that any such scheme would cause loss to some producers. Moreover, if the operation of the scheme was put in the hands of the majority of the producers, it was obvious that they might use their power to the detriment of consumers, distributors or a minority of the producers. So it is not surprising that Parliament enacted safeguards.
>
> The approval of Parliament shows that this scheme was thought to be in the public interest and in so far as it necessarily involved detriment to some persons, it must have been thought to be in the public interest that they should suffer it. But in sections 19 and 20 Parliament drew a line. They provide machinery for investigating and determining whether the scheme is operating or the board is acting in a manner contrary to the public interest.
>
> The effect of these sections is that if, but only if, the Minister and the committee of investigation concur in the view that something is being

---

5 Sadly he died at the age of eighty-four only two months after he retired.
6 [1968] AC 997 at 1030.

done contrary to the public interest the Minister can step in. Section 20 enables the Minister to take the initiative. Section 19 deals with complaints by individuals who are aggrieved. I need not deal with the provisions which apply to consumers. We are concerned with other persons who may be distributors or producers. If the Minister directs that a complaint by any of them shall be referred to the committee of investigation, that committee will make a report which must be published. If they report that any provision of this scheme or any act or omission of the board is contrary to the interests of the complainers *and* is not in the public interest, then the Minister is empowered to take action, but not otherwise. He may disagree with the view of the committee as to public interest, and, if he thinks that there are other public interests which outweigh the public interest that justice should be done to the complainers, he would be not only entitled but bound to refuse to take action. Whether he takes action or not, he may be criticised and held accountable in Parliament but the court cannot interfere.

I must now examine the Minister's reasons for refusing to refer the appellants' complaint to the committee. I have already set out the letters of March 23 and May 3, 1965. I think it is right also to refer to a letter sent from the Ministry on May 1, 1964, because in his affidavit the Minister says he has read this letter and there is no indication that he disagrees with any part of it . . .

The first reason which the Minister gave in his letter of March 23, 1965, was that this complaint was unsuitable for investigation because it raised wide issues. Here it appears to me that the Minister has clearly misdirected himself. Section 19(6) contemplates the raising of issues so wide that it may be necessary for the Minister to amend a scheme or even to revoke it. Narrower issues may be suitable for arbitration but section 19 affords the only method of investigating wide issues. In my view it is plainly the intention of the Act that even the widest should be investigated if the complaint is genuine and substantial, as this complaint certainly is.

Then it is said that this issue should be 'resolved through the arrangements available to producers and the board within the framework of the scheme itself'. This re-states in a condensed form the reasons given in paragraph 4 of the letter of May 1, 1964, where it is said 'the Minister owes no duty to producers in any particular region', and reference is made to the 'status of the Milk Marketing Scheme as an instrument for the self-government of the industry', and to the Minister 'assuming an inappropriate degree of responsibility'. But, as I have already pointed out, the Act imposes on the Minister a responsibility whenever there is a relevant and substantial complaint that the board are acting in a manner inconsistent with the public interest, and that has been relevantly alleged in this case. I can find nothing in the Act to limit this responsibility or justify the statement that the Minister owes no duty to producers in a particular region. The Minister is, I think, correct in saying that the board is an instrument for the self-government of the industry. So long as it does not act contrary to the public interest the Minister cannot interfere. But if it does act contrary to what both the committee of investigation and the Minister hold to be the public interest the Minister has a duty to act. And if a complaint relevantly alleges that the board has so acted, as this complaint does, then it appears to me that the Act does impose a duty on the Minister to have it investigated. If he does not do that he is rendering nugatory a safeguard provided by the Act and depriving complainers of a remedy which I am satisfied that Parliament intended them to have.

Paragraph 3 of the letter of May 1, 1964, refers to the possibility that, if the complaint were referred and the committee were to uphold it, the Minister 'would be expected to make a statutory Order to give effect to the committee's recommendations'. If this means that he is entitled to refuse to refer a complaint because, if he did so, he might later find himself in an embarrassing situation, that would plainly be a bad reason. I can see an argument to the effect that if, on receipt of a complaint, the Minister can satisfy himself from information in his possession as to the merits of the complaint, and he then chooses to say that, whatever the committee might recommend, he would hold it to be contrary to the public interest to take an action, it would be a waste of time and money to refer the complaint to the committee. I do not intend to express any opinion about that because that is not this case. In the first place it appears that the Minister has come to no decision as to the merits of the appellants' case, and secondly, the Minister has carefully avoided saying what he would do if the committee were to uphold the complaint.

It was argued that the Minister is not bound to give any reasons for refusing to refer a complaint to the committee, that if he gives no reasons his decision cannot be questioned, and that it would be very unfortunate if giving reasons were to put him in a worse position. But I do not agree that a decision cannot be questioned if no reasons are given. If it is the Minister's duty not to act so as to frustrate the policy and objects of the Act, and if it were to appear from all the circumstances of the case that that has been the effect of the Minister's refusal, then it appears to me that the court must be entitled to act.

It has been thought right to quote at some length from the speech of Lord Reid because he stated simply and clearly the real problem which is at issue whenever there is an allegation that an administrative authority has acted unreasonably. It is also of note that he did so by way of an exercise in legal logic, rather than by laborious reference to previous case law. Only Lord Morris of Borth-y-Gest dissented in *Padfield*, while Lords Hodson, Pearce and Upjohn all delivered speeches concurring with Lord Reid. The real core of the decision is the rejection of the whole idea of an unfettered discretion. As has been seen, Lord Reid went so far as to say that it was wrong to suggest that a Minister's decision could not be questioned if he gave no reasons, and that any reasons he did give could in any case be examined by the court because it was the duty of the Minister not to act so as to frustrate the policy and objects of the Act. Lord Upjohn went on to say that the introduction of the adjective 'unfettered' in relation to discretion was an unauthorised gloss upon the statute by the Minister, and that in any case it would probably not even have made any difference to the essential powers of the court if the word had been inserted into the Act by the draftsman! Lord Upjohn ended his speech with these words.[7]

> [A] decision of the Minister stands on quite a different basis; he is a public officer charged by Parliament with the discharge of a public discretion affecting Her Majesty's subjects; if he does not give any reason for his decision it may be, if circumstances warrant it, that a court may be at liberty to come to the conclusion that he had no good reason for reaching that conclusion and order a prerogative writ to issue accordingly.
>
> The Minister in my opinion has not given a single valid reason for refusing to order an inquiry into the legitimate complaint (be it well founded or not) of the South-Eastern Region; all his disclosed reasons for refusing to do so are bad in law.

In decisively rejecting the notion of an unfettered discretion the House of Lords had concluded that the Minister had failed to carry out his duty according to law to determine whether or not to direct that the complaint be investigated by the committee under the terms of the Act. The case was thus remitted to the Queen's Bench Division with a direction to require the Minister to consider the complaint according to law. But, as has been seen from the extract from Lord Reid's speech, the Lords clearly envisaged that it would still be possible and legal, even after reference of the complaint to the committee, and even if the committee reported in favour of the complainant, for the Minister to take the view that there are other public interests which outweigh the public interest that justice should be done to the complainants, and therefore to refuse to implement the committee's report. In the event this is what happened. The second time round the Minister referred the complaint to the committee of investigation, which duly reported in favour of the complainants. The Minister, however, then refused to take any further action in the way of making a mandatory order to the Milk Marketing Board. This latter exercise of discretion was not challenged further, so we shall never know whether there might have been grounds for alleging that the Minister was still abusing his discretion. But the distinction drawn by the House of Lords shows that an Act of Parliament may confer different levels of discretionary power, and that the standard or reasonableness may vary according to the particular discretion and the context within which it is granted.

Regardless of the final rebuff for the complainants, the actual

---

7 [1968] AC 1062.

decision of the Lords provides the strongest possible afforcement for the principle of judicial review upon the basis of unreasonable administrative activity, or abuse of power. In one sense the decision in *Padfield* does no more than reinforce and restate the powers of the courts which they have always possessed and frequently expressed since the days of Coke.[8] But Sir William Wade was surely right, in a comment on *Padfield*, when he wrote that 'English law can now match the Conseil d'Etat's famous decision in *Barel*',[9] and that 'No Conseil d'Etat, surely, could do better than their Lordships on this occasion'.[10] Perhaps the last word on the case may go to Lord Denning MR who three years later said:[11]

> The discretion of a statutory body is never unfettered. It is a discretion which is to be exercised according to law. That means at least this: the statutory body must be guided by relevant considerations and not by irrelevant. If its decision is influenced by extraneous considerations which it ought not to have taken into account, then the decision cannot stand. No matter that the statutory body may have acted in good faith; nevertheless the decision will be set aside. That is established by *Padfield v Minister of Agriculture, Fisheries and Food* which is a landmark in modern administrative law.

Padfield was followed by the Court of Appeal in *British Oxygen Co Ltd v Board of Trade*,[12] though the actual decision in that case was reversed by the Lords on a different point.[13] In *H Lavender & Son Ltd v Minister of Housing and Local Government*,[14] the question at issue was whether the Minister[15] was entitled to refuse planning permission on the ground that it was his policy that certain land should not be released for mineral working unless the Minister of Agriculture was not opposed to the working. Willis J held that although the Minister was entitled to have a policy and to decide a planning appeal in the context of that policy, a true construction of the Minister's decision letter, in which he dismissed the appeal, was that the decision, while purporting to be his own, was in fact, and improperly, that of the Minister of Agriculture. Accordingly he had failed to exercise a proper or indeed any discretion by reason of the fetter he had imposed upon its exercise. This decision is directly in line with the reasoning

---

8 *Rooke's Case* (1958) 5 Co Rep 99b.
9 (1968) 84 LQR at 168.
10 Ibid at 167.
11 *Breen v Amalgamated Engineering Union* [1971] 2 QB 175 at 190.
12 [1969] 2 Ch 174.
13 [1971] AC 610.
14 [1970] 3 All ER 871.
15 The Ministry of Housing and Local Government was shortly afterwards abolished and replaced by the Department of the Environment, with a Secretary of State.

in *Padfield*, and so is that in *Daymond v South West Water Authority*,[16] where the charges for services, etc, 'as they think fit', empowered those authorities to make charges only to those who actually used the services provided. Thus, payment of sewerage charges could not lawfully be required of persons whose premises were not connected to the main drainage system. An interesting sequel to this latter case was the passage by Parliament of the Water Charges Act 1976, providing for the refund of charges improperly made in 1974–75 and 1975–76, the years during which sewerage charges were first levied separately from general rates. The Act did not attempt to alter the principle of the *Daymond* decision, and it can be considered as an example of Parliament accepting the power and essential validity of judicial review.

Any pessimism about the weakness of English rules of judicial review is unwarranted. English law in its own peculiar way is as capable of protecting the individual from abuse of power as is the more concentrated and specialist *droit administratif* of France. It is essential to the upholding of the Rule of Law that the courts should maintain their authority in this field, and *Padfield* and succeeding cases show that this authority cannot be doubted. It should be not only lawyers who will welcome the stand on principle which the courts have taken, for all citizens should be happier that the final safeguarding of the people's rights remains in the hands of the judges rather than in those of elected politicians.[17] Let us now trace some of the most recent developments in this field.

Television licences, Skytrain, and the schools cases

At the beginning of 1975 the annual cost of a colour television licence was £12, but in March the Government announced that it would be increased by 50 per cent to £18 with effect from 1 April, and actually effected the increase by a statutory instrument, SI 1975/212. Now, as is well known, licences for television sets, as for motor vehicles, always expire at the end of a calendar month, so that a licence first taken out on, say, 15 March would actually run from 1 March till the succeeding 28 February (or 29), and one taken out on 23 April would run legally from 1 April till the succeeding 31

16 [1976] AC 609.
17 A discordant, but it is submitted misguided, note is struck by Professor J A G Griffith in his Pritt Memorial Lecture 'Administrative Law and the Judges' Haldane Society (1979) where he castigates the courts for telling Ministers they have acted wrongly in taking policy decisions on grounds disapproved by the courts. He characterises this as 'conceptual insanity'.

March. The Government had doubtless envisaged that all those whose television licences were to expire on 31 March after the announcement of the increase would dutifully go along to the Post Office and take out new licences starting on 1 April at the greatly increased fee. But they had reckoned without the resourcefulness of licence-holders faced with such a steep increase. The statutory instrument gave no power to charge the increased fee before 1 April, nor did it restrict the right to take out a £12 licence in March. Accordingly astute licence-holders anticipated the increase by taking out new licences at the old rate in the course of March, being prepared if necessary to jetison the last month or so of the running of their old licences in order to save at least a portion of the extra £6 which would otherwise have had to be paid from the beginning of April. The Home Office tried to stop the issue of licences in March to existing licence-holders, in order to compel such applicants to pay the full £18 in April. But they were too late to prevent some 20,000 licence-holders obtaining a £12 licence before this increase took effect. What the licence-holders had done was perfectly lawful, and there had been a fair amount of publicity given by the press to this legal loophole.

Now section 1(2) of the Wireless Telegraphy Act 1949 provided that 'A licence . . . may be issued subject to such terms, provisions and limitations as the [Minister] may think fit.' Section 1(4) provided that a licence 'may be revoked . . . by a notice in writing served on the holder . . .'. Once the Home Office had become aware of the successful anticipation of the increased fee they sent out thousands of letters to those who had acquired the new £12 licences demanding an extra £6 from each such licence-holder, under threat that otherwise the licences would be totally revoked. Later letters were also sent out, modifying the original threat by saying that the revocation of the licences would take place after they had run for eight months, thus making them accord with the increased fee. Mr Congreve, a City of London solicitor, was one of those who had successfully anticipated the licence fee increases, and he sought a declaration that revocation of the licence would be unlawful. In fact many of those who had obtained their licences in March had already conformed to the requirement of the Home Office that they should pay the extra £6, but Mr Congreve was representative of about 5,000 recalcitrants who refused to do so, and in the event their stubbornness was rewarded by the Court of Appeal.

In *Congreve v Home Office*,[18] it was held that, although the Home Secretary has an undoubted discretion under section 1(4) of the

[18] [1976] QB 629.

Wireless Telegraphy Act to revoke a television licence, that discretion is fettered to the extent that the courts will intervene if it is exercised arbitrarily and improperly. In this case the Home Secretary's action in demanding the extra fee under threat of revocation of the licence was held to be unfair, unjust and unlawful. A complication in the case was provided by the fact that a complaint was also made to the Parliamentary Commissioner, whose place in the law will be discussed more fully in chapter 7 of this book. In a special report the Commissioner had already condemned the conduct of the Home Secretary as maladministration.[19] As we shall see in chapter 7, the Commissioner is not supposed to investigate complaints where there is a legal remedy available in a court or other tribunal,[20] unless he thinks it is not reasonable to expect the legal remedy to be used. An action for a declaration is of course a legal remedy, and it was eminently suitable for use in *Congreve's* case, for a declaration that the Minister's action was unlawful would mean that it was void and of no effect. Nevertheless the Parliamentary Commissioner made his report and condemned the Home Secretary's action. The fact that he had so reported did not appear to inhibit the Court of Appeal in any way. As Lord Denning MR said:[1]

> The conduct of the Minister, or the conduct of his department, has been found by the Parliamentary Commissioner to be maladministration. I go further. I say it was unlawful. His trump card was a snare and a delusion. He had no right whatever to refuse to issue an overlapping licence, or, if issued, to revoke it. His original demand, 'Pay £6 or your licence will be revoked', was clearly unlawful – in the sense that it was a misuse of power – especially as there was no offer to refund the £12, or any part of it. His later demand, 'Pay £6 or your licence will be revoked after eight months', was also unlawful . . . The licence is granted for twelve months and cannot be revoked simply to enable the Minister to raise more money. Want of money is no reason for revoking a licence. The real reason, of course, in this case was that the department did not like people taking out overlapping licences so as to save money. But there was nothing in the Regulations to stop it. It was perfectly lawful: and the department's dislike of it cannot afford a good reason for revoking them.

Among the battery of arguments levelled by the court against the Home Secretary's abuse of power was the very strong point that the attempt to levy the extra £6 from the licence-holders was no less than an attempt to levy money for the use of the Crown without the authority of Parliament. It was thus contrary to the Bill of Rights 1688, and the Court of Appeal expressly followed *A-G v Wilts United*

19 HC 1974–75, No 680.
20 Parliamentary Commissioner Act 1967, s 5(2).
1   [1976] QB 629 at 652.

Dairies[2] on this point. But perhaps the most bizarre incident in the case occurred when Mr Roger Parker QC (later Parker LJ), acting for the Home Office, said in the course of his submissions that, if the court interfered with the exercise of discretion by the Home Office, it would not be long before the powers of the court would be called in question. In his judgment Lord Denning said that the court trusted that this was no more than a piece of advocate's licence, and not meant seriously. Apparently there had been no intention on the part of the Crown to threaten the court, for Mr Parker apologised at length for what he had said at the next sitting of the court.[3]

Another important decision of the Court of Appeal was *Laker Airways Ltd v Department of Trade*.[4] A United Kingdom operator wishing to operate a commercial civil air service between the United Kingdom and the United States had to satisfy three conditions under the law in force at that time. First he had to be granted an air transport licence by the Civil Aviation Authority, under section 22 of the Civil Aviation Act 1971. This Authority is an independent body, whose function is to grant or revoke such licences, after consideration of 'guidance' issued by the Department of Trade. Secondly, he had to be designated by the Department of Trade as an air carrier for the specified route between the two countries, under the Bermuda Agreement 1946, which was a bilateral agreement on the regulation of air transport services between the two countries made pursuant to the Chicago Convention 1944. And thirdly, after both the first two conditions had been satisfied, he had to gain the reciprocal operating permission from the United States authorities. Laker Airways was already a flourishing independent airline, under the chairmanship of the ebullient Mr (now Sir Freddie) Laker. Mr Laker was very anxious to expand the business of his airline by breaking into the lucrative North Atlantic air travel market, and furthermore he planned to undercut the artificially high fares charged, by common agreement, by the airlines currently working these routes. Laker Airways obtained a licence from the Civil Aviation Authority in 1972 for a cheap passenger air service to be called Skytrain between London and New York. He then obtained the required designation from the Secretary of State for Trade and Industry as an air carrier for the specified route. There was at the time a Conservative Government with its belief in free enterprise, and the Government was clearly quite content thereafter to help exert pressure upon the United States authorities to overcome the third of the hurdles facing

2 (1922) 91 LJKB 897.
3 See [1976] QB 629.
4 [1977] QB 643.

Laker Airways. The Government had in fact worked closely with Laker Airways in the planning of the new service, and partly in reliance upon this encouragement Laker Airways spent over £6 million on the project.

In early March 1974, however, the Government resigned after failing to maintain a majority in the Commons as a result of the General Election on 28 February, and the Labour Party returned to power. After at first appearing to continue his predecessor's policy, the new Secretary of State in 1975 announced a change in policy, and decided that no more than one United Kingdom airline should be licensed for any given long-haul route. The Secretary of State then instructed the Civil Aviation Authority in the form of 'guidance' that it should revoke the plaintiff's licence, and he withdrew the designation for the London–New York route. Laker Airways promptly sought declarations (1) that the new guidance was ultra vires, (2) that the defendants were not entitled to cancel the designation until the termination of the Bermuda Agreement or the lawful revocation or termination of the plaintiffs' licence, whichever was the earlier, and (3) that the defendants were estopped from cancelling the designation. The case was complicated by the fact that the Crown's power in this field was drawn partly from statute and partly from prerogative. The prerogative power is discretionary, and is exercisable by the Crown in certain areas where statute makes no other provision. The prerogative power includes that of requisitioning of property in time of war for the defence of the realm, and of making treaties with foreign powers. Where power is exercised by prerogative the courts have no authority to curtail it except in so far as statute may have curtailed the area of prerogative power or have set boundaries for it. Here the Bermuda Agreement was entered into by the Crown as part of the prerogative power to make treaties, and the Crown now maintained that the power of the Secreatry of State to withdraw the designation of Laker Airways was also part of the prerogative, and thus outside the cognizance of the courts.

At first instance Mocatta J granted the declarations asked, holding (1) that the guidance was ultra vires in so far as it purported to deprive the Civil Aviation Authority of its statutory function of granting and revoking licences, (2) that the defendants were not entitled to withdraw the designation under the Bermuda Agreement at will, as the Civil Aviation Act 1971 impliedly fettered the prerogative power of the Crown to do so, and (3) that the defendants were in any case estopped by their previous conduct (the conduct of the previous Government and Secretary of State) from withdrawing the designation in this particular case. Although the Court of Appeal disagreed with the third part of Mocatta J's judgment, for they held that successive governments must be permitted to change their policy, and that estoppel could not therefore be used to prevent such a change, they upheld the decision on the first two grounds. As Lord Denning MR concluded.[5]

> We have considered this case at some length because of its constitutional importance. It is a serious matter for the courts to declare that a minister of the Crown has exceeded his powers. So serious that we think hard before doing it. But there comes a point when it has to be done. These courts have the authority – and I would add, the duty – in a proper case, when called upon to inquire into the exercise of a discretionary power by a minister or his department. If it is found that the power has been exercised improperly or mistakenly so as to impinge unjustly on the legitimate rights or interests of the subject, then these courts must so declare. They stand, as ever, between the executive and the subject, alert, as Lord Atkin said in a famous passage – 'alert to see that any coercive action is justified in law': see *Liversidge v Anderson*.[6] To which I would add, alert to see that a discretionary power is not exceeded or misused. In this case the judge has upheld this principle. He has declared that the minister did exceed his powers. I agree with him.

So Mr Laker got his declarations, and rather than appeal further to the Lords the Secretary of State accepted this decision. The subsequent success of Skytrain was such that not only did Laker Airways flourish and build upon their services, but other airlines too were freed to reduce their international fares in order to remain competitive. The public interest thus appeared to have been served by the decision in the *Laker* case, though the eventual very keen competition between many airlines to produce the most attractive fares for passengers was a prime cause of the bankruptcy in 1982 of Laker Airways itself.

Laker Airways was no isolated instance of judicial control over this type of direct goverment exercise of discretion, nor is the English rule much different from that to be found in many other common law countries. For example, one may take the famous Canadian case of *Roncarelli v Duplessis*,[7] Duplessis was Prime Minister and Attorney-General of the province of Quebec, and he had ordered the Quebec Licensing Commission to revoke Roncarelli's liquor permit. The reason for his order was that Roncarelli had in over 380 cases acted as surety for Jehovah's Witnesses who had been charged wth distributing literature, some of which was thought to be seditious, without a licence. The Commission had revoked the permit, and indeed the discretion to so revoke such a permit was within the

5 [1977] QB 643 at 707.
6 [1942] AC 206 at 244.
7 (1959) 16 DLR (2d) 689.

powers of the Commission. But there was ample evidence that the revocation was the direct result of the instruction given by the respondent. Mr Duplessis actually stated at a press conference referred to in the report of the case that: 'It was I, as Attorney-General of the Province charged with the protection of good order, who gave the order to annul [Roncarelli's] permit. By so doing not only have we exercised a right but we have fulfilled an imperious duty. The permit was cancelled not temporarily but definitely and for always.' The Canadian Supreme Court held the revocation to be unlawful on the ground that the Commission had acted under dictation, and that it was a gross abuse of legal power expressly intended to punish Roncarelli for an act wholly irrelevant to the statute.

Probably the most overtly political of recent cases has been *Secretary of State for Education and Science v Tameside Metropolitan Borough Council*,[8] at the centre of which was that well-known political football, comprehensive education. Many may regret that the subject of children's education has become a matter for party controversy, but a moment's thought should show that all important public issues are bound to be the subject of party politics in a working democracy. Governments and oppositions must of necessity formulate their views upon such issues, and when in power attempt to bring them to fruition. In this sense education is no less political an issue than hospitals, industrial relations, foreign policy, defence and the welfare state, and we should not expect it to be.

It may be recalled from chapter 1 that the present-day local authorities in England and Wales, outside London, were created by the Local Government Act 1972, and that under that Act six metropolitan areas came into being. One of these metropolitan counties is Greater Manchester, and one of the constituent districts within that metropolitan county is Tameside. In the first elections for the new Tameside Metropolitan Borough Council, held in 1973, the Labour Party gained power, and they ruled in Tameside from the coming into effect of the 1972 Act in April 1974 until the next local elections for the district in May 1976. It had been the declared policy of the Labour Government which was in power nationally between 1964 and 1970 that the system of selection of entrants on the basis of ability for schools in the public sector[9] should be replaced over a period of time, by what has come to be known as the comprehensive education system, ie a system in which all children regardless of ability enter the same school for the area. Within such

8 [1977] AC 1014; cf *R v Secretary of State for the Environment, ex p Norwich City Council* [1982] QB 808.
9 There has never been any effort made to force such a change upon the schools in the private sector, often called preparatory and 'public' schools.

a school there may often be 'streaming' of pupils into ability ranges, but the essential difference between the comprehensive system and the selective system is that the former, unlike the latter, does not have in it different *schools* for different abilities. Under the selective system it was customary for boys and girls, after their initial few years at a primary school, to progress to grammar schools for the academically able, secondary modern schools for those less able, and secondary technical schools for those with aptitudes in the technical fields. Under the comprehensive system, however, there would tend to be much larger schools at the secondary stage catering for all ranges of ability. Obviously a change-over on a national scale to an entirely different system, involving the closing of some schools, the building and opening of others, and the merging of some, often after extensive structural alteration or addition, would be costly and time-consuming, and the Labour Government did not envisage it taking place overnight. In any case education is a direct responsibility of local, not central, government, albeit with significant support from central funds, and subject to central approval and inspection etc. Accordingly the central government could at first only encourage local education authorities to take steps to change their system in accordance with Government policy. All local plans to change over to comprehensive education had to be submitted to the Secretary of State for approval, and could only be implemented after such approval, as required by the Education Act 1944, section 13.

Perhaps inevitably the issue of comprehensive education was from its outset controversial, both on educational and on political grounds. Many parents have strong views upon how their children should be educated; educationalists have long been split upon the merits of all or part of the philosophy and practice of comprehensive education; and party politicians have often taken up stances opposed to each other on at least the details of the scheme. Broadly speaking, the Labour Party and the Liberal Party have favoured the change to fully comprehensive schooling, while the Conservative Party, though accepting the principle of equal opportunity for all children in education, has opposed the compulsory introduction of comprehensivisation against the declared wishes of individual local authorities or groups of parents. Many local authorities of varying political complexions fell in with the wishes of the Government, and in course of time introduced comprehensive schooling, though often with local variations. Not untypical of the type of variation was that adopted by the old Oxford County Borough Council in 1967 (and later maintained by the new Oxfordshire County Council) which retains two single-sex comprehensive schools alongside the coeducational ones. The present author, while at the time a University member of the old council, had the honour of seconding the introduction of that scheme.

When the Conservatives returned to power nationally in 1970 the pressure upon local authorities to 'go comprehensive' became less intense, though it should not be overlooked that the new Conservative Government continued the general encouragement to local authorities to make the change. When Labour returned to power nationally in 1974 the encouragement once more became pressure. The Tameside Council had authority in an area which included not only the usual ration of primary schools and secondary modern and technical schools, but also no less than five grammar schools, some of which had over the years achieved a high national reputation. It is therefore not surprising that the prospect of comprehensive education, involving the abolition of the prestige grammar schools, should be a matter of hot local controversy. The Labour-dominated Council elected in 1973 prepared plans for full comprehensivisation of Tameside, and submitted the proposals to the Secretary of State in March 1974. They were approved in November 1975. The Council then became entitled to implement the scheme, but were under no legal duty to do so. They determined to implement the scheme at the beginning of the school year in September 1976, and this decision became a major local issue at the local elections in May 1976. The Conservatives campaigned on a platform which included opposition to the full details of the comprehensive education plan, and in particular to the proposed phasing out of the grammar schools and their conversion to comprehensive schools. 1976 was a good local election year for the Conservatives, and they gained control of the Tameside Council by a decisive margin.

The new Council claimed to have a mandate to reconsider its predecessor's comprehensive education scheme, and they proposed to modify the scheme by retaining the existing grammar schools, but allowing completion of three comprehensive schools in the course of construction. The council wrote to inform the Secretary of State of this decision on 7 June. The immediate result was that the Secretary of State (Mr Mulley) wrote to the Council on 11 June directing them to implement the original scheme in full. Now this direction was made under section 68 of the Education Act 1944. The 1944 Act was the great charter of public education passed by Parliament during the Second World War, when R A (later Lord) Butler was Minister of Education, as the post was then called. The Act is still very largely in force, though it has been amended from time to time, and section 68 provides:

> If the Secretary of State is satisfied . . . that any local education authority

... have acted or are proposing to act unreasonably with respect to the exercise of any power conferred or the performance of any duty imposed by or under this Act, he may ... give such directions as to the exercise of the power or the performance of the duty as appear to him to be expedient.

Then, only a week after giving his direction, the Secretary of State applied for an order of mandamus to compel the Council to comply with his direction. This was granted by the Divisional Court of the Queen's Bench Division, but refused by a unanimous Court of Appeal and then by a unanimous House of Lords.

Apart from the cases already discussed in this chapter, all of which except *Laker Airways* and *Pickwell* came before the courts prior to *Tameside*, there had in recent years been a host of decisions which together had virtually disposed of the old heresy that the conferment by Parliament of a discretion upon a Minister without any express limitation placed upon it in the Act would give the Minister a subjective power. Whatever the phrase used in the statute the result had always been the same, that the exercise of the discretion must be open to objective scrutiny in the courts. Even as early as 1937 the phrase 'whenever it appears to the board' was so interpreted by the Privy Council in *Estate and Trust Agencies (1927) Ltd v Singapore Improvement Trust*.[10] The same treatment was accorded to '[as the Minister] in his discretion may determine', in *Minister of National Revenue v Wrights' Canadian Ropes Ltd* in 1947,[11] and to 'if the Minister is satisfied' in *Maradana Mosque Trustees v Mahmud* in 1967.[12] It is therefore not all that surprising that there was little attempt made to argue in *Tameside* that 'if the Secretary of State is satisfied' gave him a wide discretion to make directions according to his own subjective view of the issue at stake. What is perhaps more striking, however, is not that the jurisdiction of the court was taken for granted, but that the Law Lords made virtually no effort to assemble authorities to justify their unanimous decision. Only three cases in all were mentioned in the speeches, one of which was the *Wednesbury Corpn* case, from which the judgment of Lord Greene was cited with approval by Lord Diplock. Even *Padfield* was not mentioned at all. It may be that the speed with which all three courts dealt with the case had something to do with this, for the proceedings were heard and determined from the first instance hearing to the decision announced by the Lords within three weeks, ending on 2 August. This speed was commendable, for there was great urgency for the

10 [1937] AC 898.
11 [1947] AC 109.
12 [1967] 1 AC 13.

local education authority to know whether or not they would be able to go through the selection process for the grammar schools in time for the opening of the term in September, and then if they were authorised to do so to get on with it in the course of August. But the speed of dealing with the case was not by any means the whole reason for the lack of quoted authorities, for the House of Lords as usual took time for consideration, and the speeches of the Law Lords were written and published some considerable time after the bare decision to refuse mandamus had been announced. The real reason for the lack of quoted authorities must have been that all five Law Lords felt that the principle of the strength of judicial review on the ground of unreasonableness had become beyond question and no longer required quoted case law to justify it. Accordingly *Tameside* may well be seen as setting the seal upon the strength of the rules of judicial review.

The refusal of the Court of Appeal and House of Lords to grant the mandamus asked for by the Secretary of State was based upon the ground that he must have misdirected himself in law and misunderstood the meaning of 'unreasonably' in section 68 of the 1944 Act. It was not enough for him personally to disagree with the Council's policy: there had to be evidence that the Council was acting in a way which no reasonable Council would do. Although it had been argued on behalf of the Secretary of State that there were great administrative difficulties in the way of setting up and completing the selection procedure needed for the grammar schools before the school year opened, The Council was able to show that other education authorities had been able to overcome such difficulties elsewhere, and that they had adequate plans for coping with the problems themselves – an assertion which was well borne out in the event by their successfully completing the procedure between 2 August and the beginning of the school year just over a month later. The nub of the Secretary of State's objection to the Council's change of policy was a political disagreement. The Lords amply stated that political disagreements are a part of British public life, and that the varying political standpoints are all generally acceptable in law, unless they stray in offending against criminal law. It is perfectly reasonable for a political party, nationally or locally, to take a stand upon an issue of public importance, such as comprehensive education, and there was nothing inherently unreasonable in the Conservatives in Tameside campaigning on the issue as they did in 1976. What is more, having won their election, it was if anything doubly reasonable that they should attempt to carry out the programme on which the electors supported them. Far from the Council acting unreasonably, it was in fact the Secretary of State who had acted unreasonably in taking the view that they were unreasonable. This conundrum of double unreasonableness is a special feature of the *Tameside* case. One of the eventual side effects of the decision was that the government secured the passage through Parliament of the Education Act 1976, giving the Secretary of State stronger powers to compel recalcitrant education authorities to embrace the comprehensive principle, though it should be added that the Bill was on its way before the courts. The 1976 Act was then itself in turn repealed by the Education Act 1979, passed after the return of a Conservative Government in that year, though the end of the story so far as education in Tameside was concerned in practice came after Labour returned to power there locally in 1979. The new Council resubmitted plans for all its secondary schools to go fully comprehensive, and Mr Carlisle, the new Conservative Education Secretary, approved them in May 1980.

Yet, though the power of judicial review is now beyond doubt, the conferment of discretionary powers by Parliament is not necessarily wholly nugatory. As Lord Wilberforce said:[13]

> The section is framed in a 'subjective' form – if the Secretary of State 'is satisfied'. This form of section is quite well known, and at first sight might seem to exclude judicial review. Sections in this form may, no doubt, exclude judicial review on what is or has become a matter of pure judgment. But I do not think that they go further than that. If a judgment requires, before it can be made, the existence of some facts, then, although the evaluation of those facts is for the Secretary of State alone, the court must inquire whether those facts exist, and have been taken into account, whether the judgment has been made upon a proper self-direction as to those facts, whether the judgment has not been made upon other facts which ought not to have been taken into account. If these requirements are not met, then the exercise of judgment, however bona fide it may be, becomes capable of challenge . . .
>
> This Act, of 1944, is quite different from those which simply create a ministerial discretion. The Secretary of State, under s.68, is not merely exercising a discretion: he is reviewing the action of another public body which itself has discretionary powers and duties. He, by contrast with the courts in the normal case, may substitute his opinion for that of the authority: this is what the section allows, but he must take account of what the authority, under the statute, is entitled to do. The authority – this is vital – is itself elected, and is given specific powers as to the kind of schools it wants in its area. Therefore two situations may arise. One is that there may be a difference of policy between the Secretary of State (under Parliament) to make his policy prevail. The other is that, owing to the democratic process involving periodic elections, abrupt reversals of policy may take place, particularly where there are only two parties and the winner takes all. Any reversal of policy if at all substantial must cause

---

13   [1977] AC 1014 at 1047.

some administrative disruption – this was as true of the 1975 proposals as of those of the respondents. So the mere possibility, or probability, of disruption cannot be a ground for issuing a direction to abandon the policy. What the Secretary of State is entitled, by a direction if necessary, to ensure is that such disruptions are not 'unreasonable', i e, greater than a body, elected to carry out a new programme, with which the Secretary of State may disagree ought to impose upon those for whom it is responsible. After all, those who voted for the new programme, involving a change of course, must also be taken to have accepted some degree of disruption in implementing it.

The ultimate question in this case, in my opinion, is whether the Secretary of State has given sufficient, or any, weight to this particular factor in the exercise of his judgment.

The assertion in *Tameside* that there is nothing inherently unreasonable in a local authority carrying out the election promises of the political party in power in the Council was examined again by the House of Lords in *Bromley London Borough Council v Greater London Council*,[14] often known as the 'Fares Fair case'. In March 1981 the Greater London Labour Party issued a manifesto for the GLC election to be held in May. Among the various promises was one that 'within six months of winning the election, Labour will cut fares on London Transport buses and tubes by an average of 25 per cent'. After the Labour Party had in May won a small overall majority in the GLC they set about implementing this pledge. The GLC instructed London Transport to prepare plans for an immediate reduction of fares by 25 per cent, the shortfall in the cost of the transport undertaking to be made up by a supplementary precept by the GLC on the London boroughs, who would thus be obliged to levy supplementary rates. This was necessary because the Government block grant to the GLC was to be substantially cut as a mark of Government disapproval of the GLC's action. Bromley London Borough Council then sought judicial review by way of certiorari to quash the supplementary rate precept.

Bromley's application failed narrowly at first instance, but it succeeded in the Court of Appeal, and the House of Lords unanimously upheld the latter decision. Under section 1 of the Transport (London) Act 1969, which was then in force, London Transport had the duty to promote 'integrated, efficient and economic transport facilities'. Their Lordships considered that this obliged London Transport to conduct transport services on business principles, attempting to avoid a deficit. There were several differences between the approaches of the five Law Lords to the issue of the meaning of 'economic' in this context, and Lord Diplock

14 [1983] 1 AC 768.

in particular thought it was not necessarily unreasonable for the expectation of a grant to be taken into account. But they all considered that it was clear that such grant from the Council as could be expected after the reduction of fares would have to be so large that it would be out of all proportion to any reasonable expectation of being able to balance the books. They thus followed *Prescott v Birmingham Corpn*. Some Law Lords also took the view that the GLC was in breach of its fiduciary duties in failing fairly to balance the interests of the ratepayers and transport users, and by thrusting an inordinate burden on the ratepayers, failing to take account of the loss of grant from central government. Thus, in contrast to *Tameside*, it *was* unreasonable in this case to attempt to carry out the terms of the election manifesto because the pledge was illegal.

In a sense this latter point was only emphasised by the later decision of the Divisional Court in *R v London Transport Executive, ex p Greater London Council*.[15] In the wake of the Fares Fare case result, the GLC had given a direction to the London Transport Executive to reduce fares in accordance with a new 'Balanced Plan' which it had adopted. Although London Transport welcomed the plan it needed reassurance that it was lawful. So it sought declarations to that effect, and the Divisional Court granted them because on this occasion the Balanced Plan was in accordance with the overall duty imposed by the 1969 Act on London Transport.

It now seems clear that it is established in English law that the court will be prepared in any case to inquire whether there was any evidence upon which a Minister or other administrative authority may exercise a choice in the use of the discretion conferred upon him by Parliament. If it is found that there is no evidence upon which he can exercise his discretion, any such purported exercise of discretion will be set aside as void. So the exercise of a discretion may be held void for unreasonableness because there was no evidence upon which it could be exercised. In the United States the equivalent rule is that findings must be supported by substantial evidence on the record as a whole,[16] and the English position is narrower than this. But there would appear to be some signs that the English courts are gradually

---

15 [1983] QB 484. See also *R v Merseyside County Council, ex p Great Universal Stores Ltd* (1982) 80 LGR 639, in which judicial review of a supplementary rate demand levied by the Council to finance a cheap fares policy was refused mainly because the governing statute concerned imposed a duty to provide a 'properly integrated and efficient system', but there was no requirement that it should be 'economic'.
16 Administrative Procedure Act (USA, 1946), s 10(e); *Universal Camera Corpn v National Labor Relations Board* 340 US 474 (1951). It may be noted that the existence or otherwise of substantial evidence is more easily judged in America because of the procedural rule requiring a full record of evidence.

working their way towards something akin to a substantial evidence rule, which would only tend to reinforce the power of judicial review already established.

One final case is worthy of note, *Meade v London Borough of Haringey*.[17] The case arose (as did the *Pickwell* case, considered above) out of the considerable industrial strife during the severe winter of early 1979. The Government was attempting to hold increases in salaries and wages in the public sector to 5 per cent, with almost no success. The caretakers at over 100 schools in the London Borough of Haringey were ordered by their unions to come out on strike. They did so, and the Council, which was controlled by the Labour Party, closed the schools and kept them closed for several weeks, with the result that about 37,000 children were deprived of the teaching which they should have had. The Council did not seek to make alternative arrangements which would have enabled the schools to be kept open during the caretakers' strike, though they acknowledged that they could have done so, but claimed instead that they had just cause or excuse for not doing so on the ground that, had they done so, that would have led to further industrial action by the two trade unions which were supporting the strikers, and possibly by other unions also. A group of parents of children at the schools asked the Secretary of State for Education and Science (now Mrs Shirley Williams) to direct the education authority to reopen the schools, but she declined to do so, apparently on the ground, according to Lord Denning, that the Council's only duty was to provide school buildings and no more. As Lord Denning also remarked, if this was her reason, she had been badly advised in law. Parliament's concern in enacting the Education Act 1944 was that children should be educated, and it was for the better attainment of that object that it imposed on a local education authority a duty which it would be inconceivable that Parliament should intend to be fulfilled by the mere provision of school buildings, and did not extend to the provision of teachers and other essential personnel as were appropriate to secure the children's education. One might add that, if Lord Denning's assessment of Mrs Williams' reason for declining to intervene was correct, then her attitude differed markedly from that of her predecessor Mr Mulley when he was dealing with the local education authority in Tameside.

The parents accordingly took their grievance to the court, Mr Meade, the father of one of the pupils, seeking an injunction to restrain further breach of the Council's duty and thus to compel the Council to open the schools, on the ground that they were in breach of the Education Act 1944, section 8, in that they had failed in their

17 [1979] 2 All ER 1016.

duty 'to secure that there should be available for their area sufficient schools for providing full-time education' suitable to the requirements of the pupils. He failed at first instance, but the Court of Appeal found substantially in his favour, holding that a local education authority which 'without just cause or excuse' closes schools for which it is responsible and thereby deprives children of the education to which they are entitled under the 1944 Act acts unlawfully, and that the parents whose children are thereby deprived of education may seek a remedy through the courts, by way of either injunction or damages. The court held further that if a third party induces a local education authority to break its statutory duty to provide education, such a third party is itself acting unlawfully. Meade's complaint to the Secretary of State had been correctly made under the terms of section 99(1) of the Act, which gives parents of 'persons interested' a right of complaint to the Secretary of State against a local education authority that fails in its duty under section 8. Each of the parents suffered special damage in that their children were deprived of the education they should have had, and each of the parents whose children suffered thereby would have an action for damages. In the event, however, the remedy of injunction was not granted because the strike had ended by the time the Court of Appeal gave judgment, but Lord Denning held that Mr Meade had rightly proceeded with his application, because it was of much importance to parents, and to society at large, that the legal position should be ascertained.

Once more, therefore, the Court of Appeal has held an administrative authority, this time a local education authority, to be in breach of its statutory duty, and to have acted ultra vires; and once more the Secretary of State for Education and Science has been held to have exercised a discretion unreasonably – though on this occasion her action was only on the periphery of the matter at issue in the court. One wonders whether the Department of Education and Science has by now been compelled to re-examine its basic attitudes towards its exercise of discretions. Perhaps some notice may be found displayed in a prominent place in the Department, reading *'Remember Tameside and Mr Meade'*.

Error of law

It has been traditional to assert that there are three main grounds for judicial review of administrative action – ultra vires, breach of natural justice, and error of law. The second of these grounds, breach of natural justice, will be the subject of discussion in the next chapter of this book, while ultra vires has been discussed in the present chapter. It is not proposed to devote a separate chapter to error of law, because it is suggested that today the proper context for its consideration is within an account centred upon ultra vires. The reason for this may not at first be readily apparent, for again traditionally it has been thought that an ultra vires act is bad *ab initio* and thus does not exist at all in law, whereas an error of law committed by an administrative authority renders the decision subject to review even though the jurisdictional basis for the decision has at no stage been destroyed. In other words, error of law will be committed *within* jurisdiction, while the jurisdiction of the authority remains intact. Such a view of error of law is, however, too narrow, and has probably arisen from too close an adherence to the reasoning provided by the Divisional Court and Court of Appeal in their important decisions in *R v Northumberland Compensation Appeal Tribunal, ex p Shaw* in 1952.[18]

By the passing of the National Health Service Act 1946, which inter alia incorporated hospitals into the new National Health Service, Mr Thomas Shaw lost his employment as clerk to the West Northumberland Joint Hospital Board, but was awarded compensation in accordance with regulations made under the Act. He maintained that the amount awarded to him was too small, and he appealed to the Northumberland Compensation Appeal Tribunal, set up for the purpose of hearing such appeals under the Act, which upheld the award. Shaw then applied to the Divisional Court for an order of certiorari to quash the award on the ground that an error of law appeared on the face of the record of the tribunal's decision. Now error of law as a ground for judicial review has as lengthy a common law pedigree as ultra vires, but the superior courts had throughout its history limited it to errors appearing on the face of decisions which were challenged. Until virtually the end of the nineteenth century most powers not exercisable by the Crown were the responsibility of magistrates, so that complaints of error in the exercise of such powers were complaints against the decisions of magistrates. In the course of the nineteenth century magistrates had given up providing reasons for their decisions. This was mainly because the Summary Jurisdiction Act 1848 had provided for a standard form of conviction which omitted all mention of the evidence or the reasoning by which the justices reached their decision. The practice of the magistrates in their criminal functions spilled over into their administrative work. Accordingly the records of magistrates' decisions no longer 'spoke', and the practice of challenging decisions of administrative authorities on the ground of error of law had petered out. In 1944 the Court of

18 [1952] 1 KB 338.

Appeal had even mistakenly thought that this ground for review no longer existed.[19] In the *Northumberland* case, however, there was no problem about any record because the tribunal, without being under any compulsion to do so, had voluntarily produced the reasons for its decision and incorporated them in the written decision itself. These reasons did indeed disclose that the tribunal had erred in its implementation of the law. Both Lord Goddard CJ, in a notable review of the authorities in a judgment in the Divisional Court which was given without taking time for consideration, and Singleton, Denning and Morris LJJ in the Court of Appeal took pains to re-establish error of law on the record as a ground for review, and to disapprove of the 1944 decision which had been given *per incuriam*.

It was, however, perfectly clear that the error made by the tribunal did not go to its jurisdiction. The tribunal had a right, indeed a duty, to determine the scale of compensation which should be paid to Mr Shaw, but the actual determination was erroneous. The power of an authority to determine any issue must necessarily import the power so to decide wrongly, for no one could support the suggestion that all decisions are automatically correct. Ministers and most tribunals are now under a duty to provide reasons for their decisions, if requested, under the Tribunals and Inquiries Act 1971, section 12, which re-enacts a similar section in the earlier Tribunals and Inquiries Act 1958. Such reasons, whether written or oral, automatically became a part of the record. So that now it is often much easier to see whether there was an error of law. The belief that such errors were always within the jurisdiction conferred upon the authority concerned was fostered by the decision in *Punton v Ministry of Pensions and National Insurance (No 2)* in 1964.[20]

Two platers' helpers had claimed unemployment benefit for a period when they were out of work because the platers were on strike over a demarcation dispute. There was at the time a rule in the national insurance legislation which precluded from unemployment benefit any persons who were directly interested in a trade dispute, participating in it, or whose trade unions were directly interested or participating in it. But the rule has never been very clearly delineated, and its operation and application has often been subject to challenge. The claim went up through the special tribunal system set up for national insurance purposes, which will be referred to more particularly in chapter 6 of this book, and was eventually dealt with by the National Insurance Commissioner, the ultimate tribunal of appeal in this field. The Commissioner dismissed the appeal by the

---

19   *Racecourse Betting Control Board v Secretary for Air* [1944] Ch 114.
20   [1964] 1 All ER 448.

two claimants from the rejection of their applications. Decisions of the Commissioner, like those of all inferior tribunals, are always subject to the possibility of judicial review by the courts, and the two claimants applied for a declaration that the Commissioner's decision was erroneous in law. As will be mentioned again in chapter 5, a declaration merely states what the law on a point may be, and does not in itself actually order anything to be done. A more obvious remedy would have been an order of certiorari, which if granted has the effect of quashing the decision which has been challenged, but the applicants were out of time for certiorari under the procedural rule in force at that time. The strict time limit, six months, did not apply to the remedy of declaration, but the Court of Appeal decided that it would anyway be inappropriate because the basis of the application was that the Commissioner had merely erred in law within his jurisdiction. If this were to be proved to the court it would still only have the effect of showing that the Commissioner's decision was voidable. A declaration would be useless on such a point, because it would be pointless for the court to declare that an inferior decision was voidable without going further and ordering it to be set aside or corrected. The declaration could not so order, and thus within their discretion the court refused it.

As we shall see in chapter 5, recent reform may well have circumvented this type of procedural posturing. But *Punton* certainly emphasised that, whereas an ultra vires act would be void, an error of law within jurisdiction will only render the act affected voidable, even though Lord Denning, in an earlier hearing of the *Punton* saga,[1] had taken the view that no tribunal had any jurisdiction to decide a point of law wrongly: any such decision would be a nullity. Lord Denning may have been a little before his time on this, but a moment's thought will show that some errors at least may be so fundamental as to go to jurisdiction. Sir William Wade, in his *Administrative Law*, devotes chapter 9 to a consideration of the two types of error. He quotes Lord Goddard CJ in *R v Ludlow, ex p Barnsley Corpn*,[2] who said: 'if Parliament has chosen to make the lower tribunal or body the absolute judges of the matter before it, and to give no appeal, this court cannot interfere in a matter regarding which the lower court has been clothed with jurisdiction by Parliament'. Professor Wade himself says:[3]

> If a public authority or tribunal is given power to determine some question, its determination ought to be conclusive, whether right or

1 *Punton v Ministry of Pensions and National Insurance* [1963] 1 All ER 275.
2 [1947] KB 634 at 639.
3 At p 257.

wrong, unless statute has provided for appeal. In other words, a grant of jurisdiction inherently includes a power to make mistakes within the area of the authority granted.

But there has always been the important exception of an error on the face of the record, which may result in judicial review by a superior court even though the jurisdiction of the inferior authority may have remained valid. Where the courts are satisfied that error does not go to jurisdiction they still usually characterise the determination under review as voidable, rather than void. But in the past dozen years or so there has been a considerable movement among both judges and jurists to treat all errors of law as rendering the determination plainly void, as Wade recognises in his account.[4] This trend started with the famous case of *Anisminic Ltd v Foreign Compensation Commission*, decided by the House of Lords in 1969.[5]

The *Anisminic* case

The case arose out of the Suez adventure in 1956, when for a few days hostilities (though without any declaration of war) existed between the United Kingdom and France on the one hand and Egypt on the other. Although Suez was not in international law a war, it came very close to being such, and it certainly had results upon the relations between the participating countries and their respective subjects which strongly resembled the common attributes of war. In particular, as would have been the case in wartime, there was a tendency for Egypt to expropriate the property of British citizens and companies. The appellants, a British company, had owned a mining property in Egypt worth some £4 million. As a direct result of Suez this property was nationalised by Egypt, and then later sold to an Egyptian company which is generally referred to as TEDO. The appellants brought pressure to bear upon their former customers not to deal with TEDO and so the Egyptian Government eventually agreed to purchase the appellants' property for £500,000. However, the appellants specifically reserved to themselves any rights to compensation against any government other than the Egyptian Government. In 1959, when relations had been largely restored between the United Kingdom and Egypt, the Egyptian Government, again following the normal practice of previously warring nations, agreed by treaty to pay a lump sum to the

---

4 And see Wade's views in his article 'New Twists in the *Anisminic* Skein' (1980) 96 LQR 492.
5 [1969] 2 AC 147.

United Kingdom Governemnt as compensation for British property which had been nationalised.

Now Parliament had already set up a procedure for dealing with claims on such a fund – a procedure which had been originally designed for the aftermath of the Second World War, when many people living in the United Kingdom eventually became eligible to claim a share of the compensation funds paid over by the former Axis nations with whom the Allies had been at war. The scheme had been set up by the Foreign Compensation Act 1950, a statute which was in no sense politically controversial. The Government had agreed at that time with the opposition that it would be best to place the administration of the fund in the hands of a high-powered independent body, which would be responsible for receiving the lump sums paid over, advertising for claimants, receiving the claims and testing them, if necessary by judicial-style hearings, and then paying out such sums as it considered justified to those whose claims it considered valid. The independent body set up by the Act was the Foreign Compensation Commission, which is best thought of as a special tribunal. It was also agreed when the Act was on its way through Parliament that it was desirable for the Commission to be able to act with speed, and that as most claimants would probably have been denied compensation for property lost for several years before they were able to make a claim it was important that no further unnecessary delay should prevent them from receiving the compensation due to them. Accordingly, and again with no dissent being voiced at the time, it was decided that the Commission's decisions should be exempted from any later challenge in the ordinary courts. The actual provision to this effect was in section 4(4) of the Act: 'The determination by the commission of any application made to them under this Act shall not be called in question in any court of law'. This provision was purposely reinforced by the express exemption of the Foreign Compensation Commission from the provisions of section 11 of the Tribunals and Inquiries Act 1958, under which any provisions in earlier statutes which attempted to preclude the power of review in the High Court by such words as 'shall not be called into question in any court' were to be deemed as not preventing the court from granting orders of certiorari or mandamus. This exemption was omitted from the corresponding section 14 of the Tribunals and Inquiries Act 1971, largely because of a provision in the Foreign Compensation Act 1969. The Act of 1969 redefined the power of the Foreign Compensation Commission in the light of an agreement reached with the USSR for the payment of compensation to those living in the United Kingdom who were dispossessed by the Soviet Union in Eastern Europe during the

Second World War. By section 3 of the 1969 Act there is a right of appeal on any question of jurisdiction direct from the Commission to the Court of Appeal, though no further. This provision was inserted in the Bill during its passage through Parliament as a result of pressure from jurists and also from Law Lords in the Upper House itself.

The existence of this Commission seemed providential when Egypt eventually paid over its lump sum in compensation to those who had lost their property at the time of Suez, and the money was promptly transferred by the Government to the Commission. The appellants made a claim on the fund, but the Commission made a provisional determination that they had failed to establish a valid claim. The reason for this decision arose from the Commission's interpretation of part of the Foreign Compensation (Egypt) (Determination and Registration of Claims) Order 1962, under which the Commission was given its task to perform with the Egyptian compensation money. The Order empowered the Commission to treat a claim as properly established if they were satisfied of three matters: (1) that the application related to property which was situated in Egypt and included in a list annexed to the Order; (2) that the applicant was the owner or successor in title to the owner of such property; and (3) that the applicant 'and any person who became successor in title' were British nationals on the appropriate dates. The Commission were satisfied of the first two matters, but considered that the Anisminic Company had failed to satisfy the third qualification, because they held that TEDO was a 'successor in title' and was not a British national.

The appellants sought declarations to the effect that the provisional determination was a nullity and that they were entitled to participate in the compensation fund. They succeeded before Browne J at first instance, though the Commission's appeal was upheld by the Court of Appeal. But the House of Lords reinstated the effect of Browne J's decision, holding by three to two that the Commission had made a legal error which went to jurisdiction. Although the decision of the Lords was by a bare majority, one of the Law Lords who dissented, Lord Pearson, agreed with the majority that had he been satisfied that such an error had been made it would have gone to jurisdiction. The actual error found by the majority in the Lords was that the Commission had misunderstood the meaning of 'successor in title'. In the view of the majority, TEDO, having gained the property in Egypt from the Egyptian Government, and after expropriation, was not a successor in title, notwithstanding the subsequent payment by Egypt of £500,000, and thus in considering the nationality of TEDO the Commission had exceeded its jurisdiction by taking into account an extraneous consideration. Accordingly the purported determination of the Commission was not worth the paper it was written on – it was not a determination at all, and thus was not the sort of matter the court was precluded from reviewing by section 4(4) of the 1950 Act. It was necessary in *Anisminic* for the appellants to establish that there was not only an error of law, but also that it was a jurisdictional error and thus void, because an error merely within jurisdiction would, according to the *Punton* rule, be no use as a basis for declaration, and certiorari was not available against the Commission as a result of section 11 of the Tribunals and Inquiries Act 1958.

Mr B C Gould, in a persuasive article published in 1970, argued that the result of the Lords' decision would be that all errors of law must inevitably go to jurisdiction.[6] He bases his argument upon two wide-ranging passages in the speeches of Lord Reid and Lord Pearce, who were in the majority. Mr Gould suggests as a result that the two Law Lords have reduced almost to a vanishing point the difference between jurisdictional error and error of law within jurisdiction, but it is curious that his quotations from the speeches stop in each case just a little early, and are perhaps over-selective. Let us look at the relevant passages. Lord Reid says:[7]

> But there are many cases where, although the tribunal had jurisdiction to enter on the inquiry, it has done or failed to do something in the course of the inquiry which is of such a nature that its decision is a nullity. It may have given its decision in bad faith. It may have made a decision which it had no power to make. It may have failed in the course of the inquiry to comply with the requirements of natural justice. It may in perfect good faith have misconstrued the provisions giving it power to act so that it failed to deal with the question remitted to it and decided some question which was not remitted to it. It may have refused to take into account something which it was required to take into account. Or it may have based its decision on some mattter which, under the provisions setting it up, it had no right to take into account. I do not intend this list to be exhaustive.

Mr Gould ends the quotation here, and certainly Lord Reid has cast his net very widely in giving instances of errors which will result in the decision being a nullity. But in fact Lord Reid went on immediately to say:

> But if it decides a question remitted to it for decision without committing any of these errors it is as much entitled to decide that question wrongly as it is to decide it rightly. I understand that some confusion has been

---

6 *Anisminic* and Jurisdictional Review' [1970] PL 358.
7 [1969] 2 AC 147 at 171.

caused by my having said in *Armah v Government of Ghana*,[8] that if a tribunal has jurisdiction to go right it has jurisdiction to go wrong. So it has, if one uses 'jurisdiction' in the narrow original sense. If it is entitled to enter on the inquiry and does not do any of those things which I have mentioned in the course of the proceedings, then its decision is equally valid whether it is right or wrong subject only to the power of the court in certain circumstances to correct an error of law.

The paragraph which Mr Gould quotes from the speech of Lord Pearce runs:[9]

> Lack of jurisdiction may arise in various ways. There may be an absence of those formalities or things which are conditions precedent to the tribunal having any jurisdiction to embark on an inquiry. Or the tribunal may at the end make an order that it has no jurisdiction to make. Or in the intervening stage, while engaged on a proper inquiry, the tribunal may depart from the rules of natural justice; or it may ask itself the wrong questions; or it may take into account matters which it was not directed to take into account. Thereby it would step outside its jurisdiction. It would turn its inquiry into something not directed by Parliament and fail to make the inquiry which Parliament did direct. Anny of these things would cause its purported decision to be a nullity.

But he omits to quote the next two paragraphs:

> Further, it is assumed, unless special provisions provide otherwise, that the tribunal will make its inquiry and decision according to the law of the land. For that reason the courts will intervene when it is manifest from the record that the tribunal, though keeping within its mandated area of jurisdiction, comes to an erroneous decision through an error of law. In such a case the courts have intervened to correct the error.
>
> The courts have, however, always been careful to distinguish their intervention, whether on excess of jurisdiction or error of law, from an appellate function. Their jurisdiction over inferior tribunals is supervision, not review.
>
>> 'That supervision goes to two points: one is the area of the inferior-jurisdiction and the qualifications and conditions of its exercise; the other is the observance of the law in the course of its exercise.' (*R v Nat Bell Liquors Ltd*)[10]
>
> It is simply an enforcement of Parliament's mandate to the tribunal. If the tribunal is intended on a true construction of the Act to inquire into and finally decide questions within a certain area, the court's supervisory duty is to see that it makes the authorised inquiry according to natural justice and arrives at a decision whether right or wrong. They will intervene if the tribunal asks itself the wrong questions (that is, questions other than those which Parliament directed it to ask itself). But if it directs

8 [1968] AC 192 at 234.
9 [1969] 2 AC 147 at 195.
10 [1922] 2 AC 128 at 156.

itself to the right inquiry, asking the right questions, they will not intervene merely because it has or may have come to the wrong answer, provided that this is an answer that lies within its jurisdiction.

It is clear that Mr Gould missed out the passages in which both Law Lords affirm that it is within the jurisdiction of an inferior body to err in law without destroying its jurisdiction. This surely must stand to reason, for it is the whole basis of our appellate court structure that the lower courts may have erred in law, while remaining in full possession of jurisdiction to hear and determine what came before them. Yet Mr Gould's arguments have been reflected in a number of judgments in recent cases. It may be that this was in part because of the need to get round the ineffectiveness of the remedy of declaration where what was complained of was merely voidable, though, as we shall see in chapter 5, reforms of our system of administrative law remedies probably have rendered this effort unnecessary. Though the difference between jurisdictional and non-jurisdictional error must, in all logic, remain, we must also take account of the judicial efforts to obtain a measure of uniformity of approach towards the result of legal error.

Are all acts in error of law void?

Lord Denning has been a pioneer in the courts of the idea that all errors of law go to jurisdiction. Yet his views have not always been consistent. In 1966 he was prepared to recognise the two types of error – within and outside jurisdiction.[11] In *R v Secretary of State for the Environment, ex p Ostler*,[12] where a landowner alleged that his land had been acquired under a compulsory order in breach of natural justice, and in bad faith, he said that neither ground, if proved, would make the order void, but only voidable. It is fair to add, however, that in his book *The Discipline of Law*[13] he tenders his regrets for this *ex tempore* decision, and asserts that it would have been better to decide that acts committed in breach of such basic rules would be void.

In a 1978 case, *Pearlman v Keepers and Governors of Harrow School*,[14] the rateable value of premises was the basic issue. Section 1(4A) of the Leasehold Reform Act 1967, as amended by the Housing Act

11   *R v Paddington Valuation Officer, ex p Peachey Property Corpn Ltd* [1966] 1 QB 380 at 402; see also *James v Minister of Housing and Local Government* [1965] 3 All ER 602.
12   [1977] QB 122.
13   Page 108
14   [1979] QB 56; and see H F Rawlings 'Jurisdictional Review after *Pearlman*' [1979] PL 404.

1974, permits a tenant to apply to a County Court for a determination whether given improvements amount to structural alteration for the purpose of assessing the rateable value of premises. It is provided that such determinations shall be 'final and conclusive'. Acting under this section a County Court decided that the installation of a central heating system did not amount to 'structural alteration', and a certiorari to quash this decision was refused by the Divisional Court. The Court of Appeal, however, reversed this decision, holding that the remedy of certiorari was not excluded since the error of law made by the judge in the County Court, in misconstruing the legislation, deprived him of jurisdiction. His determination was therefore not final and conclusive. Lord Denning went so far as to assert[15] that if the High Court

> chooses to interfere, it can formulate its decision in the words: 'The court below had no jurisdiction to decide this point wrongly as it did.' If it does not choose to interfere, it can say: 'The court has jurisdiction to decide it wrongly, and did so.' Softly be it stated, but that is the reason for the difference between the decision of the Court of Appeal in *Anisminic v Foreign Compensation Commission*[16] and the House of Lords.[17]

The actual decision in *Pearlman* was by a majority, Lord Denning MR and Eveleigh LJ, Geoffrey Lane LJ dissenting. But it is nevertheless a stark and uncompromising statement of the policy of the court, which may be promoted in order to achieve uniformity in interpreting error of law as jurisdictional wherever possible. In a later case, *Re Racal Communications Ltd*,[18] the House of Lords held that the decision in *Pearlman* was wrong in that the statutory provision should have been interpreted according to its plain meaning in respect of the powers of a lower *court*. But the Lords reaffirmed that such privative enactments could not be regarded as final insofar as they apply to administrative tribunals.

This judicial policy is not limited to England. An example can be taken from the same vintage north of the border in Scotland, a decision by the Court of Session in *Watt v Lord Advocate*.[19] It has to be remembered that in Scotland the terminology of the courts and the actual remedies sought are different from those in England, but very often, as here, the substance of the issue bears a striking resemblance to that which may come before an English court. In

---

15 [1979] QB 56 at 70; and see *R v Preston Supplementary Benefits Appeal Tribunal, ex p Moore* [1975] 2 All ER 807.
16 [1968] 2 QB 862.
17 [1969] 2 AC 147.
18 [1981] AC 374; see also *South East Asia Fire Bricks Sdn Bhd v Non-Metallic Mineral Products Manufacturing Employees Union* [1981] AC 363, PC.
19 1979 SLT 137.

particular, the Scots 'pursuer' is similar to the English plaintiff or applicant, and an order for 'reduction' is equivalent to an English order to quash. Mr Watt asked for reduction of the National Insurance Commissioner's decision that he was disqualified from receiving unemployment benefit. We have already pointed out that the Commissioner is the ultimate tribunal of appeal within the tribunal system set up for the purpose of dealing with disputes concerning welfare benefits. Section 75(1) of the National Insurance Act 1965 actually contained an ouster clause to the effect that the Commissioner's decision 'shall be final'. There have been a string of English decisions in the Divisional Court and above which have made it plain that this clause does not prevent judicial review by the courts on jurisdictional grounds. The Lord Ordinary, however, who heard Mr Watt's claim at first instance, refused to allow reduction, relying on the ground that the Commissioner's decision, though possibly wrong, was nevertheless intra vires. On appeal this decision was unanimously reversed by the Court of Session, consisting of the Lord President (Lord Emslie), Lord Avonside and Lord Johnston. The Court of Session followed the House of Lords in *Anisminic*, concluding that the Commissioner's decision was ultra vires and void. In the course of his judgment, the Lord President put the judicial policy forcibly:

> When it is appreciated that what is in issue in this case is a misconstruction of the only question which the commissioner had power to determine it is as plain as plain can be that he addressed himself in the result to, and answered, the wrong question, and decided against the pursuer because he had not passed a test other than that set for him by Parliament. In these circumstances, in my judgment, he clearly exceeded his powers. There can be no doubt that, when a statutory tribunal, which quite properly enters upon an inquiry which it has jurisdiction to carry out, misconstrues the question which it is required to answer and decides some other question which was not remitted to it, its decisions will be a nullity.

It must be concluded that there still remains a difference in principle between errors of law which go to jurisdiction and errors of law which do not.[20] Unless the difference remains, the whole basis of appeals over the general field of law would crumble. It would no longer be possible to appeal in any case without also calling in question the power of the first instance court or tribunal to determine the issue originally raised before it. But granted that the difference

---

20 This view is supported by the Privy Council decision in *South East Asia Fire Bricks Sdn Bhd v Non-Metallic Mineral Products Manufacturing Employers Union* [1981] AC 363. See also *R v Knightsbridge Crown Court, ex p International Sporting Club (London) Ltd* [1982] QB 304.

continues, there are specially compelling reasons why in the context of administrative law the courts have done their best in recent years to interpret any error of law as jurisdictional as far as possible. Bedevilled as our law has been by remedies, as the *Punton* case shows, and as we must stress again in chapter 5, it is so much easier to apply an appropriate remedy if the court can conclude that what was done below was of no effect at all, that it does not need to be quashed, and that a straightforward statement of the law will lead the parties towards the desired lawful result. A decision below which is made in error of law within jurisdiction cannot be held null and void: it will remain a valid decision with full legal effect unless and until avoided by court order, and certainly no one would be safe in ignoring it, as they could at least in theory do in the case of an ultra vires decision. So not only do the courts try as far as possible to interpret an error as jurisdictional, but perhaps we should recognise that it is in the general interest of suitable development of the law they should go on doing so.

The no evidence rule

One final matter remains for consideration here. It has already been shown in the foregoing pages that the courts may be working their way towards something like the American 'substantial evidence rule'. Certainly in *Tameside* the judges were prepared to take into account whether the Secretary of State had any evidence before him on which he could legitimately make his decision to order the local education authority to act in a certain way. Put another way, an action may prove to be unreasonable, and thus ultra vires, because there is no evidence to support it. Such a conclusion is now fairly clear from the cases, but judges have rarely stated it explicitly. It is therefore worthy of note that Lord Denning, never afraid to state what he believes to be correct, whatever previous precedent may have suggested, did in 1965 put the point explicitly. It was in the case of *Ashbridge Investments Ltd v Minister of Housing and Local Government*.[1]

Stalybridge Borough Council had declared an area to be a clearance area, under the Housing Act 1957, on the ground that the houses therein were unfit for human habitation. The area included two adjoining terrace houses of similar appearance, numbers 17 and 19, Grosvenor Street, owned by the respondents. Subsequently the local authority made a compulsory purchase order for the whole clearance area, which was coloured pink on the map of the order,

1 [1965] 3 All ER 371.

and for certain adjoining land, which was coloured grey on the map. The compensation payable in respect of the pink area (unfit houses) was less than that payable in the grey area. After objections from the owners, a local inquiry was held; and after the inquiry the Minister confirmed the order with modifications. One modification was the transfer of number 19 from the pink to the grey area on the ground that it had lost its identity as a dwelling, and so was no longer a 'house' within the Act. The owners then applied under the Act for an order to quash the compulsory purchase order in so far as it affected number 17, on the ground that it too was not a 'house', or alternatively that it was not fit for human habitation. In the event the owners failed, the Court of Appeal holding that the Minister was empowered to modify the order if he was of the opinion that any land ought not to have been included in an area, and that he had evidence upon which he had validly based his eventual order. But Lord Denning helpfully drew together the strands of jurisdictional error and absence of evidence:[2]

> Seeing that the decision is entrusted to the Minister, we have to consider the power of the court to interfere with his decision. It is given in Schedule 4, para. 2. The court can only interfere on the ground that the Minister has gone outside the powers of the Act or that any requirement of the Act has not been complied with. Under this section it seems to me that the court can interfere with the Minister's decision if he has acted on no evidence; or if he has given a wrong interpretation on the words of the statute; or if he has taken into consideration matters which he ought not to have taken into account, or vice versa; or has otherwise gone wrong in law. It is identical with the position when the court has power to interfere with the decision of a lower tribunal which has erred in point of law.
>
> We have to apply this to the modern procedure whereby the inspector makes his report and the Minister gives his letter of decision, and they are made available to the parties. It seems to me that the court should look at the material which the inspector and the Minister had before them just as it looks at the material before an inferior court, and see whether on that material the Minister has gone wrong in law.

The textbooks on administrative law show that this statement of law has been followed a number of times in the courts, and perhaps most notably in *Coleen Properties Ltd v Minister of Housing and Local Government*,[3] where the Minister had rejected his inspector's recommendation that certain property ought not to be included in a compulsory purchase order for land adjoining a clearance area. No evidence had been called at the inquiry that the acquisition of the property concerned was reasonably necessary, and no additional evidence on

2 [1965] 1 WLR 1320 at 1326.
3 [1971] 1 All ER 1049.

the point had been available to the Minister. Indeed the property was in excellent condition, and the court quashed the part of the order which referred to it.[4] Lord Denning himself, in his book *The Discipline of Law*, says that his statement of the law in *Ashbridge* has never been challenged.[5] It may well be concluded that the no evidence rule forged by the courts in the past twenty years is a powerful addition to the armoury of powers of judicial review. Furthermore it opens the way for the courts in the future to recognise overtly something that so far they have only achieved from time to time covertly – that an error giving rise to judicial review need not necessarily be restricted to a point of law, but may even be a matter of fact. Once the courts assert, as it is suggested with confidence that they may well do before many more years go by, that judicial review is available on the ground of error of law or fact, the power of the courts to protect the citizen against unlawful administrative acts will be well-nigh complete.

4 On the other hand it was held by the Court of Appeal, in *R v Secretary of State for the Environment, ex p Powis* [1981] 1 All ER 788, that fresh evidence cannot be admitted on judicial review to show that the person making the decision was misled by the failure of one party to put evidence before him which would probably have led him to a different conclusion. *Tameside* was no authority for such admission of evidence at that stage.
5 Page 107.

4 Natural justice

> The quality of mercy is not strain'd,
> It droppeth as the gentle rain from heaven
> Upon the place beneath.
>
> William Shakespeare *The Merchant of Venice*

There is no area of administrative law which is so replete with recent case law as that concerned with the rules of natural justice. A cursory perusal of the volumes of the Law Reports will reveal case after case in which the essential argument before the court was that there may have been an infringement of natural justice. Stated baldly the rules of natural justice appear to be perfectly simple, for they are but two in number, and both are of a basic character. Although each is often referred to by a Latin maxim, they are equally well known by an English free translation – *audi alteram partem,* otherwise the rule that no man is to be condemned unheard; and *nemo judex in causa sua,* being the rule that no man may be a judge in his own cause. It is because of the complexity of modern life, and the difficulties inherent in obtaining and retaining jobs, that the meaning and status of these rules is so important, and that their practical application to particular circumstances so often becomes the subject of litigation. In this chapter we shall attempt to determine the place in the law occupied by these rules, and to assess the way in which they are applied in practice, without of course attempting to cover any but a small portion of the case law constantly being reported.

Judicial, quasi-judicial and administrative powers and duties

From time to time during the twentieth century the courts have held that they could only control the actions of an administrative authority if and when the authority concerned was under a duty to act judicially or quasi-judicially, and had failed in this duty. If an authority had merely an administrative duty, power or discretion, then there was no way in which the courts could interfere with the authority's exercise of its power. Thus when examining the scope of judicial control in the field of administrative law the prime distinction has often been made between bodies with judicial powers and those with only non-judicial powers. Traditional theory has it that when an authority is acting judicially it is bound by fixed legal objective standards, whereas an authority which is not under any judicial duty may act subjectively according to its own wishes. It is clear from the case law of the past twenty-five years that we have moved far from this rigid distinction, but certainly until the 1960s the courts considered it to be an essential prerequisite to the exercise of powers of judicial review to establish that an authority whose actions were called in question should have acted judicially, and that judicial review is only possible because of the failure of that authority to adhere to the procedures required by the rules of natural justice. The tone for this approach by the courts was largely set by the findings of the Report of the Donoughmore-Scott Committee on Ministers' Powers in 1932.[1]

> A true judicial decision presupposes an existing dispute between two or more parties, and then involves four prerequisites:
> (1) The presentation (not necessarily orally) of their case by the parties to the dispute; (2) if the dispute between them is a question of fact, the ascertainment of the fact by means of evidence adduced by the parties to the dispute and often with the assistance of argument by or on behalf of the parties on the evidence; (3) if the dispute between them is a question of law, the submission of legal argument by the parties; and (4) a decision which disposes of the whole matter by a finding upon the facts in dispute and an application of the law of the land to the facts so found, including where required a ruling upon any disputed question of law.
>
> A quasi-judicial decision equally presupposes an existing dispute between two or more parties and involves (1) and (2), but does not necessarily involve (3), and never involves (4). The place of (4) is in fact taken by administrative action, the character of which is determined by the Minister's free choice . . .
>
> Decisions which are purely administrative stand on a wholly different footing from quasi-judicial as well as from judicial decisions and must be distinguished accordingly . . . In the case of the administrative decision, there is no legal obligation upon the person charged with the duty of reaching the decision to consider and weigh submissions and arguments, or to collate any evidence, or to solve any issue. The grounds upon which he acts, and the means which he takes to inform himself before acting, are left entirely to his discretion . . .

The traditional nature of judicial decisions is clear if the Ministers' Powers Committee's definition is borne in mind, but it is rather more

---

1 Cmd 4060, pp 73, 81.

difficult to pinpoint the type of proceeding which may be termed quasi-judicial. The most common instance of the latter is presented by what is normally called an inquiry, and here once more the circular nature of administrative law is apparent, for inquiries must await proper examination in this book, until chapter 6. Tribunals, which usually must act judicially, and inquiries, which normally function quasi-judicially, will be considered together in that later chapter, yet both tribunals and inquiries are among the administrative authorities whose decisions or proceedings are questioned in cases considered in the present chapter. In explanation of the nature of inquiries it must suffice here to state that where a Minister is under a statutory duty to hold a public local inquiry *to inform his mind,* but then has the later and separate power to make the actual decision in the issue, a quasi-judicial proceeding within the definition put forward by the Committee on Ministers' Powers has taken place. The main object of the inquiry may be said to be to inform the Minister's mind. If the Minister or his inspector, who conducted the inquiry, refuses to hear or to consider the evidence, he is guilty of a breach of the rule *audi alteram partem,* and the eventual decision may be set aside on review by the superior court. But if, after hearing or receiving the evidence, the eventual decision takes little or no account of it, there has been no breach of the rule, and it would normally appear that no judicial review is possible. As will be seen in chapter 6, it is now much more difficult than previously for a Minister to ignore evidence that has been given at an inquiry, but that is because of the introduction of statutory rules of procedure which have nothing to do with the common law rules of natural justice.

During the decades immediately preceding and succeeding the close of the Second World War the courts seemed to take very seriously the distinctions made by the Donoughmore Report between different types of powers and duties. Indeed the courts at times appeared almost over-anxious to interpret the exercise of powers conferred upon administrative authorities as being beyond the reach of judicial scutiny. There were still some cases where the determinations of Ministers were set aside,[2] but there were perhaps more where they turned out to be judge-proof.[3] The high water-mark of this trend was seen in two celebrated licence cases, *Nakkuda Ali v M F De S Jayaratne,*[4] decided by the Privy Council in 1951, and *R v*

---

2 E g *Errington v Minister of Health* [1935] 1 KB 249.
3 E g *Miller v Minister of Health* [1946] KB 626; *Franklin v Minister of Town and Country Planning* [1948] AC 87.
4 [1951] AC 66.

Metropolitan Police Comr, ex p Parker,[5] a decision of the Divisional Court in 1953. In *Nakkuda Ali*'s case, the Controller of Textiles of Ceylon had cancelled the appellant's textile licence under his powers as contained in regulation 62 of the Defence (Control of Textiles) Regulations 1945, ie 'where the Controller has reasonable grounds to believe that any dealer is unfit to be allowed to continue as a dealer'. The Controller had in fact considered some objections to the proposed cancellation of the licence by correspondence, but in any case the Judicial Committee of the Privy Council asserted that his powers were not judicial, and that he need hold no hearing before revoking a licence. Accordingly the application for an order to quash the revocation of the licence was refused. The facts in the *Parker* case were similarly simple. The London Cab Order 1934, made under powers delegated by the Metropolitan Public Carriage Act 1869, gave the power to revoke cab-drivers' licences to the Metropolitan Police Commissioner. Having received complaints that Mr Parker, a licensed cab-driver, had been allowing his cab to be used to assist prostitutes to ply their trade, the Commissioner revoked the licence without allowing Parker to bring witnesses or friends to make representations on his behalf before the Commissioner. Again the court held that the Commissioner's powers were administrative in nature, and Parker's application for a certiorari to quash the revocation of his licence was refused.

It may be of course that the behaviour of both Mr Nakkuda Ali and Mr Parker was such that they very properly lost their licences. But the point is that neither was allowed a proper hearing at which he could try to answer any charges against him, and so it was never objectively established that he deserved to lose his livelihood. Probably the ready acceptance by the courts of this period that acts were administrative in nature and not subject to any test by objective standards was a legacy of wartime, when there were obvious reasons for upholding as far as possible anything done in the name of executive power. But the courts of the period were certainly overlooking the legal principles which had been developed over the centuries as part of the centrepiece of the common law, and they greatly underrated the function of the rules of natural justice as clearly established over the years. The stream of authority *was* clear long before the 1950s, but the courts had ignored it. To take a single example of a case which was right in the mainstream of the law, we might quote *Cooper v Wandsworth Board of Works*,[6] decided by the strong bench of Erle

5 [1953] 2 All ER 717. On both cases see Yardley 'Revocation of Licences – An English Dilemma' (1956) 1 Jur Rev (NS) 240.
6 (1863) 14 CB NS 180.

CJ, Willes, Byles and Keating JJ, in 1863. There the Metropolis Management Act 1855, section 76, had vested in the Board, which was a predecessor of our modern local government authorities, the power to demolish a house if no notice had been given by a private individual of his intention to build it. This was an early form of planning law enforcement power, but the court held that it was subject to the overriding principle of *audi alteram partem*. As Erle CJ said:[7]

> The default in sending notice to the Board of the intention to build is a default which may be explained. There may be a great many excuses for the apparent default. The party may have intended to conform to the law. He may have actually conformed to all the regulations which they would wish to impose, though by accident his notice may have miscarried; and, under those circumstances, if he explained how it stood, the proceeding to demolish, merely because they had ill-will against the party, is a power that the legislature never intended to confer ... I fully agree that the legislature intended to give the district board very large powers indeed: but the qualification I speak of is one which has been recognised to the full extent.

Lord Loreburn LC lent the weight of a House of Lords decision to this line of judicial thought when he was discoursing upon the duty of the Board of Education in *Board of Education v Rice*,[8] discussed in the last chapter:

> I need not add that in doing (deciding) either, they must act in good faith and fairly listen to both sides, for that is a duty lying upon everyone who decides anything. But I do not think they are bound to treat such a question as though it were a trial. They have no power to administer an oath, and need not examine witnesses. They can obtain information in any way they think best, always giving a fair opportunity to those who are parties in the controversy for correcting or contradicting any irrelevant statement prejudicial to their view.

It would be possible to multiply the examples of the case law developed on these lines, but it is better for present purposes to concentrate more upon the decisions of the courts during the past fifteen or twenty years. It is one of the curiosities of the decisions in *Nakkuda Ali* and *Parker* that such seminal authorities as *Cooper v Wandsworth Board of Works* were not even mentioned in the judgments. It is thus all the more important that the validity of the older authorities, specifically including *Cooper*, was reasserted and

---

7 (1863) 14 CB NS 180 at 188.
8 [1911] AC 179 at 182.

re-established in the important House of Lords decision in *Ridge v Baldwin* reported in 1964.[9]

The Chief Constable of Brighton had been tried and acquitted on a criminal charge of conspiracy to obstruct the course of justice. Two other police officers of his force had been tried with him, and were convicted. Donovan J, in sentencing them, said that the facts admitted in the course of the trial 'establish that neither of you had that professional and moral leadership which both of you should have had and were entitled to expect from the Chief Constable of Brighton'. Mr Ridge, the Chief Constable, had been quite properly suspended from duty when first arrested and charged with conspiracy, but after his acquittal the Brighton Watch Committee, which was then the police authority for Brighton, unanimously dismissed him from office, without giving him any prior notice or offering him a hearing. His solicitor then applied for a hearing, and was allowed to appear before a later meeting of the Committee, but the Committee confirmed their decision by a vote of nine to three. Mr Ridge exercised his statutory right of appeal to the Home Secretary, but his appeal was dismissed. He was particularly anxious to establish that he had been wrongfully dismissed in order to protect his police pension rights, and so he brought an action seeking a declaration that his dismissal from office was illegal, and also claiming damages for wrongful dismissal. He failed in the High Court, and again in the Court of Appeal, but the House of Lords found in his favour by a majority of four to one. The decision in the High Court had been partly on the basis of an interpretation of the police discipline regulations which are not relevant to the principles we are discussing here, but also partly on the ground that the power to dismiss the Chief Constable was administrative, and thus not subject to judicial review. The appellate courts also dealt with the effect of the regulations, but the Court of Appeal came to the conclusion that on general grounds the rules of natural justice must be adhered to before such an officer is dismissed. However, the Court of Appeal considered that, in view of the trial for conspiracy, the remarks of the trial judge about Mr Ridge, and the hearing of Mr Ridge's solicitor after the announcement of the dismissal, there was enough to conclude that Ridge must have known the nature of the charge against him, and had been given adequate

---

9 [1964] AC 40. A later decision on similar lines was given by the Divisional Court in *R v Secretary of State for the Environment, ex p Brent London Borough Council* [1982] QB 593, in which the Secretary of State was held to have denied six London Boroughs any opportunity to make representations before he exercised his statutory powers to reduce their rate support grant. See also *R v Secretary of State for the Home Department, ex p Benwell* [1985] QB 554 (dismissal of prison officer quashed for breach of natural justice).

opportunity to be heard. The majority in the House of Lords agreed that the rules of natural justice were applicable to the circumstances of Ridge's dismissal, but drew the opposite inference from the Court of Appeal as to the facts, holding that Ridge had had no adequate opportunity to know what charges he faced before the committee, and that he had thereafter also had no adequate opportunity to put his side of the case to them.

It has never been denied that ultimately the doctrine of Parliamentary sovereignty ensures that it depends upon Parliament's wish whether or not the courts may interfere with the decision of any authority. We know from such cases as *Padfield v Minister of Agriculture, Fisheries and Food*, discussed in the last chapter, that there is probably no such thing as an unfettered statutory discretion, though providing an authority keeps within the bounds of a discretion properly conferred by statute its actions will be legal. But this is not to say that a statutory provision conferring the power to make decisions concerning the rights of individuals to earn their livings in particular ways is conferring an administrative power which will not be subject to challenge in the courts. It may well be that the applicants or complainants in many twentieth century cases have been unworthy to be allowed to continue in their particular offices. It may very well be that Mr Ridge was not, as it turned out, the sort of man who should have continued to hold the office of Chief Constable of Brighton. But the error of the courts in cases such as *Nakkuda Ali* and *Parker* was that they prevented us from knowing whether this was so or not. No harm can possibly result from a proper hearing in relation to any complaints against office-holders, and the prime virtue of *Ridge v Baldwin* is that the Lords took the opportunity to redress the balance of case law by reaffirming that, in the absence of clear statutory words to the contrary, every authority having the power or duty to decide upon the merits of an issue concerned with dismissal from office is first bound to adhere to the rules of natural justice. Earlier decisions to the contrary were disapproved of, and such classic decisions as *Cooper v Wandsworth Board of Works* were expressly approved. This author was particularly pleased by the decisions of the Lords in *Ridge v Baldwin*, because he won half a bottle of claret on it, but there are even more sterling reasons for welcoming it than that.

It is a major achievement of the House of Lords in *Ridge v Baldwin* that the majority considered it no longer to be of any great significance to classify powers and duties as judicial, quasi-judicial or administrative. Instead the common law presumption is to be applied that the rules of natural justice must be adhered to in all cases where dismissal from office is being considered, unless it concerns a domestic relationship or dismissal from an office held during pleasure. As Lord Reid said,[10] 'I find an unbroken line of authority to the effect that an officer cannot lawfully be dismissed without first telling him what is alleged against him and hearing his defence or explanation.' Although the presumption may be specifically excluded by Act of Parliament in any instance, it will be applied in the absence of such exclusion, regardless of any previously understood classification of powers and duties. Thus it is now accepted that administrative functions are subject to the controlling jurisdiction of the courts without it being necessary for a court first to apply the appropriate label to any such function.

In a Scottish appeal in 1971,[11] the Lords held that a schoolteacher who by statute held his appointment 'during the pleasure' of the school board, could not validly be dismissed without a hearing. And in *R v Hillingdon Borough Council, ex p Royco Homes Ltd*,[12] already mentioned in chapter 3, Lord Widgery CJ said:[13]

> In the course of the judgments in this court reference was made to a frequently quoted observation of Atkin LJ in *R v Electricity Comrs, ex p London Electricity Joint Committee Co (1920) Ltd*[14] ... In view of that clear dictum of Atkin LJ, it is surprising that so little use has been made of the prerogative orders in this particular field, and I think that Mr Chavasse may have put his finger on the explanation when he referred to the fact that Aktin LJ's dictum required not only that the body to whom certiorari was to go should have legal authority to determine questions affecting the rights of subjects but also that the body should have the duty to act judicially, a phrase which is rather less clear and indeed very difficult of definition. Accordingly it may be that previous efforts to use certiorari in this field have been deterred by Atkin LJ's reference to its being necessary for the body affected to have the duty to act judicially.
>
> If that is so, that reason for reticence on the part of applicants was, I think, put an end to in the House of Lords in *Ridge v Baldwin* ... It is a case the facts of which are very far from the present and indeed have nothing to do with planning at all. In the course of his speech, however, Lord Reid made reference to that oft-quoted dictum of Atkin LJ, and pointed out that the additional requirement of the body being under a duty to act judicially was not supported by authority. Accordingly, it seems to me that that obstacle, if obstacle it was, has been cleared away and I can see no reason for this court holding otherwise than that there

---

10   [1964] AC 40 at 66.
11   *Malloch v Aberdeen Corpn* [1971] 2 All ER 1278.
12   [1974] QB 720.
13   Ibid at 727.
14   [1924] 1 KB 171 at 205. Atkin LJ had said: 'Wherever any body of persons, having legal authority to determine the rights of subjects and having the duty to act judicially, act in excess of their legal authority, they are subject to the controlling jurisdiction of the King's Bench Division exercised in these writs.'

is power in appropriate cases for the use of the prerogative orders to control the activity of a local planning authority. To put it the other way round, I see no general legal inhibition on the use of such orders, although no doubt they must be exercised only in the clearest cases and with a good deal of care on the part of the court.

Although in most cases since 1960 the courts have endeavoured to apply the presumption of the necessity to adhere to the rules of natural justice regardless of any classification of the powers under review, a complication has been introduced by the tendency of some judges still to refer to powers or duties which are in question as being judicial. An example is the Divisional Court case of *R v Criminal Injuries Compensation Board, ex p Lain*.[15] *Lain's* case is notable also as an example of the application of judicial review to the activities of an authority which at that time was set up and acting under non-statutory powers.[16] The applicant was the widow of a police officer who had been shot by a suspect whom he was about to question, and who, as a result of the total blindness he suffered in one eye, later took his own life. She had applied to the Board, which was charged with the duty of considering applications for compensation for crimes of violence, and which made its awards out of funds provided by the Home Office. The departmental scheme under which the Board acted required the Board to reduce the amount of any sums awarded by the amount of any payments from public funds, including, as in this case, any payments from the police pension fund. The scheme also provided that an application would normally be considered by a single member of the Board, but that a rehearing of an application could be asked for before three members of the Board. Mrs Lain was dissatisfied with the £300 awarded to her by the single member, and applied for a rehearing; but on the rehearing the three members, after making due allowance for the sums she would receive from the police pension fund, reduced the award to nil. Although her subsequent application for certiorari to quash this decision was refused, on the ground that no error had been committed by the Board, Lord Parker CJ dwelt at some length on the reasons why a non-statutory inferior authority was just as amenable to the jurisdiction of the court as a statutory body, and he concluded.[17]

> We have as it seems to me reached the position when the ambit of certiorari can be said to cover every case in which a body of persons of a public as opposed to a purely private or domestic character has to

15 [1967] 2 QB 864.
16 The Home Secretary announced in March 1984 that victims of crime are to be given a statutory right to compensation for criminal injuries in new legislation.
17 [1967] 2 QB 864 at 882.

determine matters affecting subjects provided always that it has a duty to act judicially.

This type of statement would at first sight appear to put us back to the old problem of classifying powers and duties. But it is important to realise the context of such statements by modern judges. Where they use the term 'judicial' to characterise the status of an inferior body's functions they are striving to assert that the authority is subject to review by the superior courts. Lord Parker was emphasising that a non-statutory authority is as subject to judicial review as is the more usual statutory body. Accordingly it is not justifiable to assume that the old classification of functions has been revived. Most judges will today rightly ignore the old Donoughmore Committee's classification, and stick to the common law presumption restated by Lord Reid in *Ridge v Baldwin*. Alternatively, and possibly as a comfortably verbal link with pre-1964 usage, they will characterise the functions of any inferior body whose actions are subject to judicial review as 'judicial'. But this latter term bears no relation to the stricter term adopted by the Committee on Ministers' Powers in 1932. Whichever terminology the judges adopt, the result in law is the same.

The central position of natural justice

So prominent have the rules of natural justice become since *Ridge v Baldwin* that they have virtually become the prime test of proper administrative procedure. They are the practical reminders of that somewhat abstract concept, the Rule of Law. Especially is this so with the *audi alteram partem* rule, which is far more often invoked in litigation than is the rule against bias. The reason for this latter phenomenon is not hard to find, for the standard of administrative behaviour is generally high. Members of administrative authorities are well aware of the necessity to avoid any suspicion of bias in the discharge of their functions, but it is not always so easy to guard against a complaint that a proper hearing has not been allowed. After all, every hearing must end sometime, and yet any person who finds himself dissatisfied with the eventual decision at the end of the hearing is certainly tempted to feel that he was not adequately heard, and that perhaps a longer hearing or the ventilation of further arguments, whether or not relevant, might have resulted in a different decision. The point has frequently been made that there is no need to adopt any set form of procedure in order to discharge the duty to give a proper hearing, provided that adequate notice has been given to all parties of the issues involved, and that thereafter there is adequate opportunity for each party to put his side of the case. Provided that these simple requirements are fulfilled, there is no need for an inferior authority to follow the technical rules of evidence.[18]

Common sense often indicates where the *audi alteram partem* requirement has been satisfied. In *Ostreicher v Secretary of State for the Environment*,[19] a local authority had made a compulsory purchase order under the Housing Act 1957 relating, inter alia, to houses owned by Mrs Ostreicher, and her surveyor lodged an objection on her behalf. By letter, dated 5 February 1976, the surveyor was then informed that the inquiry was to be held on 21 April. On 1 April the surveyor wrote that because of religious reasons his client was unable to attend on 21 April, and after briefly stating what her objections to the order were he asked for a special hearing to be arranged. On 7 April the Secretary of State wrote that it was not possible for a special hearing to be arranged, assured the surveyor that full account of his written objections would be taken, and pointed out that Mrs Ostreicher could be represented at the inquiry. Mrs Ostreicher was a Jew of the Chasidm congregation, and was thereby prohibited both from working and from employing anybody else to do so on the sabbath or holy days, and so she was not represented at the inquiry, nor did she or her surveyor reply to the letter of 7 April. The inquiry was duly held on 21 April, and the compulsory purchase order was confirmed, whereupon Mrs Ostricher sought an order to quash it on various grounds including that of breach of natural justice. Sir Douglas Frank QC, sitting as Deputy High Court Judge, rejected the application, holding that an opportunity to be heard had been given, and that the failure to reply to the letter of 7 April appeared to amount to acquiescence in what the Secretary of State had written. Furthermore the request for the fixing of a special date for the hearing should have been made before the hearing was fixed, and certainly not nearly two months after being notified that there would be a hearing. The Court of Appeal affirmed this decision, holding that, while any party or objector must be given a fair opportunity of being heard, this requirement had been satisfied. The applicant had been given the opportunity of being represented at the inquiry, and the inspector had her written representation before him. The applicant was very far from the only objector to be considered, and all objectors as well as the proponents of the plan had to be given an opportunity to be heard. To put off a hearing at the behest of one dilatory objector might cause great inconvenience and injustice

18 See Diplock LJ in *R v Deputy Industrial Injuries Comr, ex p Moore* [1965] 1 QB 456 at 488.
19 [1978] 3 All ER 82.

to others involved in the matter. Thus a balance of interest must be maintained, and on a general view of the whole issues there had been no breach of natural justice in failing to accede to the request for a special hearing.

A case dealing with a not dissimilar problem, but going the other way, was *Fairmount Investments Ltd v Secretary of State for the Environment*.[20] A local authority was satisfied that a group of houses was unfit for human habitation. Acting under the Housing Act 1957, it therefore declared them to be in a clearance area and, with a view to demolition, submitted a compulsory purchase order in respect of the houses to the Secretary of State for confirmation. The respondent company, who owned most of the house concerned, lodged an objection, and so a public inquiry was held, after which the inspector made a site inspection. At the inquiry the council had contended that settlement rendered the houses unfit, whereas the company had argued that they were capable of rehabilitation. However, the inspector based his recommendation that the order should be confirmed upon his opinion that the foundations of the houses were inadequate, and that rehabilitation was not a viable proposition. It appeared that this opinion must have been gained from his site inspection, for no suggestion had been made at the inquiry itself as to the inadequacy of the foundations. The Secretary of State accepted the inspector's findings and confirmed the order, whereupon the company applied to the High Court to have the order quashed. Although they were unsuccessful at first instance, the court's decision was reversed by the Court of Appeal, and the House of Lords confirmed this reversal, holding that it was contrary to the rules of natural justice to recommend compulsory purchase for the purpose of demolition on the basis of a finding which the owners had been given no opportunity to refute. The distinction between *Fairmount* and *Ostreicher* is clear, for in *Fairmount* the proper inquiry procedure had been departed from and the company had no means of knowing the basis ultimately adopted by the inspector for his recommendation to the Secretary of State.

A licensing case which admirably illustrates the way in which judicial attitudes have changed since the *Nakkuda Ali* and *Parker* decisions is *R v Barnsley Metropolitan Borough Council, ex p Hook*.[1] Mr Hook had a licence from the respondents as a stallholder in a market regulated by the Council under statutory powers. One day, after the close of the market, two Council employees saw him urinating in a side street. When they rebuked him, he used abusive language, and

20 [1976] 2 All ER 865.
1 [1976] 3 All ER 452.

the employees made a complaint to the civic amenities committee of the local authority through the market manager. The committee afforded Mr Hook a hearing, and he explained his action by saying that the call of nature was urgent and that the public lavatories had been locked for the night. The market manager was present during the hearing, but he also remained with the committee after Mr Hook's departure, and while they were deliberating upon their decision. The committee decided to revoke Hook's licence, and although they reconsidered this at a later meeting, again with the market manager present, they still decided to stick to their original decision. Hook then applied for certiorari to quash the revocation of his licence on the ground of a breach of natural justice. The Divisional Court refused his application, taking the view that the proceedings were purely administrative. On appeal, however, the Court of Appeal found that, although the control over licensing of stalls involved an administrative function, its essence was to regulate the conduct of the market, and this involved determination of matters which affected not just the contractual rights of stallholders but also the rights of subjects. The rights of the public to buy and sell in the market were common law rights deriving from the long-established rules relating to the holding of markets, and not simply from contracts entered into with those controlling the market place. Therefore the local authority's power fell within the judgment of Atkin LJ in the *Electricity Comrs* case, quoted above, as explained by Lord Reid in *Ridge v Baldwin*. Both rules of natural justice had been broken for, as well as allowing the complainant to be present throughout its deliberations while excluding the stallholder, the committee had essentially acted as judge in its own cause. Certiorari was accordingly granted, and the revocation quashed.

The three members of the Court of Appeal adopted slightly different reasons for their decision. Lord Denning considered that it was of no significance whether or not the committee's decision was characterised as administrative or judicial, for certiorari would be available in any event. Scarman LJ and Sir John Pennycuick, however, sought to describe the power exercised by the committee as judicial, thus rendering it subject to the requirement to adhere to the rules of natural justice and review by means of certiorari. If the meaning of the terminology of 'judicial' is equated with that suggested in this chapter, the views of all three judges can be readily reconciled. It is interesting also to note that Lord Denning and Sir John Pennycuick made their decisions not only on the basis of breaches of natural justice, but because of the unreasonableness of the committee's determination, in that revocation of the licence was a punishment out of all proportion to the applicant's misbehaviour.

The Court of Appeal made a similar decision in *R v Board of Visitors of Hull Prison, ex p St Germain*,[2] where again the use of the word 'judicial' can be reconciled with the view suggested in this chapter. The case arose out of disturbances in the prison in August and September 1976. A Board of Visitors, acting under powers conferred by the Prison Act 1952, heard charges against seven prisoners who had been involved in the disturbance, and made various order for their punishment, including loss of remission. The prisoners alleged a failure on the part of the Board to observe the rules of natural justice, and applied for certiorari to quash the order. On a preliminary point the Divisional Court held that there was no jurisdiction to hear the application because the Baord was sitting solely as a disciplinary body.[3] However the Court of Appeal, this time sitting without Lord Denning, held that as the Board was bound to adjudicate on questions of breaches of Prison Rules which may affect the rights, liberties or status of prisoners, it must be required to act judicially – in other words, it is subject to the supervisory jurisdiction of the High Court. The court returned the case to the Divisional Court to find whether any breach of natural justice had occured, and the Divisional Court then found that six of the prisoners had not received a fair hearing. Hearsay evidence had been admitted without an opportunity for exculpation being given, and a wrong reason had also been given for refusing to allow one prisoner to call witnesses. Thus the Board of Visitors' decisions were quashed in part.[4]

Again, in *Stevenson v United Road Transport Union*[5], very much the same point was taken. Mr Stevenson had been employed by the trade union as a full-time regional officer on terms that he would hold office for so long as he gave satisfaction to the union's Executive Committee. Unfortunately friction developed between Stevenson and other union members, and ultimately, following a report by the Divisional Officer to the Executive Committee, Stevenson was summoned to attend a disciplinary hearing. He was not given details before the hearing of the allegations against him, and his request at the hearing for the charges and relevant evidence to be put in writing, and for time to be allowed for him to prepare his defence, was refused. After deliberation the Executive Committee resolved to dismiss him from office, whereupon Stevenson brought an action for a declaration

2 [1979] QB 425.
3 This was based upon the authority of *Ex p Fry* [1954] 2 All ER 118.
4 *R v Hull Prison Board of Visitors, ex p St Germain (No 2)* [1979] 3 All ER 545. See also *R v Blundeston Prison Board of Visitors, ex p Fox-Taylor* [1982] 1 All ER 646, in which Phillips J held there was a breach of natural justice where the prison authorities had failed to ensure that all the evidence was available to the Board.
5 [1977] 2 All ER 941.

that his dismissal was illegal as being in breach of natural justice. It was argued on behalf of the union at the trial that the union was under no obligation to comply with the rules of natural justice, partly because the facts in the case were analogous to those which prevail in a relationship of master and servant. But Deputy Judge Dillon held that the analogy was false, and that the relationship of a full-time union officer to his union was not one relying wholly upon the contractual basis of pure master and servant. The office held by Stevenson conferred a status upon him, and that status could not be removed unless some misconduct has been shown on his part. Accordingly he was entitled to a hearing, and as no proper hearing had been accorded to him the purported dismissal was a nullity. The Court of Appeal upheld this decision, and stressed that the Executive Committee had not been exercising a purely disciplinary power, but had been making a decision of a judicial nature which required adherence to the rules of natural justice.

As a final example of the central and fundamental character of these rules, let us take *Metroplitan Properties Co (FGC) Ltd v Lannon*,[6] which is concerned with the less frequently invoked rule, the rule against bias. The case concerned the decision of a rent assessment committee, which is one of the tribunals that will be referred to in chapter 6 of this book. It is sufficient for present purposes to say that such tribunals hear appeals from decisions of rent officers in fixing fair rents for privately rented accommodation, and that they derive their powers and jurisdiction from the Rent Acts. The rent assessment committee concerned in the case was acting under the Rent Act 1965, though that Act has subsequently been repealed and re-enacted, with minor amendments, by later Rent Acts, the one currently in force being the Rent Act 1977. In hearing an appeal from a rent officer's decision, the rent assessment committee had reduced the rents of flats involved in the case below the figures fixed by the rent officer, and also below the figures put forward by the valuer who had given evidence on behalf of the tenants. The chairman of the committee, a solicitor, lived in a similar block of flats some miles from the flats concerned in the case, and in a different London registration area, owned by associates of the landlords in the case, and he had assisted his neighbours and his father, with whom he lived, in bringing other proceedings under the Act.

The landlords appealed against the committee's decision, under the Tribunals and Inquiries Act 1958, which has since been replaced by an Act of the same name passed in 1971, and which gave a right of appeal on law from the tribunal, and they also applied for an

6 [1969] 1 QB 577.

order of certiorari to quash the decision. The Divisional Court held that the committee were entitled to use their own knowledge and experience, and were not bound to accept expert opinion, although they were bound to hear it. Accordingly there had been no error of law. The court also decided that there was no sufficient reason for them to form the impression that the chairman had been biased, nor was there any suggestion of actual bias. Both the appeal and the application for certiorari were refused. But the Court of Appeal took a different view on the matter of bias, and on that point only reversed the decision of the Divisional Court. Although in the circumstances the Court of Appeal was prepared to find that there had been no actual bias on the part of the chairman, nevertheless the facts relating to his connection with other tenants of the landlords or their associates were such as to give the reasonable impression that he was biased. The decision of the committee was thus quashed by a certiorari, and the case remitted to another rent assessment committee for hearing. The case is particularly notable in that the Court of Appeal, consisting this time of Lord Denning MR, Danckwerts and Edmund David LJJ, clarified the nature of the test to be applied by any court in determining whether or not the rule *nemo judex in causa sua* has been broken. The court rejected the contention that the test is subjective, being a question of whether there had, in the eyes of the court, been a real likelihood of bias – a test which had previously been used in the same court in the earlier case of *R v Barnsley Licensing Justices, ex p Barnsley and District Licensed Victuallers' Association*.[7] Instead the court established an objective test of whether there was reasonable suspicion of bias. This is probably more satisfactory, and it has remained since the *Lannon* decision in 1969 as the accepted judicial test under this heading of natural justice.

The character of the rules of natural justice as the prime tests of fairness in hearings by authorities which have to determine questions between competing parties is thus clearly established. It is always open to an Act of Parliament to exclude the application of the rules, though the courts will be reluctant to accept such exclusion unless it is clearly expressed, because the rules of natural justice are basic common law presumptions. Yet there are sometimes other circumstances in which the rules are held not to be applicable, largely as a result of judicial policy. An instance of this judicial exclusion or limitation is provided by the law concerning deportation of aliens. Let us take the recent example of an American journalist, Mr Hosenball, in 1977.[8] He had been working in London, and the Home

7 [1960] 2 QB 167.
8 *R v Secretary of State for Home Department, ex p Hosenball* [1977] 3 All ER 452.

Secretary had ordered his deportation on the ground of national security, having considered the advice given him by the advisory panel maintained within the Home Office for this purpose, and also representations made on Hosenball's behalf. Mr Hosenball argued that, as the Home Secretary had failed to supply information as to the reasons for the deportation, he was unable to answer them. The Home Secretary had therefore acted contrary to natural justice. But the Court of Appeal unanimously held that the rules of natural justice had to be modified in cases such as this, and that the balance between the interest of national security and the freedom of the individual was for the Home Secretary, answerable to Parliament, to decide and not for the courts. This is a decision which is open to criticism, partly because of the court's willingness to rule that natural justice can be modified, and partly because, even if the courts ought not to usurp the prerogative of Parliament by asking the Home Secretary to account for his exercise of the power of deportation, they are not necessarily precluded from conducting surveillance of proper procedures.

Opinions may well differ as to how far the Home Secretary's power to deport should be subject to judicial review. But there can be less objection to the view of the Court of Appeal the following year that the rules of natural justice cannot be employed in order to regulate the appointment of inspectors by the Department of Trade.[9] Here Norwest Holst Ltd, a public company with thirty-five subsidiaries, had sought a declaration that the appointment by the Secretary of State for Trade and Industry, under section 165 of the Companies Act 1948, of inspectors to investigate the affairs of the company was ultra vires. Section 167 empowered the Secretary of State to appoint such inspectors where it appeared that there were circumstances suggesting that persons concerned with a company's formation or management may have been guilty of fraud, misfeasance or other misconduct, and in this case the directors or Norwest Holst Ltd objected to the appointment on the ground that no reason had been given for it. Ormrod LJ, speaking for a unanimous court, unfortunately described the appointment as an administrative function, but he then went on to say that such an appointment set in train an investigation in which all involved would have the opportunity to present their case. Provided that the Secretary of State acted bona fide within the powers granted by the Act, there was no ground upon which his action could be challenged. There was no necessary implication that there had been malpractice in the company's affairs, and the rules of natural justice would come into

9 *Norwest Holst Ltd v Secretary of State for Trade* [1978] Ch 201.

their own as the guides for behaviour in the course of the actual inquiry by the inspectors. It seems clear enough from the full context of the case that the use of the word 'administrative' in no way detracts from the force of the rules of natural justice in their proper place.

It certainly appears that in recent cases the courts have adopted a very commonsense approach to the propriety of applying the rules of natural justice. In *Lewis v Heffer*,[10] considerable internal problems had arisen within the Newham North-East Constituency Labour Party. Mr Reginald Prentice had for many years been the MP for the constituency, which was generally regarded as 'safe' for the Labour Party. He was last elected for that constituency in October 1974, but thereafter found himself more and more at odds with both the Labour Government, of which he was at one time a Cabinet Minister, and his Constituency Party, which was regarded as swinging to the far left of the Labour Party. It is common knowledge that Mr Prentice eventually resigned from the Labour Party, later joined the Conservative Party, was elected to the House of Commons in a different constituency in the General Election of 1979, and then became a Minister in the new Conservative Government. But *Lewis v Heffer* was concerned not with Mr Prentice, but with the fact that, after he had severed his connection with his old constituency party, and after a series of apparent changes in the control of the local party organisation, the National Executive Committee of the Labour Party had passed a resolution suspending the local committees and officers of the Newham North-East Party pending the results of an inquiry by the NEC. One of the local officers applied for an injunction to prevent the implementation of the suspension, claiming that the NEC had acted unlawfully and contrary to natural justice. Later the plaintiff and another officer of the local party discovered that the NEC were considering suspending them from membership of the Labour Party pending the result of the NEC inquiry, and so they also applied for injunctions to restain their suspension on grounds similar to that in the earlier action. Both sets of injunctions were refused at first instance, and this decision was upheld by the Court of Appeal. It was held that the NEC had acted lawfully in accordance with the constitution of the Labour Party which, by implication, gave them powers of suspension. There is no duty to observe the rules of natural justice when suspensions are made as a holding measure pending inquiries. The allegation that the NEC were acting with the ulterior motive of preferring one faction in the constituency to another had not been proved, though the Court of Appeal took the view that

10 [1978] 3 All ER 354.

if it had been made out this would have rendered the suspensions invalid.

Student cases

A vexed area of application of the rules of natural justice is that of students at universities and other colleges. The courts have been consistent in holding that adademic disciplinary proceedings do require the observance of the principles of natural justice, but they have equally been somewhat astute to discover reasons in virtually every case so far reported why a remedy should be denied to the applicant.[11] One instance may suffice for the present purpose. In *Glynn v Keele University*[12] the plaintiff was one of several students identified as having been seen naked on the university campus. As a result of being reported to the university authorities for this the Vice-Chancellor had fined and rusticated him. The Vice-Chancellor had acted under university statutes, but he had failed to give the student an opportunity to be heard before imposing the punishments, and had merely informed him of his right to appeal to a university appellate body. The student expressed a wish to appeal, but then went abroad before receiving notification of the appeal date, and he did not return until after the hearing, which had upheld the Vice-Chancellor's decision. The student therefore sought an injunction restraining the exclusion from residence. A small confusion in the report of the case is occasioned by the fact that his application came for decision before the Vice-Chancellor of the Chancery Division, Sir John Pennycuick, so that there were two quite different types of Vice-Chancellor involved, one judging the propriety of the actions of the other. But Sir John Pennycuick V-C dismissed the application. He did in fact hold that the University Vice-Chancellor had acted in breach of the rules of natural justice by which he was bound, because the power of expulsion or suspension from a university was more than a mere magisterial power of a tutor over a pupil. But the granting of an injunction is within the discretion of the court, and although the student had been deprived of the opportunity of meeting the charge against him and making a mitigating plea, the conduct established merited a severe penalty. Furthermore he had not been

---

11 See Wade *Administrative Law* (5th edn) p 501, and Jackson *Natural Justice* (2nd edn) pp 156–168.
12 [1971] 2 All ER 89. See also *Calvin v Carr* [1980] AC 574, in which the Privy Council held that a breach of natural justice at the stewards' inquiry in New South Wales, as a result of which a jockey was disqualified for a year, could be cured by a later fair hearing by the Appeal Committee of the Jockey Club.

deprived of his right to appeal, but had failed to make the necessary arrangements to attend the hearing of the appeal which he had himself set in motion. The student cases do highlight certain dangers in the courts' approach to the application of natural justice, but they also show an element of common sense. There is no denial that a breach of natural justice renders the behaviour complained of void, but the courts tend to insist that other available remedies should be exhausted before they are prepared to step in with the full power of their own judicial remedies.

The development of a modern rule of fair procedure

It is clear that in recent years the courts have become so used to treating the rules of natural justice as the test of fair play in any proceeding in which the interests of a person or body are at stake that they have become the hallmarks of fairness applied by the courts in their function as reviewing authorities. In a sense the courts have placed more emphasis upon the need to keep to the rules of the game than upon the actual decision reached by an inferior authority in any instance. An example of this tendency is *H Sabey & Co Ltd v Secretary of State for the Environment*.[13]

The case concerned an appeal to the High Court, under section 245 of the Town and Country Planning Act 1971, against a refusal, following a public inquiry, by the Secretary of State to grant planning permission for gravel extraction from what is called Grade I agricultural land. The policy of successive Governments to protect agricultural land of the highest quality has been well known for a long time, and at the public inquiry the applicants had devoted much of their evidence to meeting the objection that the quality of the land would be seriously reduced when it was restored to agriculture after the gravel had been extracted. The inspector reported that 'the underlying gravel by virtue of its structure is an important asset in the production of ground moisture ... The removal of the gravel and its replacement with various materials must put at risk the supply of moisture compatible with the demands of high yields which could be expected from this Grade I land'. The Secretary of State then decided fully in accordance with the inspector's findings and his recommendation that the application be refused. However, at the inquiry no evidence had been adduced on the question of moisture by any witness. The only reference to this issue in the actual

---

13   [1978] 1 All ER 586; see also *R v Leyland Justices, ex p Hawthorn* [1979] QB 283; *Chief Constable of North Wales Police v Evans* [1982] 3 All ER 141; and *R v Huntingdon District Council, ex p Cowan* [1984] 1 All ER 58.

proceedings of the inquiry was when, after a Ministry official had given evidence, and after both cross-examination and re-examination of the official, the inspector had himself asked a question in general terms, in answer to which the official had stated that 'the underlying sand and gravel strata provides water through capillary attraction to the overlying topsoil'.

The court accepted the applicant's submission that the moisture issue had arisen as a 'sidewind', and that to base the final decision upon this ground, without affording the applicants a specific opportunity to call evidence upon what was eventually seen to be the crucial issue in their application, had deprived them of what the court called a 'fair crack of the whip'. Thus the decision of the Secretary of State was quashed as having been made in breach of the *audi alteram partem* rule. It might well be thought that the decision was based upon a substantial point which could legitimately be taken as being of paramount importance by the Minister, but because it was not raised fairly and squarely in the main stream of the evidence at the inquiry the rules of the game had been broken, and accordingly a determination which may have been correct objectively was quashed for reasons of procedural irregularity.

This may seem to push the balance too far in favour of mere rules of procedure, just as in the days before the nineteenth century procedural reforms it was common for any litigant to lose his suit because of an unwise choice of remedy, regardless of the merits of the issue. But the courts are not so foolish today as to allow themselves to be easily manipulated in this way. Thus, in *McInnes v Onslow-Fane*,[14] Megarry V-C declined to intervene to enforce observance of the mechanics of natural justice or procedural fairness where he was satisfied that there was no objectively reasonable ground for doing so. Mr McInnes, who had been a Cambridge boxing blue and then had had a chequered career in the world of professional boxing, encompassing periods as a journalist, a television commentator, promoter, trainer and master of ceremonies, had all the licences that had been granted to him by the sport's controlling body, the British Boxing Board of Control, withdrawn by them in 1973 because of his alleged conduct as a master of ceremonies at a boxing tournament in Bournemouth. It is not entirely clear from the report what went wrong at the Bournemouth tournament, but apparently there were last-minute alterations to the programe, and McInnes seems to have said too much in introducing the various boxers. He later made five unsuccessful applications to the Board for a manager's licence, a type of licence which he had in fact never before held. In 1976 he applied

14 [1978] 3 All ER 211.

yet again for such a licence, asking at the same time for an oral hearing and prior notice of any case against him so that he could answer it. This application was refused without any reasons given, whereupon McInnes sought a declaration that the Board had acted unfairly and in breach of natural justice. Sir Robert Megarry refused the declaration, holding that, although the court had the power to intervene to enforce fairness and natural justice because a man's liberty to work was involved, McInnes was entitled only to have his application decided honestly by the Board. They were under no obligation to give reasons for proposing to refuse a licence nor for so doing, and there was equally no obligation to give an oral hearing. The judge even went so far as to state that the giving of reasons, in this particular issue, might have exposed the Board to unnecessary litigation at the suit of Mr McInnes.

McInnes v Onslow-Fane was decided in the same year as *Sabey*'s case, but it could be interpreted as going in a diametrically opposite direction. Yet this is not really so. In *Sabey* the applicant for planning permission had never had a chance to raise any argument concerning the question of moisture, which turned out to be vital in the refusal of his application. In *McInnes* the applicant had asked the Board to include in its procedure extra elements which it had never been under any obligation to follow. The Board was in the same sort of position as any domestic controlling body set up by those who pursue a particular occupation in order to maintain standards and to prevent abuse. A few such bodies have later been regulated by statute, as for instance those concerned with the medical and dental professions. But most remain endowed only with those powers and duties conferred upon them by the consensus of the members of the trade, business or occupation concerned. The British Boxing Board of Control was certainly not exempt from judicial review, for Megarry V-C said that any body whose powers cover a virtual monopoly upon a field of human activity, including the liberty to work in that field, is susceptible to the court's jurisdiction. It may not act capriciously and unreasonably to prevent a man from earning his living. But Megarry V-C went on to distinguish three classes of case which might arise before such a body: (1) forfeiture cases, where the decision takes away an existing right of possession; (2) application cases, where a licence or membership is refused; and (3) expectation cases, an intermediate category, where, for example, an existing licence-holder applies for renewal. The judge considered that cases within class (1) fall clearly within the scope of natural justice, and that much the same may be said for class (3), in that the deciding body must be unbiased, and that notice of charges must be given, as well as an opportunity to be heard in answer. But in the judge's view cases within class (2) do not attract the full rigour of these rules. In the plaintiff's case, which fell in class (2), the application was for a type of licence which had never been held before. The judge concluded from this that the applicant had no legitimate expectation of it being granted, and could thus have had no more than a hope that he might be successful.

Megarry V-C said that the further the situation is away from anything which may reasonably be called a justifiable question, the more appropriate it is to reject an expression which includes the word 'justice', and instead to use the word 'fairness', or a duty to act fairly. All concerned in *McInnes* accepted that the Board was under a duty to reach an honest decision, without bias, and not in pursuance of a capricious policy. The judge relied upon the authority of *R v Gaming Board of Great Britain, ex p Benaim and Khaida*,[15] where the Gaming Board, in considering an application, were required to consider 'the character, reputation and financial standing of applicants', and the court had found that fairness required that notice of relevant objections against applicants should be given. Sir Robert Megarry distinguished cases involving statutes which confer powers and impose a duty to decide upon a defined issue. In *McInnes* the British Boxing Board of Control had a much more general discretion, and refusal of a licence did not involve any slur upon the plaintiff's character. Indeed an applicant of the highest integrity may be refused a licence by the Board where there are already too many licence-holders or where he may lack some quality considered essential to an exacting occupation. The fact that no reasons had been given by the Board did not infringe the requirement of fairness. The rules of natural justice have never included an obligation to give reasons for decisions, and the only legal requirements to give such reasons have stemmed from specific statutory provisions, which in any case were absent as regards the British Boxing Board of Control. In sum, therefore, the judge found that there was no obligation to accede to the request for an oral hearing, nor to give reasons for the decision, and there was nothing else in the procedure of the Board in considering the application to suggest that there had been other than fair dealing with the application.

Granted that in *McInnes* the applicant had no rights which had to be adequately protected, it seems acceptable that the full rigours of the rules of natural justice should not be required of the Board. Yet even in this case the court was prepared to test the procedure adopted by reference to thoughts of fairness. In cases where the rules of natural justice are indeed accepted as fully applicable, the judges

15   [1970] 2 QB 417. See also *Re H K (an infant)* [1967] 2 QB 617.

have in recent years adopted the terminology of fairness. The presumptions established or re-established by *Ridge v Baldwin* are coming to be treated as the basis of fair procedure, and even where they are not applicable the courts will still strive to impose at least a lesser semblence of fairness upon the procedure of the body below. Professor Paul Jackson has suggested that Lord Hewart's famous dictum in *R v Sussex Justices, ex p McCarthy*,[16] that it 'is of fundamental importance that justice should not only be done, but should manifestly and undoubtedly be seen to be done', is perhaps a third rule of natural justice.[17] This may be placing slightly too high a reliance upon the meaning of the dictum, but its purport comes very close to the approach of the courts to all questions coming before them today.

Despite exclusions from the full force of the rules of natural justice, resulting from statutory provisions, or else from a failure to show that rights exist which require the protection of the rules, the existence of the rules of natural justice as basic to the procedural code of English law is now undoubted. In one sense it may be suggested that a breach of natural justice is merely another example of an act which is ultra vires, for the result will be the same, that whatever has been done is void. But, if for no other reason than convenience, it is best to draw a distinction between a failure to keep within the proper jurisdiction laid down, on the one hand, and on the other a failure to keep within the proper rules of procedure while otherwise discharging a jurisdiction which would be valid.

Certainly the primacy of the rules of natural justice was stressed in 1984 by the House of Lords in *Council of Civil Service Unions v Minister for the Civil Service*[18] which arose from the peremptory ruling of the Minister that civil servants employed at the Government's Communications Headquarters at Cheltenham would no longer be permitted to belong to any trade union. Although the Lords decided unanimously that her ruling had been validly made under the Royal Prerogative for reasons of national security, and that accordingly the Court of Appeal had been right to reverse the original decision of Glidewell J to grant a declaration in proceedings for judicial review that the Minister's instruction was invalid, they also concluded that there *had* been a breach of natural justice. They drew no distinction in nature between an act of the Crown done under prerogative, rather than statutory, authority, and made it clear that had it not been for the overriding requirements of national security they would have agreed with Glidewell J that the Minister's action was illegal.

16 [1924] 1 KB 256 at 259.
17 Comment [1976] PL 1.
18 [1985] AC 374.

It may be suggested also that English law pays too great an attention to procedural rules of fair dealing, to the neglect of issues of substance. Thus the courts may be said to hold a decision of an inferior body as inviolate provided that that body has made the right noises in its procedure. If the Brighton Watch Committee had given Mr Ridge due notice of its belief that his trial had disclosed his unfitness for the post of Chief Constable, and had then allowed him ample opportunity to answer such allegations before them, it may well be thought that the Watch Committee could then have dismissed him from ofice without any fear of later being impugned. So it might be deduced from that case that the courts were more concerned to enforce a proper procedure than to reach the right decision on the substance of the issue. It has already been suggested in the last chapter that there may be a great deal to be said for the introduction into English law of a substantial evidence rule, which may provide a better control of administrative power than currently exists. Yet the reasonableness rule, also discussed in chapter 3, as exemplified by such cases as *Tameside*, comes very close to the ideal. Perhaps a combination of the reasonableness rule and the rules of natural justice provide the modern courts with ample ammunition to strike down either wrong procedure or substantial injustice.

5 Remedies

> He that will not apply new remedies must expect new evils; for time is the greatest innovator.
>
> Sir Francis Bacon *Essays: Of Great Place*

In the last two chapters of this book we have explored the grounds upon which judicial review of administrative action may be sought. It is now proposed to consider the remedies which may be sought where some ground for judicial control has been alleged. In countries where, as in France, a separate system of administrative law with its own courts tailor-made for dealing only with administrative problems exists the remedies provided by the law are designed for the purposes of public law only. But this has never been the position in England. Instead the object of judicial control in administrative law has had to be met by adapting supervisory remedies first employed in the courts for the purpose of private law. And yet, having originally borrowed from private law, it is one of the greatest oddities of English administrative law that the nineteenth century procedural reforms in private law passed administrative law by. In the old days of the forms of action it was commonplace for a plaintiff to lose his suit, not because of his failure to establish the merits of his case, but simply because he had sought the wrong writ or remedy. This procedural snare spilled over into public law, and the law reports are full of cases in which the applicant for a remedy was denied by the court on procedural grounds and regardless of the actual issue in dispute. The nineteenth century brought perhaps the most sweeping collection of procedural reforms ever to be enacted in English Law, with the result that for over a century now no private litigant has needed to fear that he would be baulked from redress of whatever wrong he alleged merely because he initially asked the court the wrong question or urged it to provide him with an inappropriate remedy. All he has needed to do is to begin his action with a common form writ, attach to it a statement of claim in which the substance of his complaint is included, and then rely upon the court to provide the appropriate remedy once he has established the justice of his argument; and courts have been perfectly willing to allow amendments to the documentary impedimenta in the course of the hearing of a case if they appear to be necessary or desirable.

But these nineteenth-century reforms did pass public law by, and until recently a system very like that of the old forms of action has pervaded the rules concerning remedies in administrative law. The traditional common law remedies are, first and foremost, the three prerogative orders, originally writs, of certiorari, prohibition and mandamus. But other remedies available to persons aggrieved by administrative decisions have been the declation, the injunction, statutory appeals, adjudications in criminal proceedings, and direct actions for damages in contract and tort. None of these remedies was ever designed exclusively for the purposes of administrative law, and all are used in the more general field of English law. This is certainly the basic difference between English administrative law and the administrative law of a country such as France, for there has never been any attempt here to introduce a system of special administrative courts, and thus to exclude the ordinary courts of the land from jurisdiction in administrative law matters. The traditional remedies of English Law generally have been utilised for the purposes of administrative law, including the control of inferior tribunals and authorities. It has been a precondition for any application for a remedy that one or other or the grounds for judicial review discussed in the last two chapters of this book should be proved to exist. But it has remained the rule of English law, at least until very recently, that it is not enough just to prove the ground of complaint, and that in addition the appropriate remedy should have been sought. As will be seen in due course, this rooting of the law concerning administrative law remedies in an out-moded proceduralism may have been very largely cured with effect from 1978. But it is not possible to put the reforms of recent origin into their proper context, and to assess their effect, without first considering in profile the jigsaw puzzle of remedies with which the courts have been obsessed for centuries in this field.

The old remedies

The three prerogative orders of certiorari, prohibition and mandamus form a traditional common law machinery for the review of proceedings in inferior courts and tribunals, and of the multitudinous activities of adminstrative authorities. It is unnecessary here to describe them other than briefly, but useful accounts of the history and nature of the prerogative orders have been given from time to

The old remedies 119

time in the judgment in modern leading cases, as for example in *R v Northumberland Compensation Appeal Tribunal, ex p Shaw* , discussed in chapter 3 of this book. Ceriorari, if granted, has the effect of quashing whatever has been done by the inferior authority, and thus may be said to be negative in effect. Prohibition shares this negative characteristic, but its effect is to prevent the authority from doing whatever is complained of, rather than quashing it once it has been done. Atkin LJ, in a famous passage once remarked: 'I can see no difference in principle between certiorari and prohibition, except that the latter may be invoked at an earlier stage'[1] Bankes LJ, in the same case, went a little further still in suggesting that the objection to the issue of a writ (as it then was, before it was converted into an order by the Administration of Justice (Miscellaneous Provisions) Act 1938, section 7) because it was sought too early and nothing had yet been decided by the inferior authority would be validly raised in respect of certiorari, but not to an application for prohibition. [2] Mandamus, on the other hand, has a more positive effect, for it issues to direct the inferior authority to carry out its duty according to law.

The theory behind these prerogative orders, or writs, as they were before the purely formal change brought about the 1938 Act, is that they are remedies sought by the Crown directly against whatever inferior authority is the subject of a complaint. But the complaint is of course levelled by some other person or body, and accordingly the Crown only seeks the remedy at the instance of an actual complainant. Hence the form of name which was given to any case in which a prerogative order was sought – *R v The Wrongdoing Authority, ex p Grouse*. Hence also the procedural rule under which it was not possible to apply for a prerogative order in the same suit as any other remedy, for where other remedies are sought the actual complainants are listed as the plaintiffs. It is from the same theoretical background that other procedural disadvantages stemmed. Instead of the more general limitation periods covering the substance of various types of lawsuit, the time limit within which a certiorari has to be applied for was six months from the date of the matter in issue. The time limit did not apply to prohibition, which, in its very nature, contained an inbuilt time limit - there would be nothing left to prohibit once the matter complained of had been completed. Nor did it apply in the case of mandamus, presumably on the ground that it could be safely left to the court to determine whether or not there remained any point in ordering a duty to be carried out if the application for the

---

1 *R v Electricity Comrs, ex p London Electricity Joint Committee Co* (1920) *Ltd* [1924] 1 KB 171 at 206.
2 Ibid at 189. The judgments of both Atkin LJ and Bankes LJ were approved in the later case of *R v Minister of Health, ex p Davis* [1929] 1 KB 619.

remedy was delayed. As regards all three prerogative orders there was no proper interlocutory process, so that inter alia, neither side in the dispute would be able to obtain an order for discovery of documents. At the hearing itself evidence was given on affidavit rather than orally, and cross-examination on the affidavits was only very rarely allowed.

Certiorari was the most usual of the prerogative orders to rival what may be thought the more straightforward remedy of appeal, but it was in some respects wider than, and in other respects more limited than, appeal. At common law the High Court may by certiorari either quash completely the proceedings against which the complaint is levelled, or it may refuse to interfere at all, but it may never, upon granting a certiorari, substitute its own decision for that of the inferior body concerned. All the grounds for judicial review discussed in the last two chapters have been used as the basis for applications for certiorari, and it may seem at first sight that an alllegation of error of law within jurisdiction so clearly involves the reviewing court in an assessment of the merits of a decision below that it would be logical for that court to correct any error found in its ultimate decision. But the court has never accepted such a logical result, and instead certiorari remained an all-or-nothing remedy. Either the reviewing court would quash the proceeding below, or else it would leave its legal effect severely alone. The first statutory recognition that the court ought to possess a power to correct errors which do not go to jurisdiction came in the Administration of Justice Act 1960, though the provision it made for a change in the court's power only affected the granting of certiorari in one type of case in which a conviction before a magistrates' court was in question. Section 16 of the 1960 Act added to the power of the High Court on a certiorari the authority to vary sentence passed by the criminal court below. Although this reform was of limited effect it seems likely that the reasoning behind it may well have had some influence upon the full form of the reforms which took effect from 1978, and which will be discussed presently. The 1960 provision was a pointer to the future.

Despite this development in 1960, certiorari and appeal retained their separate purposes. As Abbott CJ said in 1821,[3] 'the rule is that, although a certiorari lies unless expressly taken away, yet an appeal does not lie, unless expressly given by statute'. Appeal has never been a common law remedy and thus no appeal is possible unless it had been provided for by statutory authority. In many instances there is no statutory provision for an appeal to the courts from the decisions

---

3 *R v Hanson* (1821) 4 B & Ald 519 at 521.

or activities of inferior authorities, and thus an injured party must turn to other remedies. Of such remedies certiorari has always been well designed as a vehicle for entertaining allegations of error of law. But this has been far less the case as regards judicial review of the proceedings of administrative tribunals since the Tribunals and Inquiries Act 1958, section 9, now re-enacted as the Tribunals and Inquiries Act 1971, section 13, gave the right of appeal on law direct from most tribunals to the High Court. The courts have consistently held that where an appeal has been expressly given by statute, that is the remedy which must be adopted, providing that the objection to be made is one suitable for the vehicle of appeal. Consequently the effect of the provision of a right of appeal from tribunals to the courts has been to render appeal the proper course in cases of alleged error of law in the decisions of such tribunals as are covered by the section, while leaving certiorari as the obvious remedy where the allegation made is of ultra vires or breach of natural justice. Furthermore, certiorari on the ground of error of law on the face of the record has become all the more accessible to a complainant in cases which do not fall within section 13 of the 1971 Act, because of the more general provision in section 12 of the Act (replacing the similar section 12 in the 1958 Act) that reasons for the decisions of tribunals covered by the Act, and also of Ministers, must be given if requested either before or at the time of the giving of the decision, and that such reasons, whether written or oral, shall form part of the record of the proceedings.

One limit upon the utility of mandamus has waned markedly in this century. In theory it has always been held that mandamus will not issue against the Crown or against any servant of the Crown in respect of duties owed wholly to the Crown. Historically the only appropriate remedy was by way of petition of right, but this procedure was abolished by the Crown Proceedings Act 1947, though the immunity of the Crown or its agents from a direct issue of mandamus was not changed, for section 11 of the Act makes a saving from the general effect of the Act in respect of acts done under prerogative or statutory powers. Nevertheless the theoretical embargo upon mandamus against the Crown has not in practice impeded those who have sought in this century to obtain orders compelling Ministers to carry out their duties. This seems to have been partly on the ground that most duties of Crown servants are not owed solely to the Crown, and partly because some bodies, like the Board of Education in *Board of Education v Rice*, discussed in chapter 3, are not solely agents of the Crown. Whatever the reason the Law Reports have been full of decisions, such as *Padfield v Minister of Agriculture, Fisheries and Food,*

122 Remedies

also discussed in chapter 3, by which the courts have compelled Ministers to conform to their legal obligations.

Judicial control of administrative action by means of adjudication in criminal proceedings is an important, though unobtrusive, form of such control. Where an administrative authority takes criminal proceedings for the enforcement of, for example, a byelaw, the resulting case is usually thought of as simply a criminal proceeding of a minor type. Yet if the court should find that the byelaw is void the result is not merely an acquittal, but also a judicial decision concerning the invalidity of the subordinate legislation itself. In this way the court may be given the opportunity to rule that the act of an administrative authority is ultra vires.

Apart from specific statutory remedies which may be provided for special purposes, and which may even be specified as exclusive so as to preclude the use of other more general remedies[4] the remaining remedies in the patchwork quilt which existed immediately before the reforms of 1978 are the actions for damages, declarations and injunctions. Just as the preogative orders could be sought either singly or in combination, so these three remedies could be employed either alone or in any permutation of combinations. Special considerations apply to actions for damages against the Crown, and these will be considered in a later section of this chapter. But for circumstances in which damages would not normally seem appropriate, the use of declarations and injunctions for purposes of judicial control of administrative action has been growing in popularity in this century. Thus, in *Barnard v National Dock Labour Board*,[5] a declaration was granted to dock workers to the effect that their suspension from work has been ultra vires, and it was fortunate for the plaintiffs that the remedy was available, because they had had no knowledge of the defect in the notices of suspension (which had in fact been issued by the wrong authority) until after the six-month time limit for a certiorari application had expired. A declaration is in essence no more than a statement by the court of the legal position in any issue brought before it. Accordingly a declaration that a suspension of workers is illegal is tantamount to a quashing of that suspension, for there can be no way thereafter in which legality of such suspension can be shown, and the suspension enforced. Cases like *Barnard* suggested that a complainant might be able to seek a general remedy by means of the declaration in any case where there was a ground for judicial control of the administration. But such a belief which had been

---

4 See e g *R v Kensington and Chelsea (Royal) London Bridge Council, ex p Birdwood* (1976) 74 LGR 424.
5 [1953] 2 QB 18.

growing, and which had been fostered by the encouragement of the future Lord Denning in his Hamlyn Lectures, *Freedom under the Law*, published in 1949, received a sharp check as a result of *Punton v Ministry of Pensions and National Insurance (No 2)*, which has been discussed in chapter 3.

As the purpose of a declaratory judgment has always been to enable a party to obtain a judicial decision upon a state of law or rights, whether or not any other substantial relief is claimed in addition, it has always seemed to be wide in scope, limited only by the court's discretion whether or not to issue a declaration in any actual case. What in *Punton* was eventually shown to be a vital drawback was not till then appreciated to be such, for the problem of enforcement had never previously arisen. The simple fact that a declaration is no more than a statement of law robs it of any coercive power. The weakness has frequently been masked by applications for ancillary relief as well as declarations, but by itself a declaration does no more than expound the law upon a point in issue, and then leave to the parties concerned whether or not they act according to the decision. Of course most parties, and in particular public authorities, are not usually intent upon breaking the law: they merely wish to know what the law is so that they may obey it. The need for coercion would therefore scarely arise. But the courts have held that they will not grant declarations on any subject as to which substantive relief would be entirely beyond the power of the court. In *Punton*, as will be recalled, it was clear that the error of law which was the subject of the complaint did not go to jurisdiction, and thus even if established it would only have rendered the decision of the National Insurance Commissioner voidable. The Commissioner at that time had no power to reverse an error of his own accord after he had already decided the case when it first came before him, and accordingly the Court of Appeal declined even to investigate further to determine whether there had indeed been an error, for a declaration would have done no more than tell everyone that an error within jurisdiction had occurred which was without any possible legal remedy.

Other disadvantages of the declaration included the rule that a person who expects to be made a defendant in an action, and who prefers to be a plaintiff, cannot as a matter of right attain his object by commencing an action for a declaration against the other prospective litigant. As Cozens-Hardy MR once pointed out, the court in the exercise of its discretion may well say: 'wait until you are attacked, and then raise your defence', and it may dismiss the action with costs.[6] But declaration does lie against the Crown, as was

---

6 In *Dyson v* A-G [1911] 1 KB 410 at 417.

established in 1911,[7] and thus does not share the disadvantage of the injunction, which, until 1978, was not obtainable against the Crown. The injunction, one of the classic equitable remedies, is a judicial order to someone or somebody to refrain from doing, or, less usually, to do, a particular act.

The problem of *locus standi* has from time to time given difficulty. As regards the three prerogative orders it seems clear that the court has always had the power within its discretion to entertain any application. The applicant need not shown any special personal right, though if a complete stranger came to court and asked for one of the remedies, the court would probably want to know why he, rather than someone connected with the matter at issue, was applying; and the court might even send him away until such time as he could bring that other person to court, either to apply on behalf of himself or to explain the unusual position. There have perhaps been few examples of prerogative orders being granted to total strangers. But one notable instance was in the case of *R v Greater London Council, ex p Blackburn*, decided in 1976.[8] In the past decade or so Mr Raymond Blackburn, former solicitor and MP, and the twin brothers Norris and Ross McWhirter, well known for their production of *The Guinness Book of Records* (and, tragically, for the assassination of Ross McWhirter by the IRA), have been in the forefront of campaigners against public indecency and obscenity. The 1976 case arose out of an application by Mr Blackburn for an order of prohibition against the GLC to prevent it from licensing indecent films by applying an unduly indulgent test of obscenity. Mr Blackburn was no more than a member of the general public applying in his capacity as a private citizen, and from motives of public interest, but the Court of Appeal found in his favour. In the course of his judgment Lord Denning MR said:[9]

> It was suggested that Mr Blackburn has no sufficient interest to bring these proceedings against the GLC. It is a point which was taken against him by the Commissioner of Police: see *R v Metropolitan Police Comr, ex p Blackburn*:[10] and against the late Mr McWhirter of courageous memory by the Independent Broadcasting Authority: see *A-G ex rel McWhirter v Independent Broadcasting Authority*.[11] On this point, I would ask: Who then can bring proceedings when a public authority is guilty of a misuse of power? Mr Blackburn is a citizen of London. His wife is a ratepayer. He has children who may be harmed by the exhibition of pornographic films.

7   In *Dyson*'s case, above.
8   [1976] 3 All ER 184.
9   Ibid at 191.
10 [1968] 2 QB 118 at 137, 149.
11 [1973] QB 629 at 648-649.

If he has no sufficient interest, no other citizen has. I think he comes within the principle which I stated in *McWhirter's* case,[12] which I would recast today so as to read:
> 'I regard it as a matter of high constitutional principle that if there is a good ground for supposing that a government department or a public authority is transgressing the law, or is about to transgress it, in a way which offends or injures thousands of Her Majesty's subjects, then any one of those offended or injured can draw it to the attention of the courts of law and seek to have the law enforced, and the courts in their discretion can grant whatever remedy is appropriate.'

The applications by Mr Blackburn and Mr McWhirter did much good. They show how desirable such a principle is. One remedy which is always open, by leave of the court, is to apply for a prerogative writ, such as certiorari, mandamus or prohibition. These provide a discretionary remedy and the discretion of the court extends to permitting an application to be made by any member of the public: see *R v Thames Magistrates' Court, ex p Greenbaum*,[13] and especially what was said by Parker LJ; and *R v Hereford Corpn, ex Harrower*;[14] though it will refuse it to a mere busy body who is interfering in things which do not concern him: see *R v Paddington Valuation Officer, ex p Peachey Property Corpn. Ltd.*[15]

In the event the court allowed Mr Blackburn's appeal against the Divisional Court's previous refusal of a prohibition and awarded him costs both in the Court of Appeal and below. But issue of the prohibition was suspended to allow the council 'time to mend their ways'. Mr Blackburn was granted leave to apply later if necessary for its issue.

The rule concerning applications for a declaration, an injunction or for damages, however, was that the applicant must be a person who is particularly aggrieved by the act of the defendant, a point directly decided in *Gregory v London Borough of Camden* in 1966.[16] Yet in the case of the injunction it is possible for a private applicant to get round the difficulties of the *locus standi* rule by a relator action, which is brought by the Attorney-General at the relation or instance of some other person. The private citizen is thus setting in motion machinery whereby the Crown exercises its power to see that public bodies are keeping within their lawful authority. However this type of action does depend upon the Attorney-General agreeing, within the exercise of his own discretion, which was gained through the Royal Preogative, to permit the relator action to proceeed, and we shall see later in this chapter that in the celebrated case of *Gouriet v*

12 Ibid at 649.
13 (1957) 55 LGR 129.
14 [1970] 3 All ER 460.
15 [1966] 1 QB 380 at 401.
16 [1966] 2 All ER 196.

Union of Post Office Workers[17] he was not prepared to allow the action to be brought.

In the decade before 1978 the indications were growing that the courts themselves were becoming impatient with the procedural impediments surrounding the different administrative law remedies. In *Chapman v Earl*[18] the Divisional Court heard an appeal on law from a decision of a rent assessment committee together with an application for certiorari on the ground of error of law on the face of the record. The appeal was refused, but certiorari was granted because of a fatal defect rendering the committee's decision a nullity; yet the most surprising aspect of the decision was that the court did not consider rejecting the whole application on the ground that it was not competent to consider an appeal along with an application for certiorari. In *Metropolitan Properties Co (FGC) Ltd v Lannon*, discussed in the last chapter, certiorari was again allowed in the same proceedings in which an appeal was made under the Tribunals and Inquiries Act (section 9 of the 1958 Act on that occasion); and in *Priddle v Fisher & Sons*,[19] where the Divisional Court was hearing an appeal from an industrial tribunal, Lord Parker CJ said that if the case had been one for certiorari rather than appeal, 'nothing would be easier than to allow the appellant to prefer a motion for certiorari'.[20] Again, in *Michaelides v O'Neill*,[1] which was a case of an appeal under the Tribunals and Inquiries Act 1971, section 13, from the decision of a rent tribunal, the Divisional Court appeared quite prepared to allow appeal and certiorari to be used interchangeably. Clearly the courts had themselves set the stage for a thorough overhaul of the machinery whereby judicial review of administrative action is obtained, though, as we shall see, the overhaul itself was eventually achieved by amending the delegated legislation, known as the Rules of the Supreme Court, by which the procedural arrangements for the courts are principally ordered.

The modern 'application for judicial review'

Dissatisfaction with various aspects of administrative law in England has been rife ever since the 1920s. As discussed in chapter 2, the main concern of the early critics was subordinate legislation and Ministers' powers. The fears on that subject were in time dispelled as a long-

17 [1978] AC 435.
18 [1968] 2 All ER 1214.
19 [1968] 3 All ER 506
20 Ibid at 508.
1 (1974) 232 Estates Gazette 199.

term result of the Report of the Donoughmore-Scott Committee in 1932. During the decade immediately following the Second World War the critics' attention was turned to possible dangers inherent in the growth of tribunals and inquiries. This topic will be examined in the next chapter of this book, and we shall find that most of the heat was taken out of the subject in the aftermath of the Report of the Franks Committee in 1957. Since then a major concern has been the unnecessary complication in the system of administrative law remedies. The Law Commission in the late 1960s engaged upon an examination of the whole area of administrative law, but decided, perhaps rather weakly, in 1969 that they would recommend to the Lord Chancellor that a Royal Commission should be set up to carry out a thorough investigation of the whole subject.[2] It was not really very surprising that this recommendation was rejected, for the Lord Chancellor may well have concluded that the Law Commission ought instead to have carried on with its own investigation.

But the Law Commission's submission was not totally abortive. They had drawn up five specific questions which they suggested as the terms of reference for the Royal Commission. Three of these questions were concerned with the issues of remedies, and were as follows:

(a) How far are changes desirable with regard to the form and procedures of existing judicial remedies for the control of administrative acts and omissions?
(b) How far should any such changes be accompanied by changes in the scope of those remedies,
    (i) to cover administrative acts and ommissions which are not at present subject to judicial control, and
    (ii) to render judicial control more effective, eg with regard to the factual basis of an administrative decision?
(c) How far should remedies controlling administrative acts or omissions include the right to damages?

Although the recommendation to set up a Royal Commission was not followed, the Lord Chancellor did request the Law Commission to make further study of the question of remedies alone, and the outcome of this request was first the Working Paper No 40, entitled Remedies in Administrative Law, published in October 1971, and then the eventual Report on Remedies in Administrative Law published in March 1976.[3] It is worth pausing for a moment to consider these two documents.

2 Administrative Law (Cmnd 4059)
3 Cmnd 6407

Both papers contain remarkably neat and lucid accounts of the law on remedies as it then was. The Working Paper is in the form of the usual Law Commission consultative document. Comments were originally requested by the end of March 1972, but in view of the delay in publication of the final Report until four years after that date it would appear that the deadline was extended. The authors of the Working Paper basically put forward two possible solutions to the need to simplify the law of remedies. First it was suggested that there should be a single remedy for judicial review of administrative action, probably to be called 'the application for judicial review'. The application for review would be available to challenge the validity of all illegal public orders or action, including ultra vires delegated legislation and decisions of inferior courts and tribunals. The applicant would be able to ask for various forms of relief - orders quashing, or enjoining the administrative authority from acting illegally, or commanding it to act according to its duty, or declaring the particular administrative action to be invalid, or declaring the applicant's legal rights or privileges. Alternatively it was suggested that, if the first proposal should not find favour, reform of the existing remedies might be achieved by retaining the use of the prerogative orders, but assimilating their procedure to that of ordinary civil proceedings.

The Law Commission's final Report, when it appeared in 1976, was rather shorter than the Working Paper had been, consisting of only twenty-nine pages, followed by a short seven-clause draft Procedure for Judicial Review Bill. Broadly it followed the main lines of the first suggestion in the Working Paper. It recommended the creation of a new form of procedure, to be called 'an application for judicial review', under cover of which an applicant could apply to the Divisional Court for any of the prerogative orders, or, where appropriate, an injunction or declaration. But this new procedure should not be exclusive, and thus it should still be open to a complainant to apply direct for any of the existing remedies according to the rules already in existence. A person applying under the new procedure should have such interest in the matter concerned as the court should consider sufficient, thus leaving the development of the principles of *locus standi* to the discretion of the courts. Except where there is a statutory time limit an applicant should not fail simply on grounds of delay unless the granting of relief would cause substantial prejudice or hardship to any person, or would be detrimental to good administration. On application for judicial review the court should have the power, if satisfied there are grounds for quashing a decision, to remit the case back to the deciding tribunal or authority for reconsideration instead of quashing. The court may also award damages in cases where such a claim is in law maintainable.

These recommendations were generally welcomed, for they were seen as proposing a fairly simple solution to the complexities of the existing administrative law remedies. Indeed they resembled in many respects earlier procedural reforms elsewhere in the Commonwealth, enacted in Ontario by the Judicial Review Procedure Act 1971, and in New Zealand by the Judicature Amendment Act 1972. The Report was almost certainly an improvement upon the first solution put forward in the Working Paper where it had been tentatively suggested that the new application for judicial review should be an exclusive remedy, not only where an administrative act or order is challenged directly, but also where it is challenged collaterally in an action for tort or breach of contract and in other cases which essentially involve the validity of the exercise of public powers. The initial proposal might have preserved an applicant's difficulty in a new guise. The Working Paper considered that the scope of the new remedy would have to be defined by statute in terms of the bodies against which it would lie. But there are many questions arising before the courts today which are on the borderline of administrative and private law. Even in the famous case of *Ridge v Baldwin*, discussed in the last chapter, the exercise of a clear administrative power by the police authority involved an effect upon the private rights of the plaintiff who had been dismissed from office, and thus gave rise not only to a declaration, but also to the award of damages. Statutory definition of the kind envisaged in the Working Paper would have been almost impossible to achieve satisfactorily, for there is no easily identified dividing line between public and private law in the English system. Since the reforms in civil procedure of the nineteenth century, starting with the Common Law Procedure Act 1852, the basic philosophy has been to eliminate exclusive forms of action, not to create them. Accordingly the suggestion in 1971 that there should be a procedural wall erected between public and private law was retrogressive. The eventual recommendation that there should be a new and simplified procedure for obtaining judicial review, but that it should be available as an alternative to the older remedies, rather than their replacement, is more flexible and sensible. There are many good reasons why an applicant should wish to apply only for one of the older remedies, for they are available over the whole area of the law. As a single instance, in the field of family law, a declaration of parental rights or as to the legal status of a purported marriage may be required, neither of which would have any great relationship with problems of administrative law. To leave all the options open for applicants and for the courts retains greater flexibility, while allowing the new application for judicial review to replace the older remedies in practice for the purposes of administrative law because of its greater convenience.

The Law Commission in 1976 clearly intended that its proposed reforms should be carried into effect by statute, and for this purpose appended its draft Bill to the final Report. But surprisingly it turned out that primary legislation was not required. The 1976 Report was accepted by the Lord Chancellor and the Government, but to implement it the device finally chosen was that of an amendment to the Rules of the Supreme Court, which of course have the force of subordinate legislation. By the Rules of the Supreme Court (Amendment No 3) Regulations,[4] a new Order 53 of the Rules was introduced, and this came into effect on 11 January 1978. It is curious that, although there was in the end no necessity for primary legislation to implement the Report in England and Wales, the enactment of largely parallel provisions for the courts of Northern Ireland turned out to require the passage of the Judicature (Northern Ireland) Act 1978. Furthermore, the importance of the reform of the law for England and Wales was subsequently recognised by the inclusion of the main principles of the new procedure in section 31 of the Supreme Court Act 1981.

Under the new Order 53, as re-enacted in the 1981 Act, as an alternative to existing remedies, an application for judicial review may ask for certiorari, prohibition, mandamus, a declaration, an injunction or damages, or for any combination of these forms of relief, whenever the issue at stake involves any matter of public law. But it is further provided that, in such issues involving public law, the new procedure by application for judicial review shall be the *only* way in which an order of certiorari, prohibition or mandamus may be sought; and the same rule applies in respect of an injunction sought under the power contained in the Administration of Justice (Miscellaneous Provisions) Act 1938, section 9, that is, to restrain a person from acting in any office in which he is not entitled to act. As regards declarations and other types of injunctions, however, the new procedure is prescribed as merely an alternative avenue for an applicant in the field of public law. But it is of interest that the Court of Appeal later in 1978 took the view that in public law cases any declaration or injunction must be applied for by means of the new procedure.

---

[4] SI 1977/1955 later slightly amended by SI 1980/2000.

The matter had arisen in *Uppal v Home Office*,[5] curiously only reported in *The Times* newspaper and the *Solicitors' Journal*. An Indian husband and wife had overstayed their permission to stay in the United Kingdom, the husband by nearly nine years and the wife by nearly three years, and deportation orders were served upon them. However they had also petitioned the European Commission of Human Rights that they should not be separated from children born in England while they themselves were living here, and they therefore applied to the Chancery Division of the High Court for a declaration that they should not be deported pending the final determination by the European Commission of their petition. Article 25 of the European Convention of Human Rights and Fundamental Freedoms, which had been ratified by the United Kingdom in 1951, imposes on countries that have declared that they recognise the competence of the Commission an undertaking not to hinder in any way the effective exercise of the right to petition the Commission. Sir Robert Megarry V-C had said at first instance that proceedings for a declaration in the Chancery Division instead of for judicial review in the Queen's Bench Division were relatively uncommon, but that he could not see why applicants should not be free to bring whatever types of proceedings they chose. But the Court of Appeal disagreed, holding that the substance of the application was really one suitable for the Order 53 Procedure, and that where a declaration is sought in such circumstances it should always be asked for by way of the application for judicial review, made to the Divisional Court which was better equipped to deal with such matters. Of course if a matter in issue is not so suitable, then a declaration may be applied for direct, under Order 15, rule 16, of the Rules of the Supreme Court, thus ensuring a full trial before a single judge.[6] But this is to stray outside the proper bounds of public law. The Court of Appeal's view was expressly followed by Goulding J in the Chancery Divison in *Heywood v Hull Prison Board of Visitors*,[7] another case arising from the Hull Prison riots of 1976, already mentioned in chapter 4. A direct application for a declaration that the Board had failed to observe the rules of natural justice in the conduct of disciplinary proceedings was refused because the plaintiff's proper remedy was to apply for judicial review under Order 53.

The issue now seems to have been put beyond doubt by the House

---

5 (1978) Times, 11 November; (1979) 123 Sol Jo 17.
6 See *R v IRC, ex p Rossminster* [1980] AC 952; *De Falco v Crawley Borough Council* [1980] QB 460.
7 [1980] 3 All ER 594.

of Lords in two cases decided in 1982. In *O'Reilly v Mackman*[8], the last chapter in the litigation arising from the riots in Hull Prison, the plaintiffs had sought declarations that the findings and penalties imposed by the Board of Visitors in respect of disciplinary offences were void as being in breach of the Prison Rules 1964 and the rules of natural justice. Three actions were commenced by writ and one by originating summons, and in the event all were struck out as being an abuse of the process of the court because the cases all involved matters of public law which is reviewable more properly by the Order 53 procedure. The reasons stated by the Lords relate not to narrow procedural arguments, but to the positive advantages of the new application for judicial review with its flexible procedure and its potential for expediting resolution of issues. And in *Cocks v Thanet District Council*[9] the Lords, similarly constituted (Lords Diplock, Fraser of Tullybelton, Keith of Kirkel, Bridge of Harwich and Brightman) and again unanimously, followed their earlier conclusions in *O'Reilly*. The case concerned an entirely different issue, proceedings started in a County Court for a declaration, injunctions and damages against a local housing authority for alleged breach of statutory duty, but these too were struck out because the plaintiff should have applied for judicial review. Conversely there has been a whole spate of recent reported cases deciding that the Order 53 procedure may not be used by litigants bringing proceedings in matters of private law.[10]

As in prerogative order cases prior to 1978, an application for judicial review will continue to be made after first applying for leave *ex parte* to a single judge or to the Divisional Court of the Queen's Bench Division. It is then provided that the court shall not grant leave unless it considers that the applicant has a sufficient interest in the matter to which the application relates. This provision as to *locus standi* appears to give the courts a wide discretion on leave, probably similar to that which had persisted in respect of the old procedure for the prerogative orders. It is certainly far less restrictive than the rules on *locus standi* for injunctions and declarations prior to 1978.[11] At any stage in the proceedings the court may grant interim relief.

8   [1983] 2 AC 237; see also *R v Huntingdon District Council, ex p Cowan* [1984] 1 All ER 58. But the House of Lords has also made it clear that the procedural changes brought about by Order 53 and section 31 of the Supreme Court Act 1981 have not removed the right of an individual who claims that his existing rights under private law have been infringed by a decision of the public authority to challenge the validity of such decisions by way of *defence* to an action brought by the public authority: *Wandsworth London Borough Council v Winder* [1984] 3 All ER 976.
9   [1983] 2 AC 286.
10 Eg *R v BBC, ex p Lavelle* [1983] 1 All ER 241; *Law v National Greyhound Racing Club Ltd* [1983] 3 All ER 300; *Davy v Spelthorne Borough Council* [1984] AC 262.
11 See eg *R v Immigration Officer, ex p Shah* [1982] 2 All ER 264.

The court may refuse leave, or may refuse any relief that has been sought, where there has been undue delay in making an application for judicial review. This provision concerning undue delay in applying is of general effect, but it is also provided that in any event the application for leave should be made within three months of the relevant proceedings complained of, unless the Court considers that there is a good reason for extending the period within which the application may be made. Thus the old six-month time limit on certiorari has now been replaced by the shorter three months. Although in exceptional cases this period can be extended, it seems more likely that the court may refuse an application even within the three month period if it is not made promptly, ie without undue delay. But the new rule also contains a specific saving of any individual statutory provision which has the effect of limiting the time within which an application for judicial review may be made. It is worth noting also that the new rule makes provision for interlocutory applications, including orders for discovery, interrogatories and cross-examination.

After leave to apply has been granted the actual application itself is to be by orginating motion to a Divisional Court of the Queen's Bench Division (or by originating summons to a judge in chambers during vacation). At the hearing anyone appearing to the court to be a proper person to be heard may be heard in opposition to the application, even though he was not served with notice. Where in the end the court grants an application, there are various special provisions concerning the effect of the remedies which do not call for note here, save for one which is particularly valuable. Where the relief sought is an order of certiorari, and the court is satisfied that there are grounds for quashing the decision to which the application relates, the court may, in addition to quashing it remit the matter to the court, tribunal or other authority concerned with a direction to reconsider it, and to reach a decision in accordance with the findings of the court. This is particularly welcome, and is indeed related in its philosophy to the provision in the Administration of Justice Act 1960, referred to earlier in this chapter, under which a criminal sentence may be varied by way of certiorari. The new provision, of general application to all certiorari cases in the field of administrative law, gives the reviewing court a discretionary power to remit a case for reconsideration, with the sort of specific direction which will avoid the necessity of a full rehearing below.

In sum, it is clear that the 1978 reform is a major shift of the emphasis of judicial review from adjective to substantive law. No longer is it likely that an applicant for judicial review may run the risk of losing his case merely because of some defect in his choice of remedy. In the field of administrative law proper it is obvious that all applicants for review will perforce use the procedure newly laid down in Order 53, either because the prerogative remedy sought must now be applied for in that way, or else because the effect of the *Uppal* case makes it essential in practice to do so. In any event there can be no advantage left in seeking any older procedure. The new Order removes the procedural defects of all the older remedies. Even the non-coercive essence of the declaration is no longer of significance because a declaration can be asked for together with any other appropriate remedy. Thus the *Punton* case, though still of importance on the difference between errors within jurisdiction and those outside jurisdiction, no longer points to a flaw in the remedy by way of declaration. It seems likely that in course of time it will be seen that the new Order 53 has brought about a major reform of administrative law remedies.

The *McWhirter* and *Gouriet* cases

The peculiar type of action known as relator proceedings has already been mentioned earlier in this chapter, and it will be remembered that it was suggested that this might be adopted as a course of action when an applicant for an injunction wishes to circumvent the difficulty of the rule concerning *locus standi* which applies to injunctions. As an injunction has always only been obtainable by a private plaintiff where he can show that his own private interest in a matter is at stake, the obstacle of standing is overcome where the Attorney-General is prepared to mount an action in his official capacity on behalf of the public interest. But this vision of an *actio popularis* suffered a serious check as a result of the decision of the House of Lords in the summer of 1977 in *Gouriet v Union of Post Office Workers*, eventually reported in the series of Appeal Cases in 1978.[12] Before considering *Gouriet* and its effect, however, it is worthwhile first to take a look at the decision of the Court of Appeal in 1973 in *A-G (ex rel McWhirter) v Independent Broadcasting Authority*,[13] which had been largely instrumental in raising the hopes of a general action for an injunction by relator proceedings.

On Monday, 15 January 1973, Mr Ross McWhirter telephoned the Attorney-General's office requesting the Attorney-General to seek an injunction to prevent the televising on Tuesday night of a film entitled 'Warhol: Artist and Film-Maker'. Newspaper previews of

12 [1978] AC 435.
13 [1973] QB 629.

the film had led Mr McWhirter to believe that the telecast would amount to a breach by the Authority of its statutory duty to satisfy itself that programmes do not offend against good taste or decency and are not likely to be offensive to public feeling. At about 2 pm on the Monday McWhirter was informed that the Attorney-General would not seek an injunction *ex officio*, but that a proper request for relator proceedings would be considered. McWhirter, feeling that there was insufficient time to obtain the Attorney-General's consent to relator proceedings, decided to proceed on his own. On the Tuesday he applied *ex parte* to Forbes J, in chambers, for an injunction, but his application was refused. He promptly appealed to the Court of Appeal, which heard him at 3.30 pm the same day. After adjourning the hearing until 5 pm to allow the Authority to be represented, the court granted an interlocutory injunction by a majority of two to one, Cairns LJ dissenting on the ground that the applicant had no *locus standi*. When the full hearing was held on 25 January, the Attorney-General had granted his consent to relator proceedings, and the hearing proceeded on that basis. In the event the applicant's assertions of failure of duty on the part of the Authority were held to be unfounded, and the injunction was accordingly discharged. The film about Mr Warhol and his work was shortly afterwards shown on the Independent Television channel, and proved to be remarkable only for its general dullness. But the Court of Appeal unanimously approved a principle enabling offences against the public at large to be drawn to the attention of the courts by any citizen, which was later restated by Lord Denning in *R v Greater London Council, ex p Blackburn* in terms which have already been quoted earlier in this chapter. Lord Denning MR, Cairns and Lawton LJJ all agreed that if at any time there should be reason to think that an Attorney-General was refusing improperly to exercise his powers to sanction relator proceedings, the courts might have to intervene to ensure that the law is obeyed. Lawton LJ thought that such a time would not be in the foreseeable future, but it was only four years before precisely this kind of issue presented itself in *Gouriet*.

In accordance with a decision taken by the International Confederation of Free Trade Unions, and supported by the British Trades Union Congress, the executive council of the Union of Post Office Workers publicly announced on 13 January 1977 that it was the intention of that union to boycott for one week, beginning on 17 January, all mail, telephone calls and telegrams to South Africa, except in any matter of 'life and death'. The purpose of the boycott was as a protest against the South African Government's policy of apartheid. The proposed boycott appeared to be contrary to the Telegraph Act 1863, section 45, and the Post Office Act 1953, section 58, which make it a criminal offence, inter alia, wilfully to delay the transmission of messages and postal packets. Mr Gouriet was secretary of the National Association of Freedom, an independent body devoted to the aim of asserting the freedom of the individual against the power of the state or of other collective organisations. In his capacity as a private citizen he applied, on Friday, 14 January, to the Attorney-General (in the then Labour Government) for his consent to relator proceedings for an injunction to prevent the boycott on the ground that it would constitute a breach of the criminal law. One may pause to wonder why Gouriet bothered to seek relator proceedings, instead of simply writing a letter to someone in South Africa, or stating his intention to send a telegram there on 17 January, thus showing that he would himself suffer special damage as a result of the boycott. But it appears that he deliberately refrained from attempting to show special damage to himself because the defendant trade union might then have sheltered behind the wide exemption from liability in tort conferred by section 14 of the Trade Union and Labour Relations Act 1974. The Attorney-General refused his consent in the following terms:

> Having considered all the circumstances including the public interest relating to the application for my consent...I have come to the conclusion that in relation to this application I should not give my consent.

The plaintiff then promptly issued a writ of summons in his own name, and applied on the afternoon of the same day to Stocker J, in chambers, for an interim injunction. This was refused on the ground that Gouriet had no *locus standi*. The plaintiff then appealed, late in the same afternoon, to the Court of Appeal. We have it on the authority of Lord Denning's own book, *The Discipline of Law*,[14] that he was on the point of leaving the Royal Courts and catching his train to go home when his clerk told him that the appeal had just been lodged. The Master of the Rolls accordingly authorised a special sitting of the Court of Appeal, in which he sat with Lawton and Ormrod LJJ on Saturday, 15 January. At the special sitting the court granted an interim injunction pending a full hearing of the issue on Tuesday, 18 January. The plaintiff was also given leave to join the Attorney-General as a defendant, and to claim a declaration that the Attorney-General, by refusing his consent to relator proceedings, had acted improperly and wrongfully exercised his discretion.

As a result of the interim injunction the union called off its threatened boycott, so that the result of the full hearing was academic

---

14 At p 137.

so far as the actual boycott itself was concerned. In any event the hearing starting on 18 January took three days, and the judges then took time for consideration before delivering their judgments after the actual week of the planned boycott had ended. At the resumed hearing the Attorney-General, Mr Sam Silkin QC, appeared and contended that the court had no jurisdiction to review the exercise of his discretion. By a majority of two to one, Lord Denning dissenting, the court held that the Attorney-General's decision to refuse consent to relator proceedings was not reviewable by the courts, and that the plaintiff himself had no *locus standi* to seek a permanent injunction against the defendant union. But the court went on to hold unanimously that the plaintiff was entitled to seek a declaration that the proposed boycott would be unlawful, and an interim injunction pending a final determination of the declaratory proceedings; and that, in the present circumstances, the declaration would be granted.

Both sides then appealed to the House of Lords. The main question before the Lords was whether, in the light of the Attorney-General's refusal to consent to a relator action, a private individual could bring proceedings to restrain others from breaking the law. There were political overtones to the case, in that it had been urged on behalf of the plaintiff that the Attorney-General's refusal had been brought about either by his own political sympathy with the aims of the union, or else by his fear of causing even more general industrial action as a result of seeming to lend his aid to Mr Gouriet's point of view. But the House of Lords unanimously reversed the main effect of the Court of Appeal's decision, and it is not beyond interest that the five Law Lords sitting included among their number Viscount Dilhorne, a former Conservative Attorney-General, who himself delivered a detailed speech supporting the inviolability of an Attorney-General's decision in such a case. The Lords supported the majority of the Court of Appeal in holding that the Attorney-General's decision to refuse consent to relator proceedings was not reviewable by the courts, and that the plaintiff had no *locus standi* to seek a permanent injunction. But they reversed the unanimous decisions of the Court of Appeal allowing Gouriet to seek a declaration that the proposed boycott was unlawful, and an interim injunction pending a final determination on the issue of the declaration. The plaintiff had claimed that if the decision went against him, it would seem that the courts were powerless to enforce the law. But the Lords pointed out that the primary means of enforcing the criminal law is by prosecuting an offender after he has committed an offence. It is not the responsibility of the civil courts to ensure that the criminal law is not broken. Lord Fraser of Tullybelton said that the only control over the exercise of this type of discretion by the Attorney-

General, stemming as it does from the Royal Prerogative, lies with Parliament.

But perhaps the main force of the Lords' decision is to be found in the following passage from the speech of Lord Wilberforce.[15]

A relator action – a type of action which has existed from the earliest times – is one in which the Attorney-General, on the relation of individuals (who may include local authorities or companies) brings an action to assert a public right. It can properly be said to be a fundamental principle of English law that private rights can be asserted by individuals, but that public rights can only be asserted by the Attorney-General as representing the public. In terms of constitutional law, the rights of the public are vested in the Crown, and the Attorney-General enforces them as an officer of the Crown. And just as the Attorney-General has in general no power to interfere with the assertion of private rights, so in general no private person has the right of representing the public in the assertion of public rights. If he tries to do so his action can be struck out.

An appeal was made to the Year Books to controvert this universally accepted proposition. Examples can be found of cases, in early times, where subjects were allowed to assert in the courts rights of the Crown (see Year Books Series Vol XVII, Ed II, 1314-15, Selden Society ed W C Bolland). But all the cases were cases asserting, through writs of quo waranto or analogous writs, claims of a nature which in modern times came to be made by prerogative writs, or cases concerned with some proprietary right of the Crown: they were not cases of individuals asserting rights belonging to the public. No instance of this can be brought forward, whether in ancient or modern times.

The plaintiff accepted that this was so but produced a number of arguments why this form of action should be departed from or modernised. The use of the Attorney-General's name was said to be fictional; the real claimant was the individual – who has to bear the costs. The introduction of the Attorney-General was a matter of practice and procedure, the subject of judicial invention; what the courts have invented, the courts can change. The Attorney-General has no real part to play in these proceedings: his functions are limited to ensuring that the action is not frivolous or vexatious. It is time to discard these fictions, or at least to remould the action for use in modern times.

My Lords, apart from the fact that to accept this line of argument would mean a departure from a long, uniform and respected series of authorities, so straining to the utmost the power of judicial innovation, in my opinion it rests on a basic misconception of the Attorney-General's role with regard to the assertation of public rights.

It can be granted that in this, as in most of our law, procedural considerations have played a part. It was advantageous to make use of the name of the King so as to gain a more favourable position in the King's Courts and to avoid restrictions by which the King was not bound:

---

15 [1978] AC 435 at 477.

see Robertson *Civil Proceedings by and against the Crown* (1908) p 464. Moreover it may well be true that in many types of action, and under some Attorney-General, the use of his name was readily granted – even to the point of becoming a formality. This was particularly the case in charity cases up to the time of Sir John Campbell A-G: see *Shore v Wilson*.[16]

But the Attorney-General's role has never been fictional. His position in relator actions is the same as it is in actions brought without a relator (with the sole exception that the relator is liable for costs: see *A-G v Cockermouth Local Board*.[17] He is entitled to see and approve the statement of claim and any amendment in the pleadings, he is entitled to be consulted in discovery, the suit cannot be compromised without his approval; if the relator dies, the suit does not abate. For the proposition that his only concern is to 'filter out' vexations and frivolous proceedings, there is no authority – indeed, there is no need for the Attorney-General to do what is well within the power of the court. On the contrary he has the right, and the duty, to consider the public interest generally and widely. . .

In so far as reliance was placed on observations of Lord Denning MR (concurred in by Lawton LJ) in *A-G v ex rel McWhirter v Independent Broadcasting Authority*, these were dicta in proceedings in which, ultimately, the Attorney-General consented to relator proceedings. The court in fact held that an individual could not apply for an injunction against a breach of the law except with the fiat of the Attorney-General. Lord Denning MR went on to express the opinion obiter than an individual member of the public can apply for an injunction 'if the Attorney-General refuses leave in a proper case, or improperly or unreasonably delays in giving leave, or his machinery works too slowly'. There is no authority for this provision and in my opinion it is contrary to principle. In any event none of the stated hypotheses apply in the present case.

The House of Lords in *Gouriet* had accordingly declined to allow the development of an *actio popularis*, by which any citizen, however remotely concerned, might obtain an injunction to prevent someone else from infringing the criminal law. Both in the *McWhirter* case, and then later in the *Blackburn* case, Lord Denning, for the most part supported by other members of the Court of Appeal, had been pressing for the assimilation and liberalisation of the various rules concerning standing as regards different remedies. In two earlier cases, brought by the same Messrs Blackburn and McWhirter, and concerned with a matter which does not demand our attention in this book (the question of whether it would be illegal for the United Kingdom to join the European Economic Community), Lord Denning had twice said that he would not object on grounds of standing to actions for declarations brought by private citizens disputing the exercise of the treaty-making power of the Crown. In

16 (1842) 9 Cl & Fin 355 at 407.
17 (1874) LR 18 Eq 172 at 176, per Jessel MR.

the later cases he had extended this view to the remedy of injunction also.[18] Sir William Wade, in his book *Administrative Law*,[19] has also drawn attention to the work of the Supreme Court of Canada in 1974 in laying down that, where a rule requires personal standing in relation to cases brought concerning regulatory legislation affecting particular persons or classes, the court may nevertheless grant declaratory relief to any citizen within its discretion if no particular persons or classes are affected more than others, and the nature of the case appears suitable for such relief.[20] Further south in 1968 the United States Supreme Court took the view that a federal taxpayer had sufficient standing to obtain relief.[1] Lord Wilberforce in *Gouriet* recognised the force in logic of the argument in favour of uniformity in the rules as to standing, yet he clung tenaciously to the old rules with their inbuilt separate effects. Lord Wilberforce and Viscount Dilhorne even mentioned without disapproval the liberal rules of standing for the prerogative orders, but still saw nothing surprising in insisting that it was a fundamental principle that only the Attorney-General should be allowed to represent the rights of the public at large.

Yet it may be suggested that the cause of legal liberalism is not necessarily lost as a result of *Gouriet*, for that decision was upon one of our battery of administrative law remedies which had not yet been affected by the new Order 53 of the Rules of the Supreme Court. As has already been pointed out, the new procedure has not abolished or replaced the older remedies; nor indeed would it be possible for a mere procedural rule so to replace them totally. But it does provide a new channel through which an applicant *must* pass if he wishes to gain the benefit of a prerogative order, and through which he *may* pass if he wishes to seek an injunction or declaration. Furthermore *O'Reilly v Mackman* and *Cocks v Thanet District Council* strongly suggest that the courts will for the future insist that no applications for injunctions or declarations in relation to matters of administrative law will be entertained other than through the new procedure. Order 53 does not deal specifically with the relator action, but perhaps this was because relator proceedings are in truth only one way in which an injunction may be sought. Accordingly the new procedure may well be equally applicable to cover those cases where an injunction

18 Thus coinciding in substance with the position in Scots law, which has no place for relator proceedings. A private individual is permitted to claim relief of this character without calling a Law Officer in aid.
19 5th edn, p 582.
20 *Thorson v A-G of Canada (No 2)* (1974) 43 DLR (3d) 1; and see P P Mercer 'The *Gouriet* Case: Public Interest Litigation in Britain and Canada' (1979) PL 214.
1 *Flast v Cohen* 392 US 83 (1968).

may hitherto have been sought by relator proceedings. The rule concerning *locus standi* under the new Order 53 is simply that the court will require an applicant to have a 'sufficient interest'. This phrase is nowhere in the Order or in the 1981 Act further explained, and it has already been suggested in these pages that the new rule as to *locus standi* would seem to be similar in effect to the liberal rules developed by the courts over the years for prerogative order cases. The House of Lords in *Gouriet* may have declined to depart from previous decisions, as it has been able to do since 1966,[2] and to establish a new uniform rule of standing in keeping with modern needs, but the new Order 53 may have done the trick instead. There were signs even before the new Order came into effect that judges may take pains to distinguish *Gouriet* so as to find that there is a sufficient interest in an issue to allow a private applicant to seek an injunction and to have his case heard on the merits.[3] But such judicial efforts may be unnecessary in future.

It is of course arguable that Order 53 does no more than allow the courts to develop their own rules on standing, and that they may preform this task by following their previous developed rules as to the different individual remedies. Professor J F Garner also raises the pertinent question whether the rules of *locus standi* are procedural or substantive.[4] If *locus standi* is a matter of substantive law, then the new Order cannot, in his view, have changed the law, and the courts will be bound by the old rules. But if the rules on standing are purely procedural, then the courts are free to decide that the new Order has changed the old rules. It is scarcely credible that a rule on standing in the courts can be other than procedural, for each application to a court will involve an assessment by the court whether it would be right to allow it to proceed. Lord Denning himself, in *The Discipline of Law*,[5] takes the view that the wording of Order 53 has had the effect of reviving his approach to standing in the *McWhirter* case, notwithstanding *Gouriet*. If the new Order, which is merely repeated word for word on the issue of standing in the Supreme Court Act 1981, is to achieve the object of providing a precedure whereby administrative law remedies may be obtained without artificial hindrance, then his view must surely be correct. All logic and

---

2   See the statement made by Lord Gardiner LC on behalf of himself and all the Lords of Appeal in Ordinary: (1966) 1 WLR 1234.
3   See eg *Kent Council v Batchelor* [1978] 3 All ER 980, in which a county council was held competent to seek an injunction to prevent breach of a tree preservation order without the need to join the Attorney-General by relator proceedings.
4   *Administrative Law* (5th edn) p 200.
5   Page 133; and see his interpretation of the *Gouriet* case in *Imperial Tobacco Ltd v A-G* [1979] QB 555 at 572–574.

convenience demands uniformity, and such uniformity can only be just if the rules on standing are also liberal.

Support for this view provided by *R v IRC ex p National Federation of Self-Employed and Small Businesses Ltd.*[6] in which the Court of Appeal (Lord Denning MR and Ackner LJ, Lawton LJ dissenting) allowed an application for judicial review by the Federation in respect of a decision by the Inland Revenue to grant an amnesty for tax evasion by casual workers in the newspaper industry, received a possible setback when a unanimous House of Lords reversed the Court of Appeal.[7] The Lords held that the Inland Revenue had in any case acted intra vires, and a majority also considered that the Federation did not have a sufficient interest to be granted a declaration that the Inland Revenue had acted unlawfully. But on this latter point Lord Diplock disagreed. He stated that there was considerable room for evolution in the application of rules concerning standing; and all the five Law Lords in the case took the view that consideration of standing need not be confined to the application for leave, but may in appropriate cases be determined after an examination of the merits. In the event, therefore, the Lords have now gone some way towards agreeing with the liberal interpretation of *locus standi* where there is an application for judicial review, and the issue must be considered as still open.

It is suggested that the only sensible view of the overall effect of Order 53, as now re-enacted, is that it provides a new procedure whereby any suitable administrative law remedy may be obtained; that the older procedures for such remedies have for all practical purposes now disappeared; that anyone may apply by the new procedure, and that the courts should exercise a wide discretion in determining whether an applicant has a 'sufficient interest'; and that the eventual remedy, if granted, will be determined by the court's assessment of the realistic needs of the case on the merits. If this proves to be correct, then we shall have already reached a position where the law has ceased to concern itself with procedural side issues, and where the courts will decide cases on administrative law according to the merit, regardless of such former procedural complexities. The end product of the Law Commission's work in this field will have been a major substantive reform which will be of immense benefit to all those with real grievances giving rise to the possibility of redress in the courts. Professor Garner and Mr B L Jones believe that the JUSTICE – All Souls Review Committee is

---

6 [1980] QB 407.
7 [1982] AC 617; and see L Neville Brown, 'The Ratepayer's Standing to Challenge Unlawful Expenditure', (1982) 7 Holdsworth Law Review 161.

likely to recommend that the grounds for judicial review should be codified, a course which they themselves favour.[8] It may well be, however, that the grounds are sufficiently well developed already, as has been suggested in the previous two chapters of this book. If this is correct, then the reform of remedies effected in 1978 has already completed the armoury of administrative remedies available in the courts to those aggrieved by administrative decisions or acts, though whether there may be any advantage in enacting a clarification of the grounds for judicial review will be examined presently.

Should there be a specialist administrative court, or a wholesale reform of judicial review?

Despite the procedural reforms brought about by the new Order 53 of the Rules of the Supreme Court, the question still arises in several quarters whether a more wholesale reform of the complete field of judicial review of administrative action is due. Order 53 may have been a long time in gestation, bearing in mind the years that went by before the Law Commission finally produced its recommendations, and then before they were substantially implemented. But it is not an isolated instance of this type of reform in a common law jurisdiction. A parallel impetus for reform, with not dissimilar results, occurred in Australia at much the same period. The Report of the Commonwealth Administrative Review Committee,[9] under the chairmanship of Sir John Kerr (later to become Governor-General of Australia), published in 1971, recommended that there should be a simple procedure by originating summons, available on any of the existing grounds for review, with the court having full power to grant whatever relief may appear appropriate. Furthermore, the task of so reviewing administrative decisions of all kinds on points of law should be given to a new court to be called the Commonwealth Administrative Court. This latter court has not in fact been set up, but procedural reforms similar to those in England have been enacted, and it is worth pausing for a moment to examine them.

The Administrative Decisions (Judicial Review) Act 1977 makes provision in Australia for a codified judicial review system. The actual implementation of the Act was somewhat delayed because its commencement was dependent upon the making of regulations to

---

8   *Administrative Law* (6th edn) p 166.
9   Australian Government Publishing Service, 1971 – Parliamentary Paper No 144. A similar type of reform was recommended in 1980 for Canada in the 14th Report of the Law Commission of Canada, entitled Judicial Review and the Federal Court.

exempt certain administrative decisions from the operation of the Act. Not unnaturally many administrators were anxious to obtain exemption for their decisions. But subject to such exemptions the Act substitutes for the previous judicial remedies a simple procedure under which an order for review is applied for. On such an application the court has a wide discretion as to the actual relief which may be granted, including referral back with directions, supervisory orders, and orders to do justice. More significantly, and going further than the English reform, the Act also codifies the grounds for review in section 5, which reads as follows:

5 (1) A person who is aggrieved by a decision to which the Act applies that is made after the commencement of this Act may apply to the Court for an order for review in respect of the decision on any one or more of the following grounds:
- (a) that a breach of the rules of natural justive occurred in connexion with the making of the decision;
- (b) that procedures that were required by law to be observed in connexion with the making of the decision were not observed;
- (c) that the person who purported to make the decision did not have jurisdiction to make the decision;
- (d) that the decision was not authorised by the enactment in pursuance of which it was purported to be made;
- (e) that the making of the decision was an improper exercise of the power conferred by the enactment in pursuance of which it was purported to be made;
- (f) that the decision involved an error of law, whether or not the error appears on the record of the decision;
- (g) that the decision was induced or affected by fraud;
- (h) that there was no evidence or other material to justify the making of the decision;
- (j) that the decision was otherwise contrary to law.

(2) The reference in paragraph (1)(e) to an improper exercise of a power shall be construed as including a reference to:
- (a) taking an irrelevant consideration into account in the exercise of a power;
- (b) failing to take a relevant consideration into account in the exercise of a power;
- (c) an exercise of a power for a purpose other than a purpose for which the power is conferred;
- (d) an exercise of a discretionary power in bad faith;
- (e) an exercise of a personal discretionary power at the discretion or behest of another person;
- (f) an exercise of a discretionary power in accordance with a rule or policy without regard to the merits of the particular case;
- (g) an exercise of a power that is so unreasonable that no reasonable person could have so exercised the power;

(h) an exercise of a power in such a way that the result of the exercise of the power is uncertain; and
(j) any other exercise of a power in a way that constitutes abuse of the power.

(3) The ground specified in paragraph (1)(h) shall not be taken to be made out unless:
(a) the person who made the decision was required by law to reach that decision only if a particular matter was established, and there was no evidence or other material (including facts of which he was entitled to take notice) from which he could reasonably be satisfied that the matter was established; or
(b) the person who made the decision based the decision on the existence of a particular fact, and that fact did not exist.

The Act also provides that a person affected by a decision may obtain the reasons for that decision without having to commence an action for review. As no special administrative court has been set up, the jurisdiction to entertain applications for judicial review is vested in the Federal Court.

This list of grounds for review appears comprehensive. But, though most carefully listed, there is practically nothing in the list which cannot already be found in the grounds for judicial review in England which have been discussed in the last two chapters of this book. Perhaps the only addition to the established grounds in England appears in section 5(1)(f), in that an error of law within jurisdiction need not appear on the record of the decision in order to give rise to an application for judicial review. Even in section 5(1)(h), and 5(3), we find that the Act restricts evidential grounds to the well-known 'no evidence' rule, rather than striking new ground and adopting a 'substantial evidence' rule, as there is some indication that the English courts might eventually do. We have already seen that Garner and Jones favour some form of detailed reappraisal of the grounds for judicial review in England, and in 1979 the JUSTICE Educational and Research Trust joined forces with All Souls College, Oxford, and set up a new Review Committee on Administrative Law in the United Kingdom, under the chairmanship of the Warden of All Souls, Sir Patrick Neill QC.

Although we still await this latest Committee's report, its terms of reference include some matters which may perhaps be regarded as already adequately reformed, such as the changes that may be desirable with regard to the form and procedures of existing judicial remedies, and the desirability of including the right to damages or compensation as a means of redressing grievances – though this latter issue may impinge upon the possible desirability of giving ombudsmen the power to award damages, which we shall consider again in chapter 7 of this book. Neither of these issues seems to require further consideration or reform, unless the present writer should turn out to be wrong in concluding that the restrictive effect of the *Gouriet* case has been largely overcome by the new rule as to *locus standi* for the procedure under Order 53. But the Committee also has among its terms of reference the question whether administrative law remedies should be extended in scope so as to provide additional grounds of review or so as to cover acts or omissions of the administration not at present subject to appeal or judicial review, and so as to render such remedies more effective. This does raise the question of expansion of the grounds for review. It is hoped that enough has been written in the last two chapters of this book to show that the existing grounds, though often stated somewhat generally, and sometimes misunderstood, are very far-reaching in effect, and provide an adequate basis for judicial review of the decisions and acts of inferior authorities. The very full exposition and restatement of the grounds for review appearing in the Administrative Decisions (Judicial Review) Act 1977 in Australia discloses virtually no substantial addition or alteration to the established grounds developed by the common law. Accordingly it is suggested here that there is probably little reason to believe that the new Review Committee can find fruitful ways in which to add to the existing grounds for judicial review. But it may well be that there is much more to be said for a statutory restatement of the grounds for review along the lines of the Australian Act. Such a development could have the beneficial effect of making the full extent of the grounds available for review better known and understood, and could also perhaps help to prevent judges from sometimes, as regrettably hitherto, interpreting the law too restrictively.[10]

Connected with the possible reform of grounds for review, and of remedies, is the belief in some quarters that there ought to be a separate administrative law court to operate the machinery of judicial review. For nearly sixty years there has been intermittent pressure for such a reform. Some of the evidence to the Committee on Ministers' Powers, which reported in 1932,[11] and to the Committee on Administrative Tribunals and Enquiries, which reported in 1957,[12] was along these lines, though it did not find favour in the Reports when published. Some critics of the law even went so far as to

10 To set against this, however, the Public and Administrative Law Reform Committee of New Zealand, in its 12th Report, considered that codification of the grounds for judicial review would not really assist the courts: see [1979] 5 CLB 420.
11 Cmd 4060.
12 Cmnd 218.

recommend the abandonment of the whole system of administrative law as it had grown up in England, and the adoption of a complete new system based upon that of France, with its separate administrative courts. The most notable of these latter protagonists, who put forward his views in a steady stream of articles and books, too numerous to mention individually here, was Professor J D B Mitchell of the University of Edinburgh. Such views of wholesale replacement of the law are too extreme for the purpose intended, particularly since the English rules of administrative law, whatever their detailed faults, do generally work. Perhaps Professor Garner in the 5th edition of his book *Administrative Law*[13] commented reasonably that the French system enjoys its high prestige in the country of its origin partly because of its history and traditions, and partly because the judges of the Conseil d'Etat are both trained lawyers and experienced administrators. As he says, 'such an institution is not, as it seems to the present writer, one appropriate for importation.'

Once more the would-be reformers have so far failed to carry their views to acceptance. The new Review Committee includes among its terms of reference the question of the impact upon administrative law in the United Kingdom of membership of the European Communities. It is well enough known that judicial review in Community law is based mainly upon the French system, but this is no reason why it should be imported into English municipal law. The most moderate suggestions have accepted that the substantive principles of English administrative law should remain much as they are, subject to reforms in detail, but that the machinery of judicial review should be operated by a separate specialist court. Professor Mitchell would have based his English Conseil d'Etat upon the Judicial Committee of the Privy Council,[14] but a more popular proposal has been that of JUSTICE in 1971,[15] that there should be created an Administrative Division of the High Court, to which would be transferred all existing jurisdiction of the superior courts to supervise subordinate administrative bodies, and also to determine statutory appeals from Ministers, tribunals or inferior courts in administrative matters. Once more we find that the specific question whether there ought to be an Administrative Division of the High Court is among the terms of reference of the new Review Committee, as well as the more fundamental question whether there should be a separate system of administrative courts.

It may be suggested here that enough has been stated already to

13 5th edn, p 118 (the passage is omitted from the 6th edn).
14 'The Causes and Consequences of the Absence of a System of Public Law' [1965] PL 95.
15 Administration under Law, a Report by JUSTICE, 1971.

reject any idea of instituting a separate system of administrative courts, with all the cost and doubtful gain in substance which would result. There is more to be said for creating an Administrative Division of the High Court. Yet even here the gains to be made would be doubtful. Apart from other areas of law which might compete with administrative law for the creation of its own Division of the High Court, it is hard to see what such a Division would achieve that cannot already be attained. The greatest argument in favour of such a change is that the judges assigned to the new Division would become administrative law specialists, instead of having to cover other areas of law as well, and thus would be more likely to build up a consistent and coherent body of administrative law, free of the occasional judicial blemishes which have occurred over the years in the past. But there is no guarantee that even specialist judges will be immune from error, and as administrative law in its nature involves contact with so many aspects of the citizen's everyday life it is hard to see the advantage in sealing off the judges in this field from other aspects of the law. The Court of Appeal said in the case of *Uppal v Home Office* in 1978, discussed earlier in this chapter, that the Divisional Court was already something of a specialist court on administrative law matters.[16] This specialism has been increased by the setting up in 1982 of a special panel of judges for the hearing of administrative law cases in the Divisional Court. The fact that it is not exclusively concerned with administrative law, and is therefore able to mingle its experience in a wider field with the questions it must answer in administrative law is probably a gain. It may be suggested that we do not require any more distinctive administrative law Division of the High Court than is already provided by the Divisional Court of the Queen's Bench Division; and since 1982 the provisions for appeals from the Divisional Court in cases that were in that court's Administrative Law List have been strengthened because the Lord Chief Justice now normally presides over such hearings in the Court of Appeal.

Crown proceedings

For largely historical reasons actions for breach of contract or in tort against the Crown itself must be considered to form a special subject within the whole area of remedies against administrative authorities. The old Royal Prerogative rules, that the King can do no wrong, and that the King cannot be impleaded in his own courts, have died

---

16 A similar point is made by H W R Wade *Constitutional Fundamentals* (Hamlyn Lectures, 1980) p 74.

hard. For a matter of centuries it remained the theory of the courts that no action could be brought as of right directly against the Crown, as the 'King' had in all reality now become, thus apparently exempting the whole national executive authority from civil liability. But of course such a position would have been intolerable unless there had been a series of fictions whereby it became in fact, though still not in theory, possible to sue the Crown, and, where an action was successful, to obtain damages or other appropriate redress. It was only when the use of the fiction as regards tort claims broke down shortly after the Second World War that the need to place the law upon a sounder basis became urgent. The result was the Crown Proceedings Act 1947, which remains today the basic authority for direct actions in contract and tort against the Crown, and which has only been amended since its passage in comparatively minor respects.

For most practical purposes the Crown is now in the same position as far as civil liability is concerned as any other defendant. This is the main effect of sections 1 (on contractual liability) and 2 (on tortious liability) of the Act. But there are some important exceptions, some specifically provided for in the Act, and others existing by implication.

Section 1 provides:

> Where any person has a claim against the Crown after the commencement of this Act, and, if this Act had not been passed, the claim might have been enforced, subject to the grant of His Majesty's fiat, by petition of right, or might have been enforced by a proceeding provided by any statutory provision repealed by this Act, the claim may be enforced as of right, and without the fiat of His Majesty, by proceedings taken against the Crown for that purpose in accordance with the provisions of this Act.

The section thus purports to introduce a general right of action against the Crown in contract, but on closer inspection one finds that this right only exists where it was possible by a different procedure to bring an action in contract against the Crown before the Act of 1947. This for the most part refers back to the former fictional method of bringing an action in contract against the Crown, which was by petition of right. There is little point here in investigating the details of the petition of right procedure, though it was in form a method of seeking the permission of the Crown to sue before actually so suing. By common practice such permission was freely given, and it was not this type of fiction which broke down after the Second World War. Nevertheless, when the fiction used for the purposes of actions in tort did break down, and the Crown Proceedings Bill was introduced into the House of Lords to remedy the defect, the Lords took the opportunity to insert an extra clause which would deal with actions in contract as well, and it was this clause which became section 1 of the Act. The stated intention was merely to provide for a direct right of action against the Crown as a substitute for the old petition of right procedure. Accordingly any types of contract action which could not hitherto have been brought by that old procedure, or under any other special statutory provision, remained outside the scope of the new direct right of action.

Before the Act it was not possible to bring an action in contract by the petition of right procedure if (1) the contract concerned would have had the effect of fettering future executive action, (2) the contract was dependent upon a future grant of money from Parliament, or (3) the contract was a contract of service with a member of the armed forces or of the civil service. The exact limits of the field covered by these exceptional contract cases have never been determined to everyone's satisfaction. *Rederiaktiebolaget Amphitrite v R*[17] is one of the few English authorities upon the first exception, though it was not by any means clear in its effect. During the First World War, the German U-boat campaign caused the sinking of many British merchantmen at sea, and this brought a severe shortage of food and other supplies to the United Kingdom. The British Government, as a consequence, had taken to requisitioning ships of neutral countries if they entered British waters. Sweden was a neutral power, and a Swedish shipowning company was anxious that its ship, the SS Amphitrite, should be able to sail to a British port, and then be released after unloading an approved cargo. Accordingly the owners sought an assurance on this point from the British Legation in Stockholm, and were given it in a letter. However, once the ship had unloaded its cargo it was refused clearance to leave. The owners therefore brought an action under the petition of right procedure for breach of contract by the Crown. The case went no further than first instance, where Rowlatt J held that there had been no enforceable contract, for the letter amounted to no more than a bare promise that the ship would be released. This must have been correct, and the judge would have been justified in leaving his decision at that. But he went on to say, obiter, that 'it is not competent for the Government to fetter its future executive action, which must necessarily be determined by the needs of the community when the question arises. It cannot by contract hamper its freedom of action in matters which concern the welfare of the State.[18]

Rowlatt J's judgment was unconsidered, and he cited no authorities, but his view of executive necessity has been accepted as

17 [1921] 3 KB 500.
18 Ibid at 503.

correct by most judges and writers since. He expressly distinguished commercial contracts, saying:[19] 'No doubt the Government can bind itself through its officers by a commercial contract, and if it does so it must perform it like anybody else or pay damages for the breach.' So the main problem since the case was decided has been to determine what circumstances will justify a defence of executive necessity raised by the Crown to absolve it from the normal legal consequences of breach of contract, where the contract is not of a commercial character. The *Amphitrite* decision was indeed criticised by Denning J in *Robertson v Minister of Pensions*,[20] and by Denning LJ in *Falmouth Boat Construction Co Ltd v Howell*.[1] But such criticism was apparently rejected by the House of Lords when the latter decision itself was approved in *Howell v Falmouth Boat Construction Co Ltd*.[2] Further support for the *Amphitrite* line of reasoning has come from as far afield as the High Court of Southern Rhodesia in 1956.[3] But perhaps the clearest seal of approval came from the Court of Appeal in *Crown Lands Coms v Page*, reported in 1960.[4] There the Crown had granted a lease of premises to Page, but later requisitioned them from him under wartime statutory powers. No rent was paid by Page during the period of the requisition, and the Commissioners brought proceedings to recover the arrears of rent. The defendant contended that there had been an implied term in the lease of quiet enjoyment, and that the requisitioning constituted an eviction in breach of it, in which case the requirement to pay rent was suspended. But both Gorman J, at first instance, and the Court of Appeal held that such a term was not to be implied into Page's lease so as to render the requisitioning invalid. A major ground for this decision was that nothing in or flowing from the lease ought to be allowed to impede the freedom of action of the Crown in time of war. As Devlin LJ said:[5]

> When the Crown, or any other person, is entrusted, whether by virtue of the prerogative or by statute, with discretionary powers to be exercised for the public good, it does not, when making a private contract in general terms, undertake (and it may be that it could not even with the use of specific language validly undertake) to fetter itself in the use of those powers, and in the exercise of its discretion.

19 Ibid at 503.
20 [1949] 1 KB 227.
1 [1950] 2 KB 16.
2 [1951] AC 837.
3 *Waterfalls Town Management Board v Minister of Housing (S Rhodesia)* [1956] R & N 691 at 697, per Murray CJ.
4 [1960] 2 QB 274.
5 Ibid at 291.

This principle has been accepted in a number of authorities. Although it must be accepted that no action for breach of contract against the Crown will succeed if the effect would be to fetter the Crown's future executive action, it now seems reasonably clear that this exception will not apply to any commercial contract and that it will be limited to the context of the need to allow the Crown freedom of action in time of war.

The second type of contract the breach of which will be exempt from redress in the courts is a contract dependent upon the future grant of money from Parliament. The rationale of this exception is that Parliament, being sovereign in law, cannot be forced by the courts to vote money for any purpose against its own will. Thus the exception will not cover contracts for which money has already been voted. The difference is well illustrated in *Churchward v R.*[6] Churchward had contracted with the Commissioners of the Admiralty, in consideration of an annual sum to be provided by Parliament, to maintain a mail service between Dover and the continent for eleven years. During the fourth year of this contract the Admiralty terminated the agreement and the Appropriation Act of that year provided that no part of the sum appropriated for the post office packet service was to be paid to Churchward after a certain date. Churchward sought to sue the Crown for breach of contract, but the Court of Queen's Bench held that the provision of funds by Parliament was a condition precedent to the enforceability of such a contract against the Crown. In *New South Wales v Bardolph*,[7] the High Court of Australia expressly followed the decision in *Churchward*, but found that such funds had on the facts before them been provided by the Parliament of New South Wales so that the action against the Crown succeeded.

It is quite possible that this exceptional type of contract could prove to be hazardous for the private party. For example, it is common for Government contracts for armaments, aeroplanes or missiles to be placed with private manufacturing companies, the goods to be delivered and the money for them to be paid over a period of several years. Again it is not uncommon for the Government to have second thoughts about its defence plans, and to cancel such contracts after they have been in existence for two or three years, but when the goods ordered have not yet been delivered, or not yet been delivered in great quantities. In such a case the company may well have gone to considerable expense in preparing machinery for the production of the goods ordered, but as the Government and

6 (1865) LR 1 QB 173.
7 (1934) 52 CLR 455.

Parliament have such a close identity of interests, with the Government party normally maintaining a majority in the House of Commons, it is unlikely that Parliament would wish to make any significant grant of money in future years to compensate the company for its losses. The company may stand to lose a vast sum of money whenever it enters into a large or long-term contract with the Government, and its workers may even stand to lose their jobs. Yet it is difficult to see how the present rule could be otherwise if the taxpayer's money is not to be wasted; and it is even more difficult to see how Parliament could ever be forced to vote money. The only remedy, and not a legal one, is to be sure that the Government is certain of its objects when it places contracts of this type and persuades Parliament to vote the first few instalments of the money due, but even then who can be sure what the future holds in store as to possible unforeseen deficiencies in the goods ordered, changes in national needs, or changes of Government?

The third type of contract still exempt from judicial enforcement is perhaps related to the second, for the rationale behind it would appear once again to stem from the necessity for the Government to be free to review and alter its defence requirements from time to time. Of course the public would not be prepared to tolerate a system which permitted the Crown to dismiss without compensation any member of the armed forces, or to fail to pay those who are still employed in such services. The reason that no disquiet over the state of the law ever seems to be voiced in this respect is that it is the invariable practice for the Crown to pay substantial gratuities to any servicemen who lose their jobs before the normal termination of their contract, and because the Crown has never attempted to default in its moral obligation to pay those still employed in the services.

As regards civil servants the law has moved on beyond the apparent void left by the Crown Proceedings Act. Under the Industrial Relations Act 1971 provision was made for cases of alleged unfair dismissal of employees to be heard and determined by industrial tribunals, which should have the power to order reinstatement or the payment of compensation. The provisions extended to a very wide area of employment, and they applied, among others, to civilian employees of the Crown. The 1971 Act was repealed and replaced by the Trade Union and Labour Relations Act 1974, which substantially re-enacted the 1971 provisions in this respect. Thus civil servants now have a right to legal redress for unfair dismissal before a special tribunal, and also a right of further appeal therefrom. But it is interesting that the exemption from legal process in the ordinary courts brought about by the Crown Proceedings Act, section 1, remains the law so far as the ordinary courts are concerned, and that no civil service plaintiff would succeed in a *court* in an action for breach of his contract of service against the Crown.

The liability of the Crown in tort is perhaps rather less complex, though section 2 of the Crown Proceedings Act looks at first sight more detailed and difficult to understand than does section 1. Section 2 reads:

> (1) Subject to the provisions of this Act, the Crown shall be subject to all those liabilities in tort to which, if it were a private person of full age and capacity, it would be subject:
>
> > (a) in respect of torts committed by its servants or agents;
> > (b) in respect of any breach of those duties which a person owes to his servants or agents at common law by reason of being their employer; and
> > (c) in respect of any breach of the duties attaching at common law to the ownership, ocupation, possession or control of property:
>
> Provided that no proceedings shall lie against the Crown by virtue of paragraph (a) of this subsection in respect of any act or omission of a servant or agent of the Crown unless the act or omission would apart from the provisions of this Act have given rise to a cause of action in tort against that servant or agent or his estate.
>
> (2) Where the Crown is bound by a statutory duty which is binding upon persons other than the Crown and its officers, then, subject to the provisions of this Act, the Crown shall, in respect of a failure to comply with that duty, be subject to all those liabilities in tort (if any) to which it would be so subject if it were a private person of full age and capacity.

There follow four other subsections, though they are ancillary and do not add anything very substantial to the main provisions of the first two subsections. Thus subsection (5) very properly exempts the Crown from any liability for torts committed by any person while discharging or purporting to discharge any responsibilities of a judicial nature vested in him; and subsection (6) makes it clear that the vicarious liability of the Crown in tort only covers those acts committed by any person who is directly or indirectly appointed by the Crown, and who at the material time was paid in respect of his duties as an officer of the Crown wholly out of the Consolidated Fund, or out of money provided by Parliament, or other funds certified by the Treasury as being of the same character.

Though the terms of section 2 are such as to refer to certain particular types of torts, or to torts committed by certain types of person, the total effect of the section really gives a far more general right of action in tort against the Crown than the right provided in the shorter, and apparently more general, section 1 concerning contracts. Subsection (1)(a) of section 2 is in truth of the widest possible extent, for it is scarcely possible to think of the commission of a tort by the Crown other than by one or other of its servants or agents, once it is conceded that sections 40 and 38 of the Act exempt the Monarch in person from liability, either in his or her private capacity, or else in right of the Duchy of Lancaster or of Cornwall. There is a slight possibility that the proviso to subsection (1) may limit the effect of the subsection somewhat, in that a very rare type of case where an ordinary employer is liable even though the servant who actually committed the tortious act cannot be sued[8] may be excluded where the employer is the Crown. Yet in a County Court case decided in 1959[9] it was held that where an action in tort was brought against the Crown and also against a servant of the Crown, but it was for some reason statute-barred against the servant, it was not so barred against the Crown.

As section 2 says at the outset, there are certain other provisions of the Act which detract from any conclusion that the section provides a total liability of the Crown for torts committed by it or on its behalf. Apart from the exemption of the Monarch personally, and the express exemption also of any prerogative or statutory powers in section 11, the main provision which has the effect of limiting the right of action in tort against the Crown is in section 10. The most important effect of section 11 is to leave untouched the immunity of the Crown from liability for acts of state. Section 10, however, makes special provisions concerning liability for torts committed by members of the armed forces on duty against other members of the armed forces.[10] Thus, where such a tort causes death or personal injury to the other serviceman, and the Minister of Defence certifies that the deceased or injured person was on duty or on service property at the time of the act involved, then there is no right of action against either the Crown or the actual tortfeasor. This may seem harsh, but the reason for the provision is that the section also provides for another certificate to be granted by the Secretary of State for Health and Social Security to the effect that the injured person shall qualify for an award from the Crown *ex gratia*. Providing that this procedure is adhered to, the lack of a right of action in tort is of no importance. There is every

---

8 *Smith v Moss* [1940] 1 KB 424, would have been an example of this type of case, in that a wife before 1962 was generally unable to succeed in an action in tort against her husband. But this gap was closed by the Law Reform (Husband and Wife) Act 1962, s 1, under which each party to a marriage has the same right of action in tort against the other as if he or she were not married.
9 *Corney v Minister of Labour*, unreported, but noted in [1959] PL 170.
10 Minor amendments to this section were made by the Defence (Transfer of Functions) Act 1964 and the Supplementary Benefit Act 1966, but they do not affect the main provisions of the section.

reason to believe that wherever a tort is committed in circumstances covered by section 10, the Crown will award a gratuity. *Adams v War Office*[11] is the solitary unfortunate example where the first of the two certificates contemplated by section 10 was granted, but the second, though at first granted, was later withdrawn, leaving the plaintiff without any judicial remedy. A reservist in a territorial battalion had been killed by a shell while engaged in an exercise on the army ranges at Bulford, and his father sued the War Office for negligence in his capacity as the administrator of the deceased's estate. He claimed damages for the benefit of the estate, and for himself and his wife by way of compensation to them for the financial loss they had suffered by the death of their son. The two certificates contemplated by section 10 were granted, but then the Minister of Pensions, who was the predecessor of the present Secretary of State for Health and Social Security, refused after all to make any grant to the plaintiff. Glyn-Jones J found that the Crown had a complete defence to the action brought by the plaintiff, even though the Minister of Pensions had apparently failed to carry out what he seemed at first to have undertaken.

The only other difficulty inherent in Section 2 lies in the provision that the Crown is only liable where the servant or agent falls within the description provided in subsection (6). It might well have been thought that there would be some fine distinctions drawn by the courts on this point. But the period of nearly forty years since the Act came into effect has proved the contrary. The exemption of Crown liability for the torts or possible torts of judges is clearly accepted, and there are no cases which show that there are hidden problems brought about by the distinction between those genuinely employed and wholly paid by the Crown in respect of the act involved and those who are not so employed and paid. Prerogative acts remain non-justiciable in British courts. But as regards other torts the general rule of vicarious liability applies. However curiously worded, section 2 of the 1947 Act has in effect brought about a near-complete liability of the Crown in tort, and on the whole this seems to be a satisfactory result.

Public interest immunity

Section 28 of the Crown Proceedings Act 1947 provides that the Crown may be required to discover documents or to answer interrogatories, but the proviso to subsection (1) of the section makes it clear

11 [1955] 3 All ER 245.

that the common law rules as to Crown privilege are left untouched. It is thus of prime importance to be sure what those rules are. They have had a tortuous history.

The problem at issue is whether or not it is open to the Crown to prevent evidence being produced in any litigation on the ground that its production would be injurious to the public interest. It has always been possible for the court to uphold the Crown's claim to privilege in this respect where it considers the claim to be a proper one, and this has been so whether or not the Crown has been a party to the actual case itself. But the liberty accorded by the courts to the Crown seemed to become excessive after 1942, when the leading case of *Duncan v Cammell, Laird & Co Ltd*[12] was decided. This case arose out of the tragedy which occurred when the submarine *Thetis* sank during her trials in Liverpool Bay shortly before the Second World War, causing the loss of ninety-nine men. Many of their dependants brought actions for negligence against the contractors who had built the submarine, and *Duncan* was treated as a test case. The ·plaintiffs called on the contractors to produce a number of important documents, including the contract with the Admiralty, the blueprints for the submarine, and the salvage reports made after the accident. These were essential if the plaintiffs were to be able to show that the defendants had been negligent in the construction of the submarine, but it is also entirely understandable in time of war that the First Lord of the Admiralty swore an affidavit that disclosure would be against the public interest, for it was of the highest importance to prevent vital construction secrets from falling into enemy hands. The House of Lords held that his affidavit could not be questioned, and so the plaintiffs, being totally unable to establish their allegations of negligence, inevitably lost their case. After the war was over it became known that the *Thetis* class of submarines had a new type of torpedo tube which could be fired in different directions, and which was in advance of any similar device known to the Germans at the time, so that the vital necessity of protecting the secret was clear.

But Viscount Simon LC, in the leading speech in *Duncan*, with which all the other Law Lords agreed, laid down a sweeping rule that the court could not question a claim of Crown privilege made in proper form, whatever the nature of the document may be. In Lord Simon's view any objection by the Crown, or by a Minister or department of state, to the production of evidence on the ground that such production would be injurious to the public interest was conclusive, though the Lord Chancellor went on to remark that the decision ruling out such documents from the case concerned is the

12 [1942] AC 624.

decision of the judge. This was a curious mixture of phrases, but it was held in many cases thereafter to amount to a complete bar to any court where a Minister claims that a document is privileged. Some mitigation of this extreme rule was provided by the case of *Broome v Broome (Edmundson cited)*,[13] where Sachs J held that the right to certify documents as covered by privilege did not always extend to all oral evidence, though his decision went little further than to say that the court will not necessarily hold itself bound by certificates in a 'blanket form' which purport to stop a witness even from going into the witness-box. So far as the law of Scotland was concerned the House of Lords itself, in *Glasgow Corpn v Central Land Board*,[14] decided in 1956, held that the court has power to override the Crown's objection to production of evidence if it is satisfied that it is not justified by the facts. This power was not actually exercised in the *Glasgow Corpn* case, though it was the following year in *Whitehall v Whitehall*,[15] and in any event its existence showed up the disadvantage of the English courts.

The *Glasgow Corpn* case provided the stepping-off point for many courts in other parts of the Commonwealth which seized the opportunity to follow the Scottish rather than the English precedent. Thus, in *Corbett v Social Security Comr*,[16] the New Zealand Court of Appeal followed the *Glasgow Corpn* case, holding that it was not bound by the House of Lords' decision in *Duncan*: only decisions of the Judicial Committee of the Privy Council, as the court of last resort in New Zealand, would be so binding. The Supreme Court of Victoria in Australia took the same line in *Bruce v Waldron*[17] in 1963, and similar decisions followed in the Queensland Supreme Court[18] and the South African Court of Appeal.[19] Lord Denning MR, dissenting in the English Court of Appeal in *Conway v Rimmer*[20] in 1967, a case shortly to be discussed, cited decisions rejecting the strict *Duncan v Cammell, Laird* rule from Scotland, Canada, Victoria, New South Wales, New Zealand, India, Ceylon and Jamaica. Clearly the English rule was becoming isolated from the rest of the Commonwealth.

Professor J D B Mitchell argued in 1963[1] that the doctrine of precedent in the field of public law has its peculiarities explicable by

13   [1955] P190.
14   1956 SC (HL) 1.
15   1957 SC 30.
16   [1962] NZLR 878.
17   [1963] VR 3.
18   *Re Tunstall, ex p Brown* (1966) 60 QJPR 146.
19   *Van Der Linde v Calitz* [1967] 2 SALR 239n.
20   [1967] 2 All ER 1260.
1   Note (1963) 79 LQR 487.

reason of the subject matter concerned, and that the decision in *Duncan v Cammell, Laird & Co Ltd* was probably satisfactory if restricted to its war-time context. Professor Goodhart, while pointing out that Viscount Simon had misunderstood the relevant Scots authorities, also suggested that the scope of the *Duncan* decision should be limited to its special facts, and that much difficulty had been caused by Viscount Simon's possibly unintentional substitution of the phrase 'public interest' for 'national security'.[2]

As a matter of practice the Crown privilege rule was modified as a result of a statement made in the House of Lords by the Lord Chancellor in 1956,[3] though this really amounted to no more than a statement of intent that the Crown would not normally claim privilege unless there was very good reason to do so. The law remained unaltered, and it was still effectively left to each Minister whether or not to enforce his right to withhold evidence. In the interest of justice many critics still felt that the question of whether or not to permit evidence to be withheld should be one for the judge and the judge alone. The disquiet felt was pungently expressed by Devlin J in *Ellis v Home Office*,[4] a case in which the plaintiff, an inmate of a prison, was unable to establish an action of negligence against the prison authorities (based upon his allegation that another prisoner had assaulted him while they were inadequately supervised by prison officers) because the Home Secretary claimed that the prison records were privileged from production before the court:

> But before I leave this case I must express, as I have expressed during the hearing of the case, my uneasy feeling that justice may not have been done because the material evidence before me was not complete, and something more than an uneasy feeling that, whether justice has been done or not, it certainly will not appear to have been done.

Only if the judge has full control over admission and disallowance of all evidence in the case before him will this 'uneasy feeling' be removed. The present writer is much in sympathy with the state of the federal law in the United States of America, where the judge certainly has this control. Professor Bernard Schwartz, in his *An Introduction to American Administrative Law*,[5] gives an admirable summary of the position, showing that it is for the judge to determine whether privilege on the ground that a 'state secret' is involved is

---

2 Note (1963) 79 LQR 153; see also D H Clark 'Administrative Control of Judicial Action: The Authority of *Duncan v Cammell, Laird*' (1967) 30 MLR 489.
3 197 HL Official Report (5th series) col 741; later extended in 1962 (237 HL Official Report (5th series) col 1191) and 1964 (261 HL Official Report (5th series) col 423).
4 [1953] 2 QB 135 at 137.
5 2nd edn, 1962, p 255.

validly claimed. Basing his account on the decision in the leading case of *Reynolds v United States*,[6] he states that the judge's inquiry extends only to seeing whether there is a reasonable basis for the assertion of privilege. If he can satisfy himself that there is such a reasonable basis from the circumstances of the case, without examining the document at issue, then he will not examine the document. On the other hand, if examination of the document itself is necessary before the judge can decide whether what might be described as a 'state secret' is really involved, then he can and should make such examination. As was stressed in the *Reynolds* case, there is no danger to the public interest in submitting the question of privilege to the decision of the courts, which will, where necessary, sit *in camera* in order to hear matter which will provide them with the background facts at issue. The judges of the United States are public officers whose responsibility under the Constitution is just as great as that of the heads of executive departments, and they can be depended upon to protect with the greatest care the public interest in preventing the disclosure of matters which may fairly be characterised as privileged.

It does not yet appear the English courts have reached a rule of practice which enables them as a matter of course to ask counsel on both sides to argue upon the background to the documents *in camera*, without the presence or the detailed knowledge of the parties to the case. Such a practice may come in time, particularly since hearings *in camera* are quite often held in cases of prosecution under the Official Secrets Acts, where state security is frequently at stake, but where it is essential for the evidence for the prosecution to be given if a conviction is to be obtained. But at least the rigour of the *Duncan* rule has now been broken in English law, as we shall see, and it is now perfectly acceptable for a judge to inspect documents covered by a privilege claim in order to determine whether it should be acceded to. In the period 1964-65 the Court of Appeal took a hand in the battle against undue use of Crown privilege to thwart the legitimate aspirations of litigants. In three cases[7] the same trio of judges, Lord Denning MR, Harman and Salmon LJJ, reviewed the authorities and found that they had been misinterpreted by the House of Lords in *Duncan v Canmell, Laird & Co Ltd*, as regards England as well as Scotland. They felt that claims of privilege should be restricted to cases concerning such matters as defence and state secrets, and they refused to accept that a claim that a document was within a 'class' which ought to be protected was conclusive to bind the court. They

6 192 F 2d 987 (3d Cir 1951).
7 *Re Grosvenor Hotel, London (No 2)* [1965] Ch 1210; *Merricks v Nott-Bower* [1965] 1 QB 57; *Wednesbury Corpn v Ministry of Housing and Local Government* [1965] 1 All ER 186.

asserted that the court had residual power to override such a claim, and to order production of a document if the public interest or the proper administration of justice so requires, although such power would only be exercised in exceptional and rare cases, and it was not in fact exercised in any of the three cases in which its existence was asserted.

In *Conway v Rimner* in 1967, a differently constituted Court of Appeal refused, Lord Denning dissenting, to accept the reasoning in this trilogy of cases, thus paving the way for an appeal to the House of Lords which by its unanimous ruling has finally freed us from the yoke of *Duncan*, and set the English courts upon a more reasonable and satisfactory course for the future, even though it makes no provision for the kind of hearing *in camera* which this author would favour. Before *Conway v Rimner* the Law Reform Committee had embarked upon an examination of the whole topic of Crown privilege, and had invited evidence on the subject. Many including the present author, responded to this invitation. But the House of Lords' decision was sufficient to cause the Committee to abandon its work on the subject. One oddity of the Lords' decision is that although their Lordships made a careful examination of a long line of English cases, there is very little reference to cases from overseas or to the trilogy of cases reported in England in 1965. This led Professor H W R Wade, while welcoming the decision, to call it 'an exercise in pure reason'.[8] It might also be noted that, although Lord Reid and Upjohn distinguished *Duncan v Canwell, Laird & Co Ltd*, Lords Morris of Borth-y-Gest and Hodson expressly declined to follow *Duncan*. Lord Pearce also impliedly took this latter line, and so *Conway v Rimmer* became the first case since the Lords' new-found freedom began in 1966 in which the House reversed a previous Lords decision.

In *Conway v Rimmer*,[9] the appellant, a former probationary police constable, had begun an action for malicious prosecution against his former superintendent. The superintendent had been instrumental in bringing a criminal charge of larceny against the appellant, who was acquitted but later dismissed from the police force. The appellent sought production of five documents in the respondent's possession, including reports on his probationary service and a report prepared in connection with the larceny prosecution. The respondent was willing to produce the documents, but the Home Secretary claimed privilege in a sworn affidavit in the following terms:

> I, The Right Honourable Roy Harris Jenkins, one of Her Majesty's Principal Secretaries of State, make oath and say as follows:

8   Note (1968) 84 LQR 171 at 173.
9   [1968] AC 910.

162 *Remedies*

> 1. On or about June 3, 1966, my attention was drawn to a copy of a list of documents delivered in these proceedings on behalf of the defendant and to the document referred to the second part of the first schedule to the said list of documents being numbered therein 38; 39; 40; 47 and 48.
> 2. I personally examined and carefully considered all the said documents and I formed the view that those numbered 38; 39; 40 and 48 fell within a class of documents comprising confidential reports by police officers to chief officers of police relating to the conduct, efficiency and fitness for employment of individual police officers under their command and that the said document numbered 47 fell within a class of documents comprising reports by police officers to their superiors concerning investigations into the commission of crime. In my opinion the production of documents of each such class would be injurious to the public interest...
> 5. I object to the production of each of the said documents on the grounds set forth in paragraph 2 of this affidavit.

The District Registrar ordered production of the documents, but this order was reversed by Brown J in chambers. The appellant's appeal was unsuccessful in the Court of Appeal, despite Lord Denning's dissent, but was successful in the House of Lords. It was held unanimously that the documents should be produced for inspection by their Lordships, and that if it was then found that disclosure would not be prejudicial to the public interest, or that any possibility of such prejudice was insufficient to justify their being withheld, disclosure should be ordered. When there is a clash between the public interest (1) that harm should not be done to the nation or the public service by the disclosure of certain documents and (2) that the administration of justice should not be frustrated by the withholding of them, their production will not be ordered if the possible injury to the nation or the public service is so grave that no other interest should be allowed to prevail over it, but, where the possible injury is substantially less, the court must balance against each other the two public interests involved. When the Minister's certificate suggests that the document belongs to a class which ought to be withheld, then, unless his reasons are of a kind that judicial experience is not competent to weigh, the proper test is whether the withholding of a document of that particular class is really necessary for the functioning of the public service. If on balance, considering the likely importance of the document in the case before it, the court considers that it should be produced, it should generally examine the document before ordering production. In the instant case it seemed to their Lordships that it was improbable that any harm would be done to the police service by the disclosure of the documents in question, which might prove vital to the litigation. Lord Reid therefore examined them, and found nothing in them which would be likely to prejudice the proper administration of the police or the general public interest if disclosed, and they were accordingly ordered to be produced for inspection by the plaintiff.

In his speech Lord Reid said:[10]

> I have no doubt that the case of *Duncan v Cammell, Laird & Co Ltd* was rightly decided. The plaintiff sought discovery of documents relating to the submarine *Thetis* including a contract for the hull and machinery and plans and specifications. The First Lord of the Admiralty has stated that 'it would be injurious to the public interest that any of the said documents should be disclosed to any person'. Any of these documents might well have given valuable information, or at least clues, to the skilled eye of an agent of a foreign power. But Lord Simon LC took the opportunity to deal with the whole question of the right of the Crown to prevent production of documents in a litigation. Yet a study of his speech leaves me with the strong impression that throughout he had primarily in mind cases where discovery or disclosure would involve a danger of real prejudice to the national interest. I find it difficult to believe that his speech would have been the same if the case had related, as the present case does, to the discovery of routine reports on a probationer constable...
>
> I would therefore propose that the House ought now to decide that courts have and are entitled to exercise a power and duty to hold a balance between the public interest, as expressed by a Minister, to withhold certain documents or other evidence, and the public interest in ensuring the proper administration of justice. That does not mean that a court would reject a Minister's view: full weight must be given to it in every case, and if the Minister's reasons are of a character which judicial experience is not competent to weigh, then the Minister's view must prevail. But experience has shown that reasons given for withholding whole classes of documents are often not of that character. For example a court is perfectly well able to assess the likelihood that, if the writer of a certain class of document knew that there was a chance that his report might be produced in legal proceedings, he would make a less full and candid report than he would otherwise have done.
>
> I do not doubt that there are certain classes of documents which ought not to be disclosed whatever their content may be. Virtually everyone agrees that Cabinet minutes and the like ought not to be disclosed until such time as they are only of historical interest. But I do not think that many people would give as the reason that premature disclosure would prevent candour in the Cabinet. To my mind the most important reason is that such disclosure would create or fan ill-informed or captious public or political criticism. The business of government is difficult enough as it is, and no government could contemplate with equanimity the inner workings of the goverment machine being exposed to the gaze of those ready to criticise without adequate knowledge of the background and perhaps with some axe to grind. And that must, in my view, also apply

10 [1968] AC 910 at 938.

to all documents concerned with policy making within departments including, it may be minutes and the like by quite junior officials and correspondence with outside bodies. Further it may be that deliberations about a particular case require protection as much as deliberations about policy. I do not think that it is possible to limit such documents by any definition. But there seems to me to be a wide difference between such documents and routine reports. There may be special reasons for withholding some kinds of routine documents, but I think that the proper test to be applied is to ask, in the language of Lord Simon in *Duncan's* case, whether the withholding of a document because it belongs to a particular class is really 'unnecessary for the proper functioning of the public service.'

It appears to me that, if the Minister's reasons are such that a judge can properly weigh them, he must, on the other hand, consider what is the probable importance in the case before him of the documents or other evidence sought to be withheld. If he decides that on balance the documents probably ought to be produced, I think that it would generally be best that he should see them before ordering production and if he thinks that the Minister's reasons are not clearly expressed he will have to see the documents before ordering production. I can see nothing wrong in the judge seeing documents without their being shown to the parties. Lord Simon said (in *Duncan's* case)[11] that 'where the Crown is a party. . . this would amount to communicating with one party to the exclusion of the other' I do not agree. The parties see the Minister's reasons. Where a document has not been prepared for the information of the judge, it seems to me a misuse of language to say that the judge 'communicates with' the holder of the document by reading it. If on reading the document he still thinks that it ought to be produced he will order its production.

But it is important that the Minister should have a right to appeal before the document is produced. This matter was fully investigated in the arguement before your Lordships. But it does appear that in one way or another there can be an appeal if the document is in the custody of a servant of the Crown or of a person who is willing to co-operate with the Minister. There may be difficulty if it is in the hands of the person who wishes to produce it. But that difficulty could occur today if a witness wishes to give some evidence which the Minister unsuccessfully urges the court to prevent from being given. It may be that this is a matter which deserves further investigation by the Crown authorities.

The documents in this case are in the possession of a police force. The position of the police is peculiar. They are not servants of the Crown and they do not take orders from the Government. But they are carrying out an essential function of Government, and various Crown rights, privileges and exemptions have been held to apply to them. . . It has never been denied that they are entitled to Crown privilege with regard to documents, and it is essential that they should have it.

The police are carrying on an unending war with criminals many of

11 [1942] AC 624 at 640.

whom are today highly intelligent. So it is essential that there should be no disclosure of anything which might give any useful information to those who organise criminal activities. And it would generally be wrong to require disclosure in a civil case of anything which might be material in a pending prosecution: but after a verdict has been given or it has been decided to take no proceedings there is not the same need for secrecy. With regards to other documents there seems to be no greater need for protection than in the case of departments of Government.

It appears to me to be most improbable that any harm would be done by disclosure of the probationary reports on the appellant or of the report from the police training centre. With regard to the report which the respondent made to his chief constable with a view to the prosecution of the appellant there could be more doubt, although no suggestion was made in argument that disclosure of its contents would be harmful now that the appellant has been acquitted. And, as I have said, these documents may prove to be of vital importance in this litigation.

In my judgment, this appeal should be allowed and these documents ought now to be required to be produced for inspection. If it is then found that disclosure would not, in your Lordships's view, be prejudicial to the public interest, or that any possibility of such prejudice is, in the case of each of the documents, insufficient to justify its being withheld, then disclosure should be ordered.

The Lords' decision in *Conway v Rimmer* effectively spelled the end of the immunity of 'class claims' for Crown privilege from judicial scrutiny, though it will be rare that a Minister's certificate will be questioned in respect of certain classes of documents, such as Cabinet minutes. In the event there have been many cases since 1968 in which the courts have continued to allow claims of Crown privilege, though they have now moved over to the more modern terminology in describing such protection of documents from disclosure as being 'in the public interest', a phase which makes clear that the judges are now excising a real discretion in determining whether or not to allow the claim to succeed. Thus in 1973, in *Rogers v Home Secretary*,[12] the House of Lords, again unanimously, held that information given to the Gaming Board by the police should not be disclosed. The documents concerned would be likely to reveal the identity of police informers. Furthermore, there was a wider ground for allowing them to be withheld in that the Gaming Board would not be able to obtain information about applicants for licences, which must often come from disreputable persons, unless the information received was immune from discovery; and without this information the Board would be unable to function. Lord Reid was again the senior Law

---

12 [1973] AC 388.

Lord sitting, and he expressed the change in terminology and emphasis aptly.[13]

> For the reasons which I have given I do not think the right to withhold the documents depends on or flows from any privilege. It arises from the public interest and the board are entitled to assert that public interest.

A similar decision of the Lords, allowing a claim of Crown privilege in respect of documents relating to the breaking of sanctions imposed against Rhodesia by the Southern Rhodesia (Petroleum Order) 1965, because the documents were relevant to a private inquiry about the matter set up by the Foreign and Commonwealth Secretary, was *Lonrho Ltd v Shell Petroleum Co Ltd*.[14] Again the new terminology was used, the public interest against disclosure being held to outweigh the general public interest that in the administration of justice the decision should be based on all relevant facts. A report to the Department of Trade resulting from an inquiry into a company held under the Companies Act 1948 was held by the Divisional Court in 1977 to be protected from disclosure by the public interest in *R v Cheltenham Justices, ex p Secretary of State for Trade*,[15] as it was information helpful to the control of crime. And the House of Lords in 1978 held that the anonymity of informers who report maltreatment of children to a local authority or protection society should be protected where the public interest so demands.[16] On the other hand, in *Burmah Oil Co Ltd v Bank of England*,[17] the House of Lords refused to uphold in full a claim that documents relating first to the formulation of Government policy, and secondly to confidential information given by businessmen to the Bank of England and to the Government upon business matters, should be withheld from disclosure in court. The documents were concerned with certain arrangements made between the Bank and the Burmah Oil Company in 1975 to assist the latter to resolve its financial difficulties. The Court of Appeal had held, by a majority of two to one, Lord Denning dissenting, that it would be contrary to public policy to allow the first category of documents to be disclosed, and that discovery of the second category might impede the giving of confidential information in future. Yet, although the Lords ordered that documents should be produced for inspection by the House of Lords they then held that none of them contained matter of such evidential value as to make an order for their disclosure to the other side necessary for disposing

13 Ibid at 405.
14 [1980] 1 WLR 627.
15 [1977] 1 All ER 460.
16 *D v National Society for the Prevention of Cruelty to Children* [1978] AC 171.
17 [1980] AC 1090.

fairly of the case, and that their significance was not such as to override the public service objections to their disclosure.

But the fact that several claims to what is now more usually referred to as public interest immunity have been allowed by the courts since 1968 does not mean that *Conway v Rimmer* was by any means a nine days' wonder. In *Norwich Pharmacal Co v Customs and Excise Comrs*,[18] the owners of a patent for a chemical compound found that it was being infringed by unknown importers, and they applied for orders to make the Customs and Excise Commissioners disclose the importers' names. Disclosure was resisted on the ground that it might cause importers to use false names and thus hamper the customs administration. But the House of Lords held that there was a duty upon those who possess information about legal wrongs to make it available to the party wronged, and that there was no valid head of public policy to set against the rights of the owners of the patent. Again, in *Campbell v Tameside Metropolitan Borough Council*,[19] the Court of Appeal ordered that reports concerning an eleven-year old school boy who was alleged to have assaulted his teacher should be disclosed. The teacher's solicitor thought she might have a claim against the local education authority because there were strong grounds for believing that the council knew the child to be of a violent disposition, and the court, after inspecting the documents, agreed they were of considerable significance to her action. Although the council claimed that the reports were confidential and that those who made them would be inhibited in future it they realised that such reports might be used in legal proceedings, the court decided that it had to balance the public interest in justice being done against the public interest in keeping the documents confidential, and that in the instant case the former should prevail. There is always likely to be conflict between the interest of the administration and private rights. But what the decision in *Conway v Rimmer* has achieved, and what later decisions have underlined, is that the courts are no longer allowing the Crown to prevent disclosure of relevant evidence in those cases where the

18 [1974] AC 133; cf *Alfred Crompton Amusement Machines Ltd v Customs and Excise Comrs (No 2)* [1974] AC 405 (Crown claim to withhold documents accepted on the ground that disclosure would be harmful to the efficient working of an Act of Parliament.
19 [1982] QB 1065; see also *Williams v Home Secretary* [1981] 1 All ER 1151. cf *Air Canada v Secretary of State for Trade* [1983] 2 AC 394, in which the House of Lords ruled by three to two that a court should not automatically have the right to inspect documents for which public interest immunity is claimed. The party seeking disclosure ought at least to satisfy the court that the documents are very likely to contain material which would give substantial support to his contention on an issue which arises in the case. In the event the court could not be satisfied, and disclosure was not allowed.

Crown is satified that it is desirable. A much fairer balance has been struck. All claims to withhold evidence are being assessed by the courts on their merits, and by an application of an objective assessment of what in the round is 'in the public interest'. The present writer still rather hankers after the American flexibility, including the possibility of hearings *in camera*. But it is clear that the state of English law on what may now be only archaically referred to as Crown privilege is infinitely more healthy than before *Conway v Rimmer*.

Before closing this chapter it might be well to glance at certain developments in Australia. The Commonwealth Administrative Review Committee, under the chairmanship of Sir John Kerr, recommended in 1971 that the rules for Crown privilege, along the lines settled in *Conway v Rimmer*, should be statutory. This has now been substantially achieved by The Freedom of Information Act 1982 (Cth). This places all departments of state and statutory organisations under a duty to identify and index internal documents and to publish the results. Members of the public are entitled to obtain copies, subject to limited exceptions on grounds of national security, foreign relations and defence.[20] Any further claims by Ministers that documents ought not to be produced for reasons of confidence or sensitivity of the subject matter may be tested in the courts. In recent years there has been considerable political pressure for the enactment of a similar measure in the United Kingdom, but it remains to be seen if and when this object will be achieved.

Before the Australian reforms had been enacted a considerable *cause célèbre* was provided by the case of *Sankey v Whitlam* in 1978.[1] The case arose out of informations laid by a private citizen, Mr Sankey, against Mr Gough Whitlam, lately the Prime Minister of Australia, and three of his former ministerial colleagues for various crimes of conspiracy. Sankey also demanded discovery of a veritable sheaf of documents which included Cabinet papers and memoranda on matters of Government policy. Not unnaturally this demand was resisted by the defendants, who were able to obtain the support of their successors in claiming Crown privilege. The High Court of Australia unanimously held that, in pursuance of the reasoning of the House of Lords in *Conway v Rimmer*, which they adopted, there is no class of documents which is protected from the possibility of disclosure in court. All are subject to the overall discretion of the court, which may determine whether or not to allow them to be withheld. This is in line with the reasoning of Lord Reid and his

---

20 Citizens are also entitled to have any misleading or incomplete personal references expunged from such documents, if necessary by court order.
1   (1978) 53 ALJR 11.

colleagues, though Lord Reid had stressed that judges would be likely to hold that Cabinet minutes ought not to be produced until they are of only historical importance. In *Sankey v Whitlam*, however, the High Court of Australia effectively cast aside the notion that there may be any class of documents which should not be produced in judicial proceedings. The court ruled that all documents regardless of source were subject to the test of the weight of public interest. In pursuance of this view it then went so far as to order the production of all the documents concerned, including Cabinet minutes, executive council minutes and ministerial correspondence, even though less than three years old.

Sankey v Whitlam expressly followed *Conway v Rimmer*, but it went further. It is not without interest that some Government circles in Australia were convinced that it went too far. In New South Wales the backlash took the form of an Act which in effect restored for the State of New South Wales much of the force of the old rules in *Duncan v Canmell, Laird & Co Ltd*,[2] a curious back-tracking on the progressive developments of the last few years. But this enactment can probably be treated as an isolated, and perhaps temporary, aberration. For the most part the development of the common law has been clear, and in the interests of objective justice. It has rounded off the rapid progress made in the latter part of the twentieth century to bring our administrative law remedies up to date.

---

2 Evidence (Amendment) Act 1979.

6 Tribunals and inquiries

> Nothing is more remarkable in our present social and administrative arrangements than the proliferation of tribunals of many different kinds. There is scarcely a new statute of social or economic complexion which does not add to the number. Many existed before the Second World War, but since then they have multiplied rapidly.
>
> Sir Carleton Allen *Administrative Jurisdiction*

It is a notable feature of our public life in the present century that no longer is all, or even the great bulk, of our judicial business carried out by judges in the ordinary courts of the land. Progressively and inexorably a considerable proportion of the decision-making which in former centuries would as a matter of course have had to be discharged by the courts, if indeed the problems at issue counted among those which were recognised as justiciable, has been handed over to specially constituted bodies of citizens from all walks of life who sit in judgment upon their fellow-citizens in the so-called administrative tribunals. This appellation is to some extent unfortunate, because the powers of the various tribunals are mainly judicial rather than administrative. 'Special tribunals' might well be a less misleading description, but the traditional term is so well established that it would only serve to confuse to attempt in this book to adopt any more accurate title for them.

It has frequently been asked why there is any need to have such tribunals, particularly since administration is normally in the hands of the Crown and its servants or agents, or else carried out by those other authorities which we have already discussed in chapter 1, while judicial decisions would normally be obtainable through the ordinary courts. The reason is that under modern circumstances, just as there is far too much legislation required at any given time for Parliament to be able to cope with the load (so that we are bound to need delegated legislation, as was discussed in chapter 2), so also there are too many problems of mixed law and administration, or of law concerned with the administration, for the courts to be able to deal with them effectively and speedily. We have only to realise the ramifications of one major aspect of modern life, the welfare state, to understand how the courts cannot possibly provide an adequate or suitable judicial service for its purposes. Under current welfare state legislation, virtually all of which now dates from the period since the Second World War, there is provision on the one hand for the collection on a compulsory basis of insurance contributions from all those living in the country who earn income, and on the other hand for the payment of a whole battery of different types of benefit covered by this compulsory insurance scheme. The actual identity of these benefits will be considered presently when we deal with social security appeal tribunals. Qualifications for the payment of any one of such benefits will depend upon a variety of factors, including the relevant contribution record or conditions; whether the circumstance intended to be covered by the benefit has actually occurred; and whether the claim was made within the requisite time limit, and if not whether the proviso that a claim made out of time may be allowed if continuous good cause for the delay can be proved has been satisfied. These are only a few of the problems which arise constantly under the welfare state insurance scheme, but all require a judicial-type investigation or trial before the relevant legal answer can be arrived at. Sometimes the problems at issue are complicated by questions as to the eligibility of dependants to enable claimants to obtain increases of benefit, or, in the case of unemployment benefit the question whether a claimant is disqualified from benefit because he has lost his employment by virtue of his involvement as an interested party in a trade dispute at his place of employment. In a nation which has become accustomed to an overall unemployment figure approaching three millions it is clear that the burden of judicial decision related to unemployment benefit alone is heavy.

It must be admitted that the welfare state provides perhaps the most obvious and weighty example of a field of administrative law which requires a special decision-making process outside the ordinary courts. But there are many other areas of modern life which throw up a similar need. Problems of law or mixed law and administration inevitably arise from the process of civil aviation licensing, the fixing of rents in privately let accommodation, together with the ancillary question of security of tenure in some types of such accommodation, rating valuation appeals, applications and references by patients under the Mental Health Act 1959 and later statutes and allegations of unfair dismissal from employment; and these again are only examples taken virtually at random from a vast patchwork quilt of what Sir Carleton Allen called 'Administrative Jurisdiction'. The courts could never cope with them unless they were greatly increased in number. But even such an expansion of the court system would not suffice, for the prime requirements in dealing with the problem arising in this whole area of administrative law are speed, cheapness, a special aptitude for the particular type of problems concerned (a quality which is provided for by the composition of each tribunal), lack of formality and forms, and the provision of a type of justice which often involves a fair degree of compromise, thus contrasting with the normal court decision whereby one party or the other becomes successful at the expense of the other.

It has been found more and more in the course of this century that tribunals of various kinds are far more readily adapted to these needs than are the ordinary courts, and it is now for the most part accepted that they are able to perform their tasks to the best advantage of all parties. Administrative tribunals have not been without their critics, and severe criticism led to the setting up in 1956 of a particularly influential committee, the Committee on Administrative Tribunals and Enquiries, under the chairmanship of Sir Oliver Franks (later Lord Franks), whose Report, published in 1957,[1] has had a profound effect upon general thought and attitudes towards administrative jurisdiction. We shall consider this Report presently, but it is as well to bear in mind at the outset that one of its greatest achievements was to sweep away the attitudes of ignorance and prejudice against the work of the tribunals which had been clearly evident before the Report appeared. In this the Franks Committee performed a service in this area of the law not dissimilar from the overall achievements of the Donoughmore-Scott Committee Report twenty-five years before in relation to delegated legislation.

Where it has been decided by Parliament to entrust the power to decide problems within the area of administrative law to some body which is independent of the administration, the power will normally be conferred upon an administrative tribunal. But the Crown still retains a considerable area of decision-making within its own hands, and exercises it through the decisions of Ministers and Secretaries of State. Yet even here it has long been recognised that a decision should only be made after first following a procedure which is intended to enable those who will be affected by the decision to make their views known; and this type of procedure is an inquiry. The most common inquiries are concerned with proposals which affect property rights. Thus inquiry procedures are used in connection with schemes to create new towns, or in relation to appeals to the Secretary of State against refusal by a local planning authority of proposals to develop land, and where there are proposals to acquire private land compulsorily for housing, or in order to build airports or new motorways.

---

1 Cmnd 218.

Administrative tribunals 173

The actual inquiry is conducted by an inspector, whose duty it is to allow all objectors a fair chance to put their case, after which he must make a report and recommendations to the Minister. In essence this process is intended to enable the mind of the Minister who decides a particular issue to be properly informed before he comes to his decision, while not requiring him necessarily to arrive at his determination in accordance with the weight of the evidence brought to his attention. But we shall see that in recent years Ministers have not been so free as to the courses they may take in their decisions as they were formerly, and this again is a development achieved in the aftermath of the Franks Report. In comparing tribunals and inquiries with the ordinary court system, one may be reminded of the advice believed to have been given by Winston Churchill during the Second World War on measures for assisting the maintenance of physical health in a time of constant exhausting effort while directing the war effort. Never stand up if you can sit down, and never sit down if you can lie down. Applied to the adjudicating process in administrative law, one might say that the philosophy which pervades the system is now that matters for decision should never be left in the hands of the administration alone if it is acceptable that an inquiry procedure can be held beforehand; that they should never be left with the administration anyway, if it is acceptable that they should be entrusted to independent tribunals; and that they should not be left to tribunals if it is reasonable that the courts should, in the circumstances, continue to discharge their traditional role.

Administrative tribunals

As has already been indicated, the diversity of types and variations of tribunals is considerable, and it is not intended to attempt to catalogue them in this book.[2] There has been no general legislative attempt to classify the different tribunals or procedures, though the Tribunals and Inquiries Act 1971, re-enacting and consolidating earlier Acts of the same name of 1958 and 1966, does provide for a more effective control and supervision of the procedure and functioning of most tribunals than hitherto. For the present let us look at just a few examples of tribunals as they operate today.

(a) *Tribunals concerned with rent regulation.*[3] Accommodation rented for living purposes may be divided naturally into that which is let in

---

2   A useful discussion of many of the different bodies and procedures is to be found in G Ganz *Administrative Procedures.*
3   For an interesting account, see H Street *Justice in the Welfare State* (Hamlyn Lectures, 1968) ch 2.

the public sector by local authorities and that which is let privately by other owners. Ever since the First World War it has been the consistent policy of successive governments to exert an element of control over the level of rents charged for such accommodation, the purpose being to prevent the normal market forces in an age of rapidly increasing population and housing shortage causing such a rise of rents as would be beyond the reasonable scope of tenants. In the public sector undue increases in rents have been prevented throughout this century by the legislation binding local authorities, and the resulting financial constraints imposed upon them. But in the private sector it has been necessary to create a tribunal structure to provide the machinery for determining disputes arising between landlords and tenants within the context of legislation which is designed to place a restriction upon the freedom of landlords to increase rents at their own will. The very first intervention of Parliament in this field was a merely temporary war-time measure of rent control, the Rent and Mortgage Interest (War Restrictions) Act 1915. But after the conclusion of the First World War it was replaced by a series of statutes, starting in 1920, all intended to be of more permanent application. Today rent regulation in the private letting sector is governed by the Rent Act 1977, a measure which has consolidated certain earlier statutes, notably the Rent Acts 1968 and 1974, as well as making a small number of changes in the law which it has consolidated, and by the Housing Act 1980. Most, but not quite all, private lettings or tenancies are covered by the 1977 and 1980 Acts, the exceptions being long leases and tenancies of large properties which are above the relevant rateable value limit.

Rent regulation law has been something of a tangled web, with constant changes in direction. There are today three types of private tenancy subject to the Acts – regulated tenancies, restricted contracts and shorthold tenancies. But this division of private lettings only dates from the Rent Act 1974, now replaced by the 1977 and 1980 Acts. Formerly there were also some controlled tenancies which were, broadly, the poorest types of unfurnished lettings, and their control went right back to the original 1915 Act. Tenancies which were originally controlled have now, however, been progressively decontrolled and have become regulated tenancies. One of the types of tribunal under the present system, rent assessment committees, has had a role to play where tenancies have been transferred from the controlled to the regulated category, as we shall see presently. Under the Furnished Houses (Rent Control) Act 1946 provision was made for the first time for determining the level of rents for private furnished accommodation, and under that Act a landlord or a tenant of such accommodation, or indeed the local authority within whose area the property was situated, was given the right to refer the fixing of what the rent should be to a new body called a rent tribunal. In 1949 these tribunals were given power to determine rents for some unfurnished accommodation too, though it was taken away again in 1957. But the Rent Act 1965, later consolidated in the Rent Act 1968, established rent assessment committees and rent officers alongside the rent tribunals, and gave them the duty of regulating unfurnished rents, apart from the very largest properties and those which remained within the controlled tenancy field. The distinction between furnished and unfurnished accommodation was nothing like as clearcut as many might have supposed, and there often appeared to be an overlap in jurisdiction between the two lines of tribunals. The distinction was for most purposes abolished by the Rent Act 1974, and a new division between rented accommodation in property also occupied by the landlord (restricted contracts) and dwellings not so shared (regulated tenancies) replaced it. This present distinction between regulated tenancies and restricted contracts is more satisfactory, but far from foolproof. But it was always doubtful, to say the least, whether it was satisfactory that there should remain two different types of tribunal for determination of disputes concerning the fixing of rents, one for regulated tenancies and the other for restricted contracts.

Under the 1977 Act the Secretary of State for the Environment must draw up panels of persons to act as chairmen and other members of rent assessment committees for such registration areas of England and Wales as he may from time to time determine. Each area panel must contain a number of persons appointed by the Lord Chancellor who are thus empowered to act as chairmen of the committees, and a number of persons appointed by the Secretary of State, after consultation with the Council of Tribunals, who may sit as members of such committees. One of those appointed by the Lord Chancellor must be nominated by the Secretary of State as President of the panel, and one or more others from the Lord Chancellor's list must be nominated by the Secrtetary of State as Vice-Presidents. The panel as such never sits in any adjudicatory capacity, and all its actual work of rent regulation is done by the rent assessment committees set up by the President of the panel in each area as they may be needed, and by the rent tribunals whose chairmen and members must also be members of the relevant panel. Clerks and other staff of the panel are appointed by the President, with the approval of the Secretary of State, and the Department of the Environment is responsible for providing suitable offices for each panel and for booking hearing rooms etc. In practice there are three classes of panel members – lawyers, valuers and laymen, the latter term being taken to mean anyone else who is not a lawyer or valuer. All lawyers on each panel are there by virtue of being on the Lord Chancellor's list, and thus empowered to act as chairmen. It is, however, quite common for either the President of the panel or one of the Vice-Presidents not to be a lawyer, and thus also to be qualified to sit as a chairman. When the Thames Valley Rent Assessment Panel was first set up in 1966, the present writer had already been chairman of the Thames Valley Rent Tribunal (then called the Oxford and Reading Tribunal) for over three years. The two bodies were kept distinct in those days, and while I continued as chairman of the tribunal (and indeed remained as such until my necessary resignation from the panel when I became an ombudsman in the autumn of 1982), the new panel had as its President a Professor of Agricultural Economics, and as its two Vice-Presidents a practising solicitor and a chartered surveyor. Later on the agricultural economist retired, and was succeeded as President by the solicitor, whose place as Vice-President was taken by myself.

The provisions concerning membership of rent tribunals, though now included in the consolidating Rent Act 1977, and altered in minor respects by the Housing Act 1980, have remained substantially the same as they were when first enacted in the Furnished Houses (Rent Control) Act 1946. Although the members of each tribunal must now be members of the relevant rent assessment panel, and the chairman of each tribunal is actually now normally appointed by the President of the panel from among those on the Lord Chancellor's list, the work of the tribunal remains in principle quite distinct from that of its associated rent assessment committees. A very curious section of the Housing Act 1980, section 72, actually purports to abolish rent tribunals, and to transfer their functions to rent assessment committees. But this is intended only to effect a total amalgamation of the personnel and staff of both bodies, and to make common provisions concerning quorums; and section 72(3) then goes on to provide that a rent assessment committee when carrying out the functions previously conferred on a rent tribunal shall be known as a rent tribunal.

Despite the method of appointment to panels it cannot be stressed too strongly that all rent assessment committees and tribunals are entirely independent of the executive in the exercise of their functions. Their duty is to interpret the law in each case before them, and although they are provided with the payment of fees and allowances, and with copies of relevant statues and other documents sent by the Department, they are in no way subject to dictation from the Department as to how they should carry out their functions. Each appointment is made by the Secretary of State for a fixed period, now usually two or three years, subject to an overriding retirement age prescribed by statutory instrument, which is currently seventy-two. But there is no evidence which has ever been produced to suggest that any member has not been reappointed because of dissatisfaction with the manner or content of his decisions, save in the one instance where the High Court seriously criticised the propriety of a chairman's actions, in the case of *Metropolitan Properties Co (FGC) Ltd v Lannon*,[4] which has been discussed in chapter 4 of this book. With the modern assimilation of the personnel of the rent assessment committees and rent tribunals, however, together with their sharing of offices and staff, the time was ripe, or even overdue, for total amalgamation of the two types of body, a process now virtually completed by the Housing Act 1980.

Let us now consider the jurisdiction and work of these tribunals. Rent assessment committees are essentially appellate bodies, and their duty is normally to fix rents – regulated rents, as defined by the Rent Act 1977.[5] The reason they are appellate bodies is that the cases with which they deal are always appeals from rents fixed by rent officers. Rent officers, like rent assessment committees, were first created by the Rent Act 1965, and they are also independent tribunals, though consisting of just one person acting as such in each case. Rent officers are appointed for specific areas, and there are usually several such distinct areas within the area covered by each rent assessment panel. The task of rent officers is to determine regulated rents at first instance in all cases referred for regulation within their areas. Thereafter it is open to either the landlord or the tenant to appeal from the decision to a rent assessment committee. A rent assessment committee must have a quorum of two, though normally it consists of three persons. The jurisdiction of the rent assessment committee (and of the rent officer) covers all regulated tenancies, which are defined by the Rent Act 1977, section 18, as all protected private sector tenancies which are neither controlled tenancies nor restricted contracts. Accordingly it is necessary to determine a little more precisely what are the latter types of tenancy.

A controlled tenancy was usually one where the rateable value of the dwelling-house concerned on 7 November 1956 did not exceed £30, or in London £40, *and* where the tenancy was created by a lease or agreement coming into operation before 6 July 1957. Section 17 of the 1977 Act also specified certain other lettings which fell within the definition of a controlled tenancy, but it is enough for

---

4   [1969] 1 QB 577.
5   In recent years, however, certain other duties have been given to them, eg the settlement of the purchase price for the freehold of property being purchased by the holder of a long lease if that price is disputed by the parties. Under the Housing Act 1980, ss 141 and 142 the tribunal is for this purpose designated as a leasehold valuation tribunal.

present purposes to state that all such lettings can be grouped together as having formed the poorest section of the private letting sector. The Act also specified circumstances in which many controlled tenancies could be converted to regulated tenancies after improvements had been effected, and where the rent officer, or on appeal the rent assessment committee, had subsequently determined a new fair rent for the accommodation. Controlled tenancies have been gradually eliminated, and several reports in recent years recommended their total abolition.[6] The Housing Act 1980 finally converted all remaining controlled tenancies to rent regulation.

The most significant area of private lettings which does not fall under the jurisdiction of rent assessment committees (unless they are operating as rent tribunals, under section 72 of the Housing Act 1980) is that of restricted contracts. A restricted contract is defined by sections 19 and 20 of the 1977 Act as a contract whereby one person grants to another, in consideration of a rent, the right to exclusive occupation of at least one room in a dwelling occupied by the lessor, whether or not there is any entitlement to use in common with any other person other rooms or accommodation in the house. There are some fine distinctions covered by the Act, notably the exemption of holiday lettings from the provisions of the Act, and the provision that even if a landlord is resident in the building other tenancies in the building are regulated tenancies if the building is a purpose-built block of flats; but it is scarcely necessary to deal with them here. The main distinction for our present purposes is that where there is a letting in a dwelling where the landlord is also resident it is a restricted contract, and may be referred to a rent tribunal, and not a rent assessment committee; whereas other lettings, within the rateable value laid down by the legislation, whether furnished or unfurnished, are regulated tenancies. The rateable value limit is £750, or £1,500 in Greater London, on 1 April 1973. The Housing Act 1980 added a new form of tenure, the shorthold tenancy, whereby the lessor and lessee agree to a short fixed term letting of premises for one to five years which would before the 1980 Act have been a regulated tenancy. The main purpose of the tenure is the certainty of its term, thus avoiding litigation about security of tenure; but a shorthold tenancy may have its rent fixed by a rent officer or, on appeal, a rent assessment committee according to the 'fair rent' formula in the Rent Act 1977 if the tenant so wishes.

Another curious distinction is provided by the different criteria laid down for the fixing of rents by the two sets of tribunals. Rent

6   Eg Report of the Committee on the Rent Acts (Cmnd 4609, 1971), generally referred to as the Francis Committee Report because the chairman of the Committee was Mr Hugh Francis QC.

tribunals, in fixing rents for restricted contract lettings, are bound to fix *reasonable* rents, which have never been defined in any of the legislation from 1946 to 1980, and which must thus be assessed upon ordinary objective criteria. But rent officers and rent assessment committees, in fixing rents for regulated and shorthold tenancies, are bound by section 70 of the 1977 Act to fix *fair* rents, and fair rents are defined with much more particularity in the section. The section lays down that, in determining what rent is or would be fair, regard must be had to all the circumstances (other than personal circumstances), and in particular to the age, character, locality and state of repair of the dwelling-house, and, if any furniture is provided for use under the tenancy, the quantity, quality and condition of the furniture. But is must also be assumed that the number of persons seeking to become tenants of similar dwelling-houses in the locality on the terms (other than those relating to rent) of the tenancy is not substantially greater than the number of such dwelling-houses in the locality which are available for letting on such terms. There must also be disregarded any disrepair or defect attributable to the tenant's neglect or default, and any improvement carried out by the tenant other than in pursuance of the terms of the contract. Accordingly in fixing a fair rent the rent assessment committee is bound to ignore any inflation in rental value which has been caused by scarcity of the type of property under review, and thus the committee in every case is likely to be assessing an artificial figure.

One other important difference between the two types of tribunal is that, whereas rent officers and rent assessment committees are solely concerned with the fixing of rent, rent tribunals have had the ancillary task of determining whether or not a lessee should be allowed to have a period of security of tenure. Tenants in regulated tenancies enjoy automatic security of tenure which can only be broken by order of the County Court on the basis of the landlord proving to the satisfaction of the court one of a number of grounds for such termination. It is unnecessary here to go into such grounds, but they include a number of fairly obvious matters, such as failure of the tenant to pay rent or the need of the landlord or his family to occupy the premises as their own dwelling. In the case of a restricted contract, however, it is not unreasonable that the tribunal which must adjudicate upon any dispute as to rent may also be charged with the requirement of determining how much security of tenure the lessee should have, because the existence of a dispute as to rent will so often only be a manifestation of some more deep-seated unease between the two parties, both of whom are living under the same roof. The Act provides that a rent tribunal shall have a complete discretion in deciding what, if any, security of tenure there may be, subject to an upward limit of six months at a time. The rent tribunal may also thereafter decide later applications for either extension or reduction of security without reopening the issue of the amount of rent, though an application for reduction or security may only be entertained upon certain specific grounds, such as failure to pay rent regularly, nuisance or breach of the terms of the contract of letting. In practice disputes coming before rent tribunals today are more usually concerned with problems of security of tenure than with the rents involved in the letting, so that the original ancillary power of the tribunals provides their prime *raison d'être*. Where, however, with effect from 1980, a shorthold tenancy has been created security of tenure is irrelevant, for the security is, so to speak, provided for the period of the fixed term tenancy, and no further. Furthermore, from the coming into force of the Housing Act 1980, any new restricted contract, while remaining subject to the possible fixing of a reasonable rent by a rent tribunal, is no longer subject to such a tribunal's jurisdiction over security of tenure. Instead the lessor can apply direct to a County Court for possession after service of a notice to quit. Rent tribunals thus now retain jurisdiction over security of tenure only in cases concerned with the old pre-Housing Act 1980 restricted contracts.

The actual procedures for rent assessment committees and for rent tribunals are laid down by statutory instrument. The procedure for the committees was laid down in an instrument made in 1971,[7] while that for rent tribunals was first provided by the Furnished Houses (Rent Control) Regulations 1946,[8] both of which have been subsequently amended. But in their basic essentials the two procedures are similar, and the variations are largely peripheral. The actual form of an application to a rent tribunal, which unlike an assessment committee is a first instance tribunal, is that of a 'reference'; and the same device is adopted for appeals to rent assessment committees, for the rent officer from whose decision an appeal is taken is obliged to 'refer' the case to the committee. Both statutory instruments lay down the forms to be used by the parties in applying and in providing the information required concerning the property in question, such as its character, description, the services or furniture provided, and other relevant matters, and in the case of the rent tribunal the relevant information about any notice to quit which may have been served. There are prescribed periods of notice to be given by the clerk of

---

[7] Rent Assessment Committee (England and Wales) Regulations 1971, SI 1971/1065, amended especially by SI 1981/1493.
[8] SR & O 1946/78.

each tribunal to the parties of the date and time of the hearing, and of any inspection. Although a hearing must be held unless neither party requires it, inspections of the premises are not obligatory. But in practice inspections are always made of the premises involved, except in those cases before rent tribunals where the issue at stake is solely an extension or reduction of security of tenure. Although there is no specific quorum laid down for those conducting an inspection on behalf of either type of tribunal, it is normal for the chairman and members all to attend, together with their clerk.

Because of the practice of inspecting premises concerned in any case, both rent tribunals and rent assessment committees are peripatetic. The clerk to the tribunal will endeavour to arrange inspections and hearings of a small group of cases from the same district within the tribunal's area to be dealt with together on the same day. In some large urban areas it is possible to hold all hearings in the same central place, and this is the normal practice in the London area. But elsewhere the actual hearing of any case will be held in some convenient public room which has been booked for the purpose by the clerk, often in the council chamber or a committee room of a town hall or local council offices. At the hearing a party to the contract may appear in person, or else be represented by counsel or a solicitor or by any other representative he chooses, and he may be accompanied by any person whom he may wish to assist him. Subject to these provisions, the regulations effectively place the conduct of the hearing in the hands of the chairman, who is thus able to combine an orderly disposal of business with a considerable measure of informality. The regulations for rent tribunals prescribe that the hearing may be held either in private or in public, but the more recent regulations for rent assessment committees specify that a hearing should be in public, unless there is some very good reason why the committee should exercise its discretion to sit in private. This latter provision is in line with the recommendation of the Franks Committee Report that all tribunal hearings should be held in public, except in cases where considerations of public security are involved, or intimate personal or financial circumstances have to be disclosed, or the hearing is a preliminary investigation of a case involving professional capacity and reputation.[9] In practice it is now extremely rare for any case before either a rent assessment committee or a rent tribunal to be heard in private. Applications for private hearings are not infrequently made by parties, but the present writer, sitting as chairman of a rent tribunal, was involved in granting no more than

---

9 Cmnd 218, paras 77–81.

182 *Tribunals and inquiries*

one such application while sitting in this capacity during the period 1963–1982. Hearings take the form of a full consideration of all the facts and law concerned. But they are often quite short, and in a substantial number of cases the parties expressly decline to avail themselves of the right to be heard personally or by representatives, and content themselves with submitting written representations.

The decision of either tribunal may, if necessary, be by a majority, and when it is composed of only a chairman and one member the chairman has a casting vote. But in practice it is extremely rare for decisions in either tribunal to be other than unanimous, which suggests that nearly all problems coming before these tribunals are capable of agreed solution after discussion. The decision of a rent tribunal is stated in writing, signed by the chairman, though there is no provision on the set form on which such decision is recorded for any reasons to be included: instead it is now the common practice of the chairman to give the reasons orally to the parties present at the hearing. There is no similar set form on which the decision of a rent assessment committee is recorded, but the regulations prescribe that the decision must nevertheless be recorded in a document signed by the chairman. It must not, however, contain any reference to the decision being by a majority if that be the case, or to any opinion of a minority. It is usual for the decision to be written after the hearing by the chairman, after first agreeing its terms with the other members. In my own case I always wrote the decision immediately after the hearing, and before the committee dispersed, using a common form of reasoned decision which had been worked out over the years in the Thames Valley area as a basis, thus ensuring as far as possible that all relevant matters were covered, and also saving time. Decisions given by either of these tribunals must then be sent as soon as possible to the parties to the contract.

Like the vast majority of inferior tribunals of all kinds, rent assessment committees and rent tribunals come under the general supervision of the Council on Tribunals, as regulated by the Tribunals and Inquiries Act 1971. The Council, which will be examined more particularly later in this chapter, has no power to review any specific cases decided by tribunals, but it may make reports and recommendations upon any matters concerning their functions and procedure. From time to time in the Council's Annual Reports recommendations have been made about procedural matters, and in fact the rules of procedure made in 1971 for rent assessment committees were made after consultation with the Council. The Franks Committee in 1957 was disturbed at the amount of freedom from consistent procedural regulations attaching to the rent tribunals, which at that time were of course the only tribunals existing for the purpose of rent regulation.[10] The Committee was particularly concerned that there was then no right of appeal to any court from a rent tribunal decision, although review by way of the prerogative orders was available. The Council on Tribunals took up this criticism, and conducted a detailed investigation.[11] The Council certainly found that the methods of arriving at the calculation of a reasonable rent varied from tribunal to tribunal, but it concluded that the varieties were often dictated by local need and circumstances, and that the resulting conclusions of all rent tribunals were usually similar for cases where any form of comparison could be fruitful. The Council found that all the tribunals appeared to take into account such factors as must be relevant to the calculation of a reasonable rental, such as the capital value of the premises, the value of the furniture provided, the amount of electricity and gas supplied, insurance of the premises, amenities, decoration, the cost of repairs, and reasonable profit. The Council also found that the tribunals were usually careful to inspect the premises in person, and to afford all parties adequate opportunity to air their own cases in any dispute. Altogether they concluded that the difficulties of assessment, and the enormous variety in the circumstances presented in the varying cases, rendered it impossible to determine any one standard procedure which would be suitable for all cases. Still less did the Council feel that it was possible or desirable to attempt to lay down any standard form of valuation and assessment of rents.

The Council considered that on the whole rent tribunals were discharging a difficult task quite well, and that the feeling of the Franks Committee that there should be a right of appeal from their decisions, not only on points of law (this right of appeal was, as we shall see, instituted in 1958), but also on the merits, was not justified. Rent tribunals, by virtue of their experience built up over a period of time, become expert tribunals in the problems which face them, and an appeal on the merits to a judge in a County Court sitting with a valuer as an assessor, as the Franks Committee had suggested,[12] could only mean that the decision of an expert tribunal would become subject to review by a less expert tribunal. Furthermore, tenants might have a strong inducement to appeal because it would become necessary to extend automatically the period of security of tenure while the appeal was pending.

A specific right of appeal on a matter of law from a rent tribunal or a rent assessment committee, as well as from a long list of other types of tribunals, was given first by the Tribunals and Inquiries Act

10 Cmnd 218, paras 165–166.
11 Annual Report for 1962, paras 40–50.
12 Cmnd 218, para 166.

1958, section 9 and Schedule I, now replaced by the Tribunals and Inquiries Act 1971, section 13 and Schedule I. Such appeal lies direct to the Divisional Court of the Queen's Bench Division of the High Court. Although there is still no similar appeal on fact, it may be remembered that in the case of a rent assessment committee's decision there will already have been one appeal to the committee from the rent officer, and it is the practice of rent assessment committees to conduct their hearings in the form of a complete rehearing of all fact and law involved in any issue. In addition to the right of appeal to the High Court on law, there is always the possibility of review after an application for judicial review, as discussed in chapter 5 of this book. This type of review exists in respect of all inferior authorities, including the decisions of magistrates' courts, of Ministers and of administrative tribunals. As we have seen in chapters 3 and 4, the grounds for such review are ultra vires, breach of natural justice, and error of law on the face of the record. As regards the last of these three grounds it will be remembered that rent assessment committees are bound by their rules of procedure to give reasons for decisions, so that any error of law should be apparent on the face of the record. But there is an additional provision, again first enacted in 1958, and now contained in the Tribunals and Inquiries Act 1971, section 12, under which any administrative tribunal is required to give reasons if so requested by a party to the proceedings either before or at the time of giving the decision. There is a clear overlap between the procedure for review on the ground of error of law and that of appeal under section 13 of the 1971 Act, but in practice it has been found in recent years that complaints of error of law within jurisdiction are normally dealt with on appeal under the 1971 Act, while the remedy of certiorari or mandamus is sought (by way of the new procedure instituted in 1978) where the complaint concerns a breach of natural justice or goes to jurisdiction.

Having considered tribunals concerned wth rent regulation at some length, it may be noted that many aspects of their procedure are equally applicable to other tribunals. This is particularly so as regards informality, appeal and review.

(b) *The Lands Tribunal.* This tribunal was set up by the Lands Tribunal Act 1949. The general purpose of the Act is well stated in its long title:

> An Act to establish new tribunals to determine in place of official arbitrators and others certain questions relating to compensation for the compulsory acquisition of land and other matters . . .

Thus the tribunal was not constituted for the purpose of dealing with a completely novel type of business, but was to be a new body exercising old functions. The change from the past lay mainly in the collection for the one new tribunal of a number of different jurisdictions which had previously pertained to several older bodies or institutions. The tribunal consists of a President and other members. The President must either have held judicial office under the Crown or be a barrister of at least seven years' standing. The number of other members of the tribunal lies within the discretion of the Lord Chancellor, though it has usually amounted to four or five, and they must be either barristers or solicitors or else have had experience in the valuation of land, the latter being appointed after consultation with the President of the Royal Institute of Chartered Surveyors. All members, including the President, are appointed and dismissible by the Lord Chancellor, and they take office for such time as he shall think fit. Any one member of the tribunal may sit alone to hear disputes brought before it, although it is usual that two or three shall sit if the issue appears likely to raise any particular difficulty, and in these latter instances the lawyers and valuers are normally equally represented.

It is clear from the method of appointment of the President and members, and also from the restricted groups of persons who are eligible for appointment, that the Lands Tribunal is one of the more superior of the many administrative tribunals, even though, like all such tribunals, it remains inferior to the ordinary courts, and thus subject to review by them. The importance of the tribunal is also emphasised by the type of work which comes within its jurisdiction. Its exact jurisdiction has been altered several times since 1949. But broadly it today covers such matters as: the resolution of disputes concerning the level of compensation for compulsory acquisition of land; the hearing of appeals from the Commissioners of Inland Revenue as to the value of real or leasehold property for capital transfer tax purposes; the determination of applications for the discharge or modification of restrictive covenants; and the hearing of appeals from the decisions of Local Valuation Courts (which are first instance special tribunals) as to the rateable value of premises. This latter jurisdiction accounts for the majority of the business brought before the tribunal, and accordingly the Land Tribunal is for the most part an appellate tribunal. But there is provision for jurisdiction over virtually any matters relating to valuation to be conferred upon the tribunal from time to time by Order in Council. Thus the tribunal holds itself out, so to speak, as a body of experts ready and willing to take on the task of resolving disputes in a wide variety of matters similar in scope to any of its already existing jurisdictions.

Under the Lands Tribunal Act the President is given power to make directions of binding force upon the procedure of the tribunal, though the procedure has occasionally been altered by direct intervention of a later Act of Parliament, as happened, for example, under the Arbitration Act 1950. According to the present procedure the tribunal is, like rent tribunals and rent assessment committees, peripatetic, and as a normal practice it views disputed land *in situ*, and then hears arguments sitting in public. Unlike most inferior tribunals, the Lands Tribunal is empowered to hear evidence on oath, but is not bound to do so; and affidavit evidence is allowed by consent of the parties or by order of the President. Such formality indicates that, again unlike most inferior tribunals, the Lands Tribunal is dealing with matters often of great financial import, and that it consists of a more high-powered type of personnel. Another peculiarity is that evidence of any kind may be summoned by the tribunal even if the parties or their representatives have expressed no wish for it. Decisions of the tribunal must be written and reasoned. These decisions are then published and circulated among interested persons and bodies, with the result that a considerable corpus of precedent has been built up. Although this precedent is not binding upon the tribunal itself in later hearings, it does have the effect of making all members of the tribunal aware of previous decisions, and it is thus an aid to consistency. Another indication of the importance attached to the Lands Tribunal is that, although appeals on law lie from most administrative tribunals to the Divisional Court of the Queen's Bench Division, under section 13 of the Tribunals and Inquiries Act 1971, there has always been such a right of appeal by any person aggrieved by a decision of the Lands Tribunal direct to the Court of Appeal, by way of case stated.

.There has been general agreement that the Lands Tribunal has worked smoothly and well. The publication of decisions has been very successful in providing guidance for the future, and comparatively few cases have gone further on appeal to the Court of Appeal. The Franks Committee expressed itself in virtually eulogistic terms on almost every occasion that it mentioned the tribunal. Thus it considered the arrangements for the remuneration of members,[13] evidence[14] and the use of the oath,[15] the balance between formality and informality in proceedings,[16] the award of costs,[17] and the system of appeals to the Court of Appeal[18] as beyond reproach; and it even suggested that the business of the Lands Tribunal could be suitably expanded by

13 Cmnd 218 (1957), para 57.
14 Para 90.
15 Para 91.
16 Para 64.
17 Para 97.
18 Para 115.

the absorption of other tribunals.[19] The Committee concluded: 'We have received little evidence about the Lands Tribunal and virtually no criticism of it.[20]

(c) *Mental Health Review Tribunals.* Mental Health Review Tribunals were first created by section 3 of the Mental Health Act 1959, though this and amending Acts have now been consolidated by the provisions of the Mental Health Act 1983. Their purpose is to deal with applications and references by and in respect of any patient where there is a complaint concerning the treatment or care of mentally disordered persons, or in respect of their property or affairs. The jurisdiction of the tribunals is wide, and it includes the consideration of applications to obtain the release of patients who are subject to compulsory treatment for mental disorder. The tribunals are composed of 'legal members', who are appointed by the Lord Chancellor, and other members, including 'medical members', who are appointed by the Lord Chancellor after consultation with the Secretary of State for Health and Social Security.

The Mental Health Review Tribunal Rules 1983[1], replacing earlier rules dating from 1960, prescribe the procedure to be followed in proceedings before the tribunals. A copy of every application must be sent to the authority responsible for the patient's care, and this authority must then supply the tribunal with full information about the patient. A copy of this information must also be sent by the tribunal to the applicant, though the tribunal has power to exclude any part of the statement from disclosure to the applicant if it is deemed to be in the patient's interest to do so. The patient may be examined by a medical member of the tribunal; and the tribunal may itself interview the patient, and must do so if the patient asks for an interview. Unless a formal hearing of an application to reconsider a patient's mental health is requested, a tribunal may determine an application in whatever manner it considers appropriate. Where the patient is himself the applicant and has asked for a formal hearing, but the tribunal is satisfied that such a hearing would be detrimental to the patient's health, the application will be determined informally. In contrast to the proceedings of most other types of tribunal, the tribunal will thus sit in private except in some cases when the applicant has asked for a public hearing. In such a case the tribunal, before acceding to the request, must be satisfied that this would not be detrimental to the patient's interests and would not for any other reason be undesirable; and, except insofar as the

---

19 Paras 137–139.
20 Para 159.
1 SI 1983/942.

tribunal may direct, the names of persons concerned in the proceedings are not to be made public. Thus, although the practice of normally hearing cases in private is exceptional when compared with the practice of most other tribunals, it is nevertheless in full conformity with the views of the Franks Committee, for intimate personal circumstances are involved.

Notification of the tribunal's decision in any case must be given to all persons concerned, including the patient where he is not himself the applicant; and both the applicant and the responsible authority have the right to request the tribunal to give the reasons for its decision. This latter provision is of course similar to that contained in section 12 of the Tribunals and Inquiries Act 1971, which is itself a re-enactment of the provision contained in the similar section 12 of the Tribunals and Inquiries Act 1958. On this point the Rules in 1960 were bringing Mental Health Review Tribunals into line with the other tribunals covered by the 1958 Act.

(d) *Social Security Appeal Tribunals.* The welfare state is often regarded as a purely twentieth-century phenomenon. This is incorrect. As has been shown in the classic work on the subject of social security, A I Ogus and E M Barendt, *The Law of Social Security*,[2] one aspect of social security, war pensions, can be traced back as far as classical Greek times, and in Britain as far back as the days of King Alfred. And the first statutory provisions, for the payment of benefit to soldiers and sailors from the local rates, were made in measures passed towards the end of the sixteenth century. Further Acts of Parliament were passed in the nineteenth century to make what today would seem rudimentary provisions for service pensions, the notorious poor law, and workmen's compensation for injury or death resulting from employment risks. But the common belief is easy to excuse, for it was not till the present century that the foundations for what we now understand to be the welfare state were well and truly laid, initially by legislation which was the brainchild of two statesmen who have gone down to posterity as the leaders of their country in the days of peril during the two World Wars, David Lloyd George and Winston Churchill. When they laid these foundations, before the First World War, they occupied the posts respectively of Chancellor of the Exchequer and President of the Board of Trade.

---

2   2nd edn, 1982, p 337. Special studies of local tribunals can be found in H Street *Justice in the Welfare State*, especially ch 1; and K Bell, P Collison, S Turner and S Webber 'National Insurance Local Tribunals' (1974) 3 J Soc Pol 289, and (1975) 4 J Soc Pol 1; L Neville Brown 'Formality or Informality: A Case-Study of British National Insurance Local Tribunal Procedure and Practice' (1982) 23 *Les Cahiers de Droit* 625. See also Sir R Micklethwait *The Natioanl Insurance Commissioners* (Hamlyn Lectures, 1976).

Their pioneer work was built upon by successive governments during the inter-war years, and then the great surge of welfare state legislation which we currently recognise started after the Second World War, notably by such measures as the National Insurance Act 1946, the National Insurance (Industrial Injuries) Act 1946, and the National Assistance Act 1948.

It is unnecessary for our present purposes to concern ourselves with any of the individual statutes currently in force, though the legislation of the 1940s has for the most part been replaced or updated. It is sufficient to relate that there is now a mass of modern legislation, both primary and secondary, and that the most striking and important of the Acts currently in force is the Social Security Act 1975. Under this and a host of other enactments there now exists a right, in appropriate circumstances, to a wide range of social security benefits. It is equally unnecessary for the purposes of this book to discuss the identities and details of these various benefits, but the following are included in a list which is long and constantly being altered or added to: unemployment benefit, sickness benefit, invalidity benefit, severe disablement benefit, attendance allowance, invalid care allowance, mobility allowance, retirement pension, graduated retirement benefit, non-contributory pension, widow's benefit, death grant, maternity grant, maternity allowance, guardian's allowance, special hardship allowance, war pension, war widow's pension, child benefit, supplementary benefit and family income supplement. All of these benefits and pensions are subject to differing rules concerning eligibility, contribution conditions, possible increase in benefit because of dependants, and termination. It is obvious, therefore, that these benefits, which are at the centre of the philosophy of the welfare state, are likely to give rise to a considerable amount of dispute, and the determination of such disputes has been very largely shifted off the shoulders of the responsible government departments on to those of independent tribunals.

All applications for any of the above benefits are made in the first instance to the appropriate government department, which is the Department of Employment in respect of unemployment benefit, and the Department of Health and Social Security for all other benefits. Thereafter the consideration of applications for attendance allowance go to the Attendance Allowance Board, with a right of appeal to the Social Security Commissioner. The consideration of all other applications, however, is initially in the hands of an adjudication officer in the appropriate department, though his duty is to act judicially rather than just as an agent of the administration. For example, one of the reasons why many applicants are disqualified from receiving benefits, at least for a period, is that they have made claims which are out of time. All the various benefits have specific time limits set by the relevant legislation within which valid claims must be made, and these time limits are of widely differing duration. Thus a person who claims a retirement pension must do so within three months of retirement in order to ensure that it is payable from the date of retirement. One who applies for unemployment benefit, on the other hand, must apply on the first actual day of unemployment itself in order to gain benefit for that day. If any relevant time limit has been exceeded by the claimant he will lose the benefit for the period which is outside the time allowed unless he can show that there was continuous good cause for his late claim. 'Good cause' has not been defined by any of the legislation concerning welfare benefits, but the Social Security Commissioners, who hear second-tier appeals in social security cases,[3] and whose decisions in practice bind the lower tribunals, have described it as some fact which having regard to all the circumstances, including the claimant's state of health and the information which he had received and that which he might have obtained, would probably have caused a reasonable person of his age and experience to act, or fail to act, as the claimant did. Thus, when an adjudication officer is faced with a late claim he must exercise a discretion in determining whether or not continuous good cause has been shown. In performing this task he must act as far as possible as a one-man independent tribunal, and not merely apply administrative convenience.

From the decision of any adjudication officer the claimant has a right of appeal to a local social security appeal tribunal, which will consider afresh the whole issue at stake in any case. And from the decision of the tribunal a further appeal lies, at the instance of either the claimant or the department,[4] to a Social Security Commissioner. The Commissioners, who must be barristers or solicitors[5] (or in Scotland advocates) of ten years' standing, are appointed by the Crown, and act as full-time judges of these second-tier appeals. They are distinguished lawyers, and there are currently twelve of them for England and Wales, including a Chief Commissioner, and two for Scotland.[6] They sit singly, though the Chief Commissioner may at

---

3 The Social Security Act 1980 introduced for the first time a further right of appeal from decisions of the Commissioners direct to the Court of Appeal.
4 But only with leave, either of the chairman of the tribunal or of the Commissioner, if the tribunal's decision was unanimous.
5 Under the Social Security Act 1979 appointment as a Social Security Commissioner is opened to solicitors as well as barristers.
6 In 1984 a new Chief Social Security Commissioner was appointed who also holds the appointment of a Circuit Judge. This was in line with the new policy of the Lord Chancellor to show the close relationship between the courts and tribunals. The first President of the social security appeal tribunals is also a Circuit Judge.

his discretion convene a tribunal of three Commissioners to sit where an appeal involves a question of law of special difficulty. Two of the Commissioners normally sit in Edinburgh, and one in Cardiff, while the remainder sit in London. In addition to the hearing of appeals from appeal tribunals, they hear appeals on points of law from medical appeal tribunals (which in turn hear appeals from medical boards, whose task is to assess degrees of disablement on medical grounds) and from the Attendance Allowance Board.

But for the purposes of present illustration it is the social security appeal tribunals with which we are primarily concerned. Before March 1984 they were called national insurance local tribunals, but the Health and Social Services and Social Security Adjudications Act 1983 merged these older tribunals with the former supplementary benefit appeal tribunals, and created the new social security appeal tribunals with a President and Regional Chairmen, together with other full-time and part-time chairmen. Each sitting of such tribunal consists of a chairman and two lay members. The chairman must have been appointed to the Lord Chancellor's panel of chairmen. There is no legal obligation for all chairmen to be lawyers, but in practice they almost invariably are. The lay members who sit with the chairman are drawn by the clerk of the tribunal from two panels made up of representatives of employers and employees respectively. Members are appointed to these panels by the Secretary of State for Health and Social Services, usually after he has first asked interested organisations of employers and employees to put forward names of possible members. Each panel will consist of anything up to two dozen members, and it is normal for the clerk to call on members more or less in rotation, though this is of course subject to availability. It is intended in the near future to amalgamate these two panels. Although a few appellants may be under the impression that the lay members are intended to represent the interests of employers and employees respectively, this is not so. They are expected to exercise the same impartiality as the chairman, and it is the duty of the chairman, where necessary, to make this clear both to his members and to appellants. In the event the vast majority, certainly 95 per cent, of all appeals are decided unanimously, so that the theory of impartiality would seem to be borne out in practice. Indeed, far from there being much evidence of difficulty in obtaining agreement between representatives of employers and employees, a recent study has shown that the chairman dissents more often than do his lay members.[7]

Unlike some other tribunals, such as rent tribunals and rent

---

7   Bell et al, above, 3 J Soc Pol at 303–304.

assessment committees, social security appeal tribunals are not peripatetic. Hearings are held in the same place, and normally in a room which is not part of any offices owned or rented by the Departments of Health and Social Security or Employment. The clerk is an officer of the Department of Health and Social Security, and is responsible for convening tribunal sittings, and arranging for the papers to be sent to the tribunal chairman and members, as well as to the appellants and adjudication officers, both of whom are entitled to appear at the hearing. Appellants may also be represented by anyone else of their choice. Some bring legal representatives with them, and rather more are represented by trade union officers, but the great majority either appear alone (or accompanied by a husband, wife, near relative or friend) or else choose not to appear at all. It is sometimes thought that those who do not appear in person may be at a disadvantage, but this is doubtful. The tribunal always has before it the written appeal form, and is able to consider the written representations. Furthermore, although there is a higher incidence of success for appellants who appear at the hearing than for those who do not, a powerful contributory reason for this is that often claimants who have exercised their statutory right to appeal against a refusal of benefit find when they receive the appeal papers that the full reasoned adjudication officer's decision discloses that they have little or no chance of success in their appeal. For example, a wife may have been disallowed the award of child benefit after her marriage has split up, the children are living with her husband, and she is not contributing to their upkeep. In such circumstances she may well feel aggrieved that she is no longer receiving child benefit, but there is no way in law that a tribunal could reverse the adjudication officer's disallowance, for the whole basis of her previous entitlement has been destroyed. Again, mobility allowance is intended for those who are disabled and require their own transport in order to get to work. Accordingly it is not available for a person who is over retirement age, and who has not qualified for the allowance before retirement. There are many cases where elderly people who have recently become infirm apply for mobility allowance long after reaching retirement age. They feel aggrieved that their applications are turned down by the adjudication officer, and thus appeal. But they rarely appear at the subsequent tribunal hearing, probably because the full case papers have shown them that they cannot possibly be brought within the group of people eligible for such an award. Nevertheless in all cases the adjudication officer is present at the hearing, or is represented by another presenting officer from the Department, and will put the case against the appellant. It is noteworthy, however, that adjudication officers who appear at tribunal hearings are usually of a high standard both of competence and objectivity. When new evidence at a hearing puts a different complexion upon the issue before the tribunal it is quite common for the adjudication officer to support the appeal in the light of the new information.

The conduct of the hearing is once more in the hands of the chairman. It has been a practice in recent years for the chairmen of tribunals to meet togerther for one-day conferences from time to time, and one desirable result of these conferences has been the achievement of a great measure of uniformity in the approach to procedure in hearings. This trend is assisted by the new presidential organisation of the tribunals. There is considerable informality throughout, though the chairman will always endeavour to keep control to prevent loss of temper, interruptions of evidence or any practice which may tend to upset an appellant who may well be nervous of the proceedings. The chairman will introduce each case by explaining the task of the tribunal, and its impartiality, and then, where necessary, explaining to an appellant precisely what he must prove in order to succeed in his appeal. An appellant who is not represented will usually be helped to present the facts and his arguments by the chairman's encouragement and questioning. He will also be given adequate scope to call any other evidence which he may wish to present, either in the form of further documents or else by means of actual witnesses who have come with him to the hearing. Thereafter the chairman will give his lay members an opportunity to ask the appellant and his witnesses any relevant questions, and the adjudication or other presenting officer will be given an opportunity both to question the appellant and his witnesses, and also to make any oral representations in addition to his written submissions. All those present at the hearing will be seated round a table, or in some similar fashion, and like other inferior tribunals there are no rules of evidence which need to be observed. After the hearing the parties must withdraw, and then the tribunal will deliberate, and come to a decision. This decision must be written, reasoned, and signed by the chairman. There is a very convenient form provided by the Department, on which the chairman will enter the names of those appearing, and then his notes of the evidence, and the written decision. There is also provision on the form for entering a note of any minority view in the event of the tribunal coming to a majority decision.

Three other features of the procedure may be briefly noted. First, hearings must normally be in public. But the chairman alone has a discretion to allow a hearing in private in certain circumstances, a discretion which is scarcely ever exercised in practice.[8] Secondly, the chairman again has a discretion to secure the assistance of a medical assessor at a hearing. Tribunal chairmen vary in their attitude to this discretion, and some are loath to call upon medical assessors. Others, including the present writer during the period 1969–1982 when he was chairman of a national insurance local tribunal, are often very glad to call upon them to assist with cases which involve distinct medical questions. A typical example of a case where such an assessor may be of value would be a claim by a housewife for severe disablement benefit to pay for help in running her home on the basis that she is physically unable to do so; or again where there is doubt whether a particular injury was caused or materially contributed to by an industrial accident. The medical assessor takes no part in the deciding of any case, but his advice upon medical questions is often of great assistance to a tribunal. Thirdly, in a few cases the adjudication officer may be unable to make up his mind whether a claim should be allowed or not. In such a case the officer is entitled to refer the case for decision by the tribunal, who will thus act as a tribunal of first instance. Such references are fairly rare. Ogus and Barendt refer to the figures in England and Wales for 1979, when tribunals heard over 40,000 cases, of which only about 1,350 were references.[9] The advantage to an adjudication officer of being able to refer a case in this way is that the tribunal, unlike the officer sitting alone in his office, is able to test the evidence in a hearing. But the jurisdiction of appeal tribunals over such references shows that tribunals sometimes have a mixture of first instance and appellate functions.

Inquiries

The main distinguishing feature between tribunals and inquiries is that the former type of body has conferred upon it the full power to determine the issue before it, whereas the latter has not. At an inquiry there will be a full investigation of the points at issue, but the eventual resolution of these matters need not necessarily accord with the balance of the evidence adduced at the inquiry, and is in any case provided by a Minister or other authority outside the actual inquiry procedure. In the next section of this chapter we shall consider the work of the Franks Committee and its effect. But whereas it is possible

8   It is also a matter for the chairman alone to determine whether or not to grant leave to appeal to the Commissioner where the tribunal has been unanimous in its decision.
9   *The Law of Social Security* p 587.

to deal first with the tribunal system, as we have just done, and then to move on to improvements of detail effected as a result of the work of the Franks Committee, the very nature of most inquiry procedures was altered in the aftermath of the Franks Report. Accordingly we may here anticipate the next section insofar as it would otherwise have been concerned with inquiries.

The most far-reaching reform stemmed from the provision, now in the Tribunals and Inquiries Act 1971, section 11, that the Lord Chancellor may make rules regulating the procedure to be followed in inquiries held on behalf of a Minister. Under this section, and its predecessors in the Tribunals and Inquiries Acts 1958 and 1966, rules have been made covering a number of the most common types of inquiry, particularly those held before a Minister decides on the merits of appeals to him against refusal of planning permission by local planning authorities. This development was a direct result of the first *cause célèbre* to come within the purview of the Council on Tribunals, the advisory body set up by the Tribunals and Inquiries Act 1958, and now regulated by the 1971 Act, which will be referred to more closely in the next section of this chapter.

A firm of sand and gravel producers applied in 1958 for planning permission to dig chalk from their land. The local planning authority, which was Saffron Waldon Rural District Council acting on behalf of the Essex County Council, refused permission, and the company appealed to the Minister of Housing and Local Government (a predecessor of the present Secretary of State for the Environment) under section 16 of the Town and Country Planning Act 1947. An inspector of the Ministry held a public local inquiry at Saffron Waldon on 13 November 1958, and at the inquiry the appellant company and the local planning authority were heard. In addition Major A L Buxton of Stansted, Essex, who was a neighbouring landowner, and three other neighbouring landowners were heard and produced expert evidence in support of their objections to the planning application. The inspector recommended that the appeal should be dismissed on the ground that the production of chalk from the site was likely to result in dust being blown onto the objectors' adjoining land, with serious detriment both to agriculture and to amenity. The Minister rejected the inspector's recommendation and decided to allow the appeal. It transpired that the Minister, in rejecting the inspector's finding of fact, had relied upon certain subsequent advice and information given to him by an expert in the Ministry of Agriculture without affording the local planning authority or the objectors any opportunity of correcting or commenting upon it. Accordingly the objectors applied to the High Court, under the Town and Country Planning Act 1959, to have the Minister's decision quashed. But they failed, because the court held that they were not technically 'persons aggrieved' within the meaning of the Act, and so the merits of their case could not be considered by the court.[10] The local planning authority would have been a 'person aggrieved' because it was a party to the actual planning application, but the objectors had merely been permitted to appear at the inquiry as a courtesy extended to them by the inspector within his discretion.

Having thus failed to gain any judicial remedy, being defeated by the essentially private philosophy which lies behind all planning applications, Major Buxton then asked the Council on Tribunals to look into the circumstances of the case. As will be seen presently, the Council has no executive power, and thus was powerless to do anything to reverse the actual decision of the Minister concerning the application that was before him. But the Council outlined the main facts and issues in the affair in its Annual Report for the year 1960, and went on to make a special report to the Lord Chancellor upon the principles at stake in April 1962. This special report provides the genesis for the modern system of inquiries, and accordingly it is worth pausing to consider what it recommended.

The Council on Tribunals took the view that the practice of accepting new factual evidence after the close of a public inquiry was unjust unless an opportunity was given to challenge it. Thus the Council recommended that new rules for statutory inquiries should be made, and in particular it proposed two new rules: (1) that where a Minister proposes to disagree with the recommendation of an inspector who has held a public inquiry, either because of some factor not considered at the inquiry or because he differs from a finding of fact made by the inspector, he should notify the parties of his disagreement and of the reasons for it, and afford them an opportunity for making comments and representations in writing before finally making his decision; and (2) that where the Minister proposes to depart from the inspector's recommendation, either (a) because of fresh evidence on a question of fact or (b) because of fresh expert evidence, including expert advice, or (c) because of the introduction of a fresh issue, the inquiry should, if any of the parties so desire, be reopened and the new evidence or issue should be produced at the reopened inquiry.

The special report of the Council stated that the number of cases where the inspector's recommendation had been rejected by the Minister was small, and that it appeared that the most satisfacory general rule might be for the Minister to refer back to the parties for their comments in every case in which he proposed to differ from the

10 *Buxton v Minister of Housing and Local Government* [1961] 1 QB 278.

inspector's recommendations. On the request of any party whose comment he rejected, the inquiry could be reopened. But it would not be reopened where the Minister disagreed with the inspector because the recommendation conflicted with general ministerial policy. This concession recognises that governments must govern, and that it is therefore reasonable to permit a Minister to reject a recommendation which conflicts with government policy, which is in itself distinct from expert evidence or any other issue of fact. In examining the whole problem the Council considered that it had been guided by four general principles:

(a) If the public is to have confidence in the procedure laid down by Parliament, it must be made clear that inquiries are not just an incident in the administrative process.
(b) The public regards an inquiry as a requirement by Parliament that before the final decision is reached local feeling and local facts must be taken into account by the Minister. Thus complaints understandably arise where a Minister rejects the recommendations of an inspector who has both heard the evidence and seen the site, if (i) the rejection is based on ministerial policy which could or should have been made clear before the inquiry or (ii) the Minister takes advice after the inquiry from persons who neither heard the evidence nor saw the site, but yet controverted the inspector's findings as to the facts of the local situation.
(c) As recommended by the Franks Committee, to be considered presently, every effort should be made to make ministerial policy clear before the inquiry.
(d) Proper respect should be paid to an inspector's findings of fact and recommendations about the particular case in its local aspects, otherwise parties will naturally feel that they have wasted their time and money.

The Lord Chancellor accepted the Council's recommendations. At the same time he also accepted the recommendations in another special report made by the Council concerning the importance of an adequate code of procedure for planning inquiries generally.[11] The result was that there have now been a whole series of statutory instruments made, starting in 1962, under which the procedures for most of the common types of statutory inquiries are more clearly and satisfactorily laid down than hithero. Not only do these rules of procedure cover such matters as the procedure before inquiries, including the necessary periods of notice, but it is also provided that for most inquiries any persons interested have the right to inspect

11   See Annual Report of the Council on Tribunals for the year 1961.

documents and to appear and give evidence or make written representations. The inspector who conducts an inquiry must, in making his report to the Secretary of State, include his findings of fact and his recommendations, if any, or reasons for not making recommendations. Most importantly, where the Secretary of State differs from the inspector on a finding of fact, or after the close of the inquiry receives new evidence (including expert evidence on a matter of fact), or takes into consideration any new issue of fact (not being a matter of government policy), and is in consequence disposed to disagree with any recommendation made by the inspector, he must not come to a decision at variance with the recommendation without first giving the parties who appeared at the inquiry an opportunity of making representations, or (if the Secretary of State has received new evidence or taken a new issue of fact into consideration) of having the inquiry reopened. Finally, the Secretary of State must notify his decision and reasons to the parties, and to any other person who appeared at the inquiry and who has asked to be notified.

It is clear that these rules of procedure have completely altered the pattern and original plan for inquiries. No longer can they be regarded merely as methods of informing the mind of the Minister before he makes a decision in which he is entitled to ignore the facts or merits of any issues raised at the inquiry. If the Minister's decision in what has come to be called *The Chalkpit* had been made at a time when such rules were in force, he would have been obliged to disclose the advice he received from his alkaline experts about the likely effect of chalk dust upon neighbouring properties. As it was Major Buxton was left without redress against the Minister's decision, though his possible subsequent right of action in nuisance against the developers was left unaffected. Today the Secretary of State's hands would be largely tied. Unless he was disposed to accept the inspector's recommendations he would have to give Major Buxton and other objectors a chance to rebut the fresh evidence before him at the reopened inquiry. His only effective right to reject the inspector's recommendation without giving the objectors a second bite at the cherry would be if there was some issue of government policy by which his decision could be supported, such as perhaps an overriding government policy that as much chalk must be produced as possible regardless of all obstacles.

Nor is the requirement that the Secretary of State must give a reasoned decision to be taken lightly. In *Givaudan & Co Ltd v Minister of Housing and Local Government*[12] the Minister's decision to dismiss an appeal against refusal of planning permission was quashed because

---

12 [1966] 3 All ER 696.

the reasons he had given were unintelligible. Again, in *Earl Iveagh v Minister of Housing and Local Government*,[13] a case which concerned the more general provision in section 12 of the Tribunals and Inquiries Act 1958 (now section 12 of the 1971 Act) that a Minister must give reasons for any decision made by him after the holding of a public inquiry, and that his reasons, whether written or oral, form part of the record, Lord Denning MR said:[14]

> The whole of that enactment is to enable the parties and the courts to see what matters he has taken into consideration and what view he has reached on the points of fact and law which arise. If he does not deal with the points that arise, he fails in his duty, and the courts can order him to make good the omission.

The result of this restriction of ministerial discretion after inquiries brought about by the Tribunals and Inquiries Acts and the various statutory instruments providing rules of procedure in respect of inquiries has been to open up more clearly the avenues for judicial review which we have already explored in chapters 3, 4 and 5 of this book.

The Franks Committee and after

Tribunals and inquiries have quite often been the subject of adverse criticism. So far as inquiries are concerned the criticism has mainly been on the ground that the Minister's mind has been made up and that the inquiry is no more than a charade. But the increasing realisation of the strength of the new rules of procedure for inquiries, and of the very limited room for manoeuvre now permitted to a Minister making a decision after an inquiry, has brought about a greater acceptance of the ingredient of judicialisation which has now been introduced into the process of decision-making. There remain instances of inquiries concerning proposed new trunk roads and motorways which are disrupted by protestors, but these are caused more by deep-seated antagonism towards road-building than towards the inquiry system as such.

Adverse criticisms of administrative tribunals have on the whole not been against any individual tribunals, but against the tribunal system, and these criticisms have been largely stilled since the publication of the Franks Committee Report. Up to that time the opposition to the system was for the most part under three main heads: (i) that tribunals were unnecessary; (ii) that they should be

13 [1964] 1 QB 395.
14 Ibid at 410.

replaced by separate administrative courts, probably modelled on the French administrative courts; and (iii) that all administrative procedures should be standardised, as in the USA, where there is a federal Administrative Procedure Act 1946. Criticisms under head (i) were mostly motivated by prejudice and ignorance, and have virtually disappeared since the Franks Report which, after a searching examination, concluded that tribunals were absolutely necessary, and even desirable, in modern conditions,[15] as has been indicated at the beginning of this chapter. But the Franks Committee was not content to issue just a crushing rejoinder, and it recommended a number of ways of strengthening the review of tribunals' procedures and decisions.

It may be recalled from Chapter 2 that a distinction was drawn between the production and reception of the Report of the Donoughmore-Scott Committee on Ministers' Powers in 1932 and that of the Franks Committee on Administrative Tribunals and Enquiries, published in July 1957. Apart from the peculiarity in spelling in that the Franks Report was about Tribunals and Enquiries, and that all subsequent legislation has been about Inquiries, it has had a consistently better press and more direct impact than the Donoughmore Committee Report. As was mentioned in chapter 2, the Franks Report was produced more quickly, in the life of the same Parliament during which it was set up, and was framed in less legalistic language. It touched the emotions of the Conservative backbenchers in the Commons who were thus able to press their own Government into action, and it was published at a time when the whole tide of reasoned lay thinking was favourable to a report which was at the same time both palliative and constructive in reaching towards the perfection of a recognisably raw system. Tribunals were seen to be basically useful and even essential, but capable of much improvement. So critical study was channelled into the achievement of such improvement, rather than wholesale destruction and replacement. The keynote of the Franks Report was struck by the coining of three popular words. After the Committee had recognised that the requirements in meeting the new social and economic problems raised by the settlement of disputes connected with such manifestations as the welfare state were speed, cheapness, expert knowledge, flexibility and, in many cases, a degree of informality, the Committee found that there were other prime characteristics of these procedures. As the Report ran:[16]

   it is clear there are certain general and closely linked characteristics which

15   Cmnd 218, paras 403, 406
16   Cmnd 218, para 23.

should mark these procedures. We call these characteristics openness, fairness and impartiality.

It has been generally recognised that these three watchwords have usually been followed by tribunals in the past. But insofar as tribunals and their members have needed to be reminded of their general duty since the Franks Report the general recognition of these characteristics has been of salutary effect since the Report was published. 'Openness' means that tribunal hearings should be held in public, unless there is some compelling reason, as spelt out by the Franks Committee, to the contrary; and that all documents and other information submitted to a tribunal shall be made available to all parties to the case concerned. 'Fairness' is a general description of the rules of natural justice, which we have considered in chapter 4. 'Impartiality' characterises the essential independence of tribunals from the government departments with which they are connected by reason of their particular subject matter. Provided that a tribunal always remembers that it must remain open, fair and impartial, there is little chance that it will seriously err in its conduct of proceedings.

Criticisms under head (ii) have been largely abandoned since the Franks Report, particularly since the avenues of direct appeal to the High Court on matters of law have been opened by the Tribunals and Inquiries Act 1958, now re-enacted in 1971, as was mentioned above in relation to rent tribunals and rent assessment committees. But there remains a considerable body of opinion among English lawyers which favours, not the replacement of our whole administrative law by something resembling the French *droit administratif*, but the creation of an Administrative Division of the High Court.[17] Yet, however desirable this might be for the purpose of ensuring that the development of administrative law is more consistent and just, it is unlikely that such a view will prevail. If for no other reason than that it is obvious that the claims of administrative law for a separate division of the High Court are no better than those of other branches of English law. In any case the Divisional Court of the Queen's Bench Division, as has been suggested in chapter 5, in many way resembles such an Administrative Division, and it seems more realistic to work towards a more consistently stable membership of this Divisional Court in administrative law cases than towards its replacement.

The movement under head (iii) for standardisation of all administrative procedures received a setback from the Franks Committee Report, for the Committee found that individual tribunals often had entirely different types of task to perform from others. Even the American Administrative Procedure Act has only been partly

17 See e g Administration under Law (a Report by JUSTICE, 1971).

successful, because of the diversity of work covered by administrative agencies. It is possible that the sting from this type of criticism of tribunals was drawn by the two main recommendations for change made by the Franks Committee, namely the setting up of a Council on Tribunals and the institution of direct appeals on law from many tribunals to the High Court. Let us further briefly consider these two measures.

The Council on Tribunals

The Council on Tribunals was set up by the Tribunals and Inquiries Act 1958 substantially along the lines suggested by the Franks Committee. Its composition and powers are now regulated by the first six sections of the Tribunals and Inquiries Act 1971. Broadly it advises the Lord Chancellor as regards England and Wales, and the Lord Advocate as regards Scotland, upon the general supervision and procedure of tribunals and inquiries, and it makes annual reports to them upon its work, and may make other special reports as and when it thinks fit. But a careful perusal of the relevant sections of the Act reveals the fact that the Council has virtually no real *powers*, in the sense that it cannot order anything to be done or undone. Just as the Franks Committee was set up at a time when there was general popular dissatisfaction with or misunderstanding of the activities, or supposed activities of administrative authorities, and of statutory tribunals in particular, so the Council was created by the 1958 Act on a wave of popular belief that its watchdog character would bring about any necessary reform of the composition, powers or practices of administrative tribunals.[18] Curiously attention was mostly focused at that time upon the Council's relations with tribunals, as its official title would suggest, and it was not until the Tribunals and Inquiries Act 1966, now consolidated and replaced by the 1971 Act, that its supervisory functions in relation to inquiries were put upon a par with those relating to tribunals.

The institution of the Council was a new departure in British constitutional history for it received a statutory constitution, and was expected to have a marked effect in bringing about an element of standardisation of tribunal procedures, while at the same time having no power to do anything more than offer advice. The Council consists of not more than fifteen and not less than ten members, appointed by the Lord Chancellor and the Lord Advocate, and one of these members is also appointed as chairman. In addition the Parlia-

---

18 For a strong contrary view, however, see J A G Griffith 'Tribunals and Inquiries' (1959) 22 MLR 125.

mentary Commissioner for Administration, whose office will be discussed in chapter 7 of this book, is an *ex officio* member. Either two or three of the Council's members are designated by the Lord Advocate as members of the Scottish Committee of the Council (and one of them as chairman of the Scottish Committee), and the Lord Advocate must also appoint either three or four other persons, not otherwise members of the Council on Tribunals, to this Scottish Committee. Apart from the general function of supervision over the proceedings of tribunals and conduct of inquiries, the Council is specifically empowered to advise the appropriate Minister upon appointments to membership of tribunals, and is encouraged to advise upon the substance of any proposed rules of procedure.

The Annual Reports of the Council indicate the nature of the work it has undertaken. Much time was taken up in its early years with preliminary inspections of and investigations into the actual practice and procedure of tribunals and inquiries, including such problems as the suitability of accommodation. But soon the Council was in a position to make recommendations upon more substantial matters. The practice of attending to individual complaints was established, despite the absence of any power to provide any direct remedy. The lack of such a coercive power certainly does not seem to have detracted from the usefulness of the Council's interest in specific cases, as the outcome of its investigation into *The Chalkpit* has shown. The key to the Council's success has lain in the co-operation of the Lord Chancellor and other Ministers in agreeing to implement the substance of any Council recommendation. The result of the investigation into *The Chalkpit* is only the most striking of the Council's achievements, but there have been countless instances in the period of over twenty years since the Council started work when the Ministers have agreed as a result of Council recommendations to make new or amended rules of procedure for tribunals or inquiries. It may seem remarkable that successive Ministers have proved so compliant, yet this has proved to be the case and the only instances of ministerial refusal to implement Council recommendations have been over matters of detail, and even then the Minister has not infrequently complied with the original suggestion at a later stage. Thus in 1962, when the Council issued a report under the title Report of Council on Tribunals on the position of 'third parties' at Planning Appeal Inquiries,[19] Lord Dilhorne LC refused to agree to the recommendation that third parties should be given the *right* to appear at such inquiries, though he stressed that there was already a practice, by administrative concession, whereby all persons with a genuine interest

19 Cmnd 1787.

204 *Tribunals and inquiries*

in an application were permitted to appear and take part in an inquiry. Yet seven years later the substance of the 1962 recommendation was conceded and included in new rules of procedure.[20]

There has been an unbroken period since the Council's inception of harmony between itself and the Lord Chancellor and other Ministers. But should these harmonious relations deteriorate the Council has a secret weapon in its armoury, for it has full power to release statements or special reports to the press. Under present practice such reports are released a few days after their submission to the Lord Chancellor and the Lord Advocate, but the power to release reports in this way could doubtless be used to embarrass a government department if necessary. There may well be major advantages in a body with little formal power but a statutory constitution, for it can do many effective, even surprising, things, yet it can only be disbanded by the extreme and formal measure of an Act of Parliament, a step which would need to be justified in Parliament and to the public at large.

Appeals under the Tribunals and Inquiries Act 1971

As has already been mentioned, section 13 of the 1971 Act provides that any party to proceedings before any one of a stated list of tribunals who is dissatisfied in point of law with a decision of that tribunal may appeal therefrom to the High Court (in fact to a Divisional Court of the Queen's Bench Division) or require the tribunal to state and sign a case for the opinion of the High Court. Thus a new and direct judicial remedy was introduced (originally by section 9 of the 1958 Act) for a party aggrieved by a decision of any one of the tribunals affected, and a body of case law was built up from these appeals. The Act did not seek in any way to encroach upon the field occupied by the older remedies, and we have already discussed in chapter 5 the relationship between all these remedies, and their reform by the creation of the new application for judicial review. But, as was suggested in chapter 5, the practical effect of the new direct appeals under the Tribunals and Inquiries Act was to make this the normal channel for challenge on grounds of error of law of any decision by a tribunal subject to this method of appeal. Yet the Act's provisions for direct appeal are limited, for not all tribunals are covered by this new procedure. The Act extends the right of appeal only to cases concerned with tribunals listed in part of Schedule 1 to the Act. Among tribunals from which no such direct

20   Town and Country Planning (Inquiry Procedure) Rule 1969, SI 1969/1092.

appeal to the court will lie are some of the strongest or most high-powered, such as the Immigration Appeal Tribunal, Mental Health Review Tribunals, and the Social Security Commissioners. From certain other tribunals there is a right of appeal under other statutes, as in the case of the Lands Tribunal (and now also the Social Security Commissioners) from which an appeal will lie direct to the Court of Appeal. Yet not all tribunals by any means are subject to the possibility of appeal on law to one of the ordinary courts of the land. So far as such tribunals' decisions are concerned, therefore, any person wishing to appeal would be driven back to applying for one or more of the traditional remedies by way of an application for judicial review. Such applications have been facilitated by the provision in section 12 of the 1971 Act that reasons for decisions of nearly all tribunals, and of Ministers after holding statutory inquiries, or where such inquiries could have been demanded must be given if requested; and that any such statement of reasons becomes part of the decision and of the record. Thus any error is bound to appear upon the face of the record. Of course most parties to disputes before tribunals never bother to ask for detailed reasons for decisions, but they can always obtain them if they wish, so that any person who in any way feels himself aggrieved now has the means to discover whether there is any substance in his disquiet. But more than that, the spirit of section 12 has caused most tribunals to give proper reasons for their decisions as a matter of course, even if not compelled to do so by their rules of procedure. Thus, of those examined earlier in this chapter, social security appeal tribunals are obliged by their rules of procedure to provide written reasoned decisions, whereas rent tribunals and rent assessment committees are bound only to give written decisions, whether or not reasoned. Nevertheless, as was stated earlier, it has become the practice of chairmen of rent tribunals since the Franks Report was published to give full oral reasons for the tribunals' decision as well as to sign the written decision.

Yet it may be alleged that a tribunal has made an error of fact rather than law. Although we have suggested in chapter 3 that the courts are working towards an expansion of their power to review on the ground of error of law to cover also error of fact, there is no authority in the Tribunals and Inquiries Act for a direct appeal to the court from any of the tribunals covered by the Act on fact or merits. The Franks Committee has recommended that the structure of appeals relating to tribunals should be as follows: (a) a right of appeal from all except the very strongest first instance tribunals on law, fact or merits to appellate tribunals; and (b) a right of appeal on law from an appellate tribunal to the court. In effect the Tribunals and Inquiries Acts implemented the second of these recommendations, though not for all appellate tribunals, and yet they also extended it to cover some first instance tribunals, such as rent tribunals. But the Acts have not implemented in any consistent way the first recommendation, and neither Parliament nor the Franks Committee envisaged any right of appeal *to the courts* on facts or merits.

Some have wondered whether Parliament should take the kernel of the Franks Committee's first recommendation on appeals from first instance tribunals and carry it on further to introduce a general right of appeal on fact or merits from all tribunals to the Divisional Court - or, according to some arguments that have already been referred to earlier, to a new Administrative Division of the High Court. On a superficial basis it may seem attractive to provide for a method of correcting any type of error in the High Court. But the present writer would urge that such a uniform change might prove regrettable. Let us revert to one instance of a common inferior tribunal, far from exceptionally strong in membership, and from which at present there is no right of appeal to any appellate tribunal, but only the statutory right of appeal on law under the Tribunals and Inquiries Act. Such a tribunal is a rent tribunal. As will be recalled, the tasks of a rent tribunal are to fix reasonable rents for restricted contract lettings, and where relevant to determine what, if any, security of tenure shall run in favour of the lessee. The tribunal is bound by certain basic requirements, such as the necessity to hear all parties to a dispute, and the minimum period of notice which must be given to parties of the date, time and place of a hearing. Accordingly the tribunal will form its own opinion on the state of the premises, the area in which it is situated, the cost or likely cost of the services provided, the value to be placed upon any furniture provided, the value of the unfurnished accommodation provided, including any parts of the house shared in common between the lessor and lessee, and the most reasonable apportionment between the parties of the cost of insurance and other outgoings. Furthermore the tribunal will draw its own conclusions as to the reliability and character of the parties and their witnesses, and form its own opinion in the light of all that it has seen and heard of the best way to tackle the often vexed question of security of tenure. In the end the tribunal will solve both its tasks by a combination of mathematical calculation, general impression, and an assessment of the human needs and hardships involved so far as security of tenure is concerned.

If there were to be an appeal on fact or merits from the decision of a rent tribunal it is hard to see how it could be operated other than as a rehearing before another tribunal at which all the foregoing matters would have to be considered afresh. There clearly should be another inspection, and the parties or their representatives would be well advised to appear once more before the appellate tribunal. The clear result of this would be the destruction of several of the merits of the tribunal system praised by the Franks Committee, namely speed and cheapness, as well as a fair measure of informality. Many lessees might be encouraged to appeal merely in order to secure delay in the resolution of the question of security, and there would inevitably be considerable delay in reaching a final disposition of all the issues in a case. Yet there would be no guarantee that the decision of the appellate tribunal or of any court[1] hearing an appeal on fact or merits would be any better than that of the first instance body. The possible benefits of instituting appeals on the merits as a general rule from the first instance tribunals might turn out to have been dearly bought.

Other reforms

The two major legislative achievements of the Franks Report were the creation of the Council on Tribunals and the institution of appeals on law from any tribunals direct to the Divisional Court. But there were many other marked effects upon the whole flavour of the system of administrative tribunals and inquiries. The great majority of the ninety-five detailed recommendations of the Committee were promptly accepted by the Government of the day, and a number of others were later accepted either in whole or in part. Only a mere handful were in the end rejected or simply not carried into effect. But as many of the recommendations which were accepted were on matters of detail, rather than principle, it was possible to implement them without resorting to legislation. For example, the recommendation that all chairmen of rent tribunals should have legal qualifications[2] has been effected as a matter of practice without altering either the primary or the secondary legislation concerning the tribunals. Again, the emphasis placed by the Committee upon the requirements of openness, fairness and impartiality has been reflected usually not in subsequent legislation, but by a change in general attitude by those tribunals which had not previously appreciated the full import of these characteristics. As was mentioned earlier, the statutory instrument which governs the procedure of rent tribunals dates from 1946, though it has since been amended in some

1 The hearing of an appeal by a judge in a County Court sitting with an assessor (as suggested by the Franks Committee) could even give rise to positive injustice, for the appellate judge would not even have seen the premises.
2 Para 163.

respects, and that instrument permits tribunals to sit either in private or in public at their own discretion. Before the Franks Committee Report it was quite common for rent tribunals to sit in private, and to exclude the press, but since the Franks Report chairmen of rent tribunals have realised the importance of sitting in public unless there is some really compelling reason to sit *in camera*. Accordingly, as was stated earlier, it is now common practice to sit in public unless persuaded to do otherwise by the principles already stated.

A host of other reforms have been achieved by changes of administrative practice. Many of these are concerned with the detailed procedure of individual tribunals or types of inquiry, and need not be considered here. But among the most prominent we may perhaps list three:

(a) Appellate tribunals now customarily publish selected decisions as guidance both for themselves in later cases and for first instance tribunals. Thus decisions of rent assessment committees are circulated to all members of the relevant panel, and to all rent officers within the panel area. Also, and perhaps of greatest importance in this context, the decisions of the Social Security Commissioners are published by Her Majesty's Stationary Office, and circulated to all adjudication officers, all chairmen of social security appeal tribunals, and to selected libraries. These decisions, though not of quite the same binding precedent value upon other tribunals in the social security field which would attach to a decision of the High Court, are nevertheless considered by adjudication officers and tribunals as generally binding upon them, so that a consistent body of social security tribunal case law is built up. Furthermore, a highly authoritive Digest of Commissioners' Decisions, compiled by a retired Commissioner, Mr Desmond Neligan OBE, and also published by the Stationery Office,[3] is of the greatest assistance in helping to establish this consistent body of precedent. The Digest is kept up to date by a regular loose leaf service.

(b) Legal representation is allowed before almost all tribunals, but it is a matter for each party whether he avails himself of such representation. The Franks Committee has recommended that the legal aid scheme should be extended to the more formal or expensive tribunals, and to final appellate tribunals.[4] The right to legal representation is generally recognised, and is sometimes specifically stated in rules of procedure. Also the legal advice scheme has been progressively extended in the years since the Franks Report so that it is now available to cover advice before hearings in any tribunals. But the

3 The Digest was first published in 1979, and replaces an earlier Digest written by Mr Edgar Jenkins OBE, and first published in 1964.
4 Para 89.

scheme has not yet been generally extended to cover the cost of legal representation, though it may be noted that it was extended to representation before mental health review tribunals by the Mental Health (Amendment) Act 1982. This may well be largely because of the cost to the public purse which it would entail. But other reasons probably include doubts about whether solicitors, who would be the more likely practising lawyers to appear at most inferior tribunal hearings, are adequately equipped to cope with the specialist law which is dealt with. Certainly in proceedings before tribunals in the social security field the experience of the present writer as chairman of an appeal tribunal suggests that trade union officers usually make more effective advocates for appellants than do lawyers.[5] So parties are welcome to retain lawyers to represent them in almost all tribunal proceedings, but normally only at their own expense.

(c) Chairmen of tribunals must usually now have had legal training, and must normally be selected by the appropriate Minister from a panel of persons appointed by the Lord Chancellor, or in Scotland by the Lord Advocate.[6] This helps to ensure that the person who chairs any tribunal proceedings is qualified to appreciate the importance of a full disclosure of all material facts to all parties before the hearing takes place,[7] and that an adequate opportunity is given to all parties to attend the hearing (and any inspection which may be involved).[8] Furthermore, the legal qualifications of the chairman should help to ensure that a proper watch is kept from the chair to see that the rules of natural justice are followed in the course of the hearing, and that any questions are put from the chair to parties to elicit facts or arguments which are relevant, but which may not have been sufficiently presented without such prompting. This latter function of a chairman probably more than makes up for any absence of actual legal representation of a party at the hearing.

As has been explained in chapter 2, the overall effect of the publication of the Report of the Donoughmore-Scott Committee on Ministers' Powers was to remove the great majority of the previous fears and apprehensions about delegated legislation; but it took many years for this effect to be appreciated, and decades before Parliament acted upon any of the Committee's detailed recommendations. The effect of the Franks Report was far more immediate. The first Tribunals and Inquiries Act received the Royal Assent only a year

5 For two opposing views on the subject, we see Alec Samuels 'Legal Aid and Rent Control Tribunals' (1970) 114 Sol Jo 4; and D C M Yardley 'Legal Aid and Rent Control Tribunals: a Reply' 114 Sol Jo 24.
6 As recommended in the Franks Committee Report, paras 48, 51, 53-55 and 58.
7 As recommended, Franks Report, paras 71-72.
8 As recommended, Franks Report, para 74.

after the Report was published, and indeed a number of the administrative changes recommended by the Committee were already in train by that time. The overall effect upon the climate of opinion was also much quicker, and by the time the Council on Tribunals embarked upon its work in 1959 there was already a general belief that any defects were being ironed out.

Nevertheless it is always wise to keep our minds open for any means of further improving our system. Accordingly it is welcome that the JUSTICE-All Souls Review Committee on Administrative Law in the United Kingdom, set up in 1979 though it has yet to report, has included in its terms of reference a consideration of whether the present system of tribunals and inquiries could be improved. And the Report of the Royal Commission on Legal Services, published in the same year,[9] has recommended that the procedures of all the main tribunals need to be reviewed by the Council on Tribunals.[10] Such a review may well be due, as it is now over a quarter of a century since the Franks Committee did its work. There is obvious merit in keeping such procedures under periodical scrutiny, and perhaps this should be accomplished about every thirty years or so. It may well be that most, if not all, such procedures will come through with a clean bill of health, but public confidence in a system which is so important at the grass-roots of the law can only be maintained as a result of constant vigilance.

Developments in Australia

Before closing this chapter, and because we have already put forward the view that it is salutary to keep our minds open for the future, and to consider further possible improvements in our system, it may be useful to glance briefly at some related reforms which have been taking place in recent years in Australia. It may be recalled that in chapter 5 we gave some consideration to the possible enactment of our principles of judicial review in statutory form. The ideas presented were based upon a series of recommendations made in 1971 by the Commonwealth Administrative Review Committee,[11] under the chairmanship of Sir John Kerr. The main burden of these recommendations were enacted for Australia by the Administrative Decisions (Judicial Review) Act 1977. The same Review Committee had given

---

9   Cmnd 7648
10 Recommendation 15.1. Another recommendation (R. 15.2), that advice and representation by lay agencies for applicants before tribunals should be encouraged, certainly accords with the views of the present writer.
11 Parliamentary Paper No 144.

its attention also to problems concerned with tribunals. The system of administrative tribunals in Australia at the time was much less well developed than in England, and it was not subject to such careful judicial control. But the Review Committee was anxious to make up for lost time, and it produced a series of recommendations which together, if followed, would amply do so, and would also provide for an even more clearcut and consistent procedure for judicial review. The majority of these recommendations were implemented by an earlier Act of 1975.

The Kerr Committee had proposed the creation of a general Administrative Review Tribunal to review all administrative decisions for which no appeal structure on questions of merits already existed. The Administrative Appeals Tribunal Act 1975 established just such a high level review tribunal, under the name Administrative Appeals Tribunal. The tribunal does not have quite such a general jurisdiction as the Kerr Committee had envisaged, but it does have jurisdiction to review specified types of administrative decision. These are decisions which are for the most part made by Ministers or government departments, rather than by tribunals as we would understand them in England. Thus the type of discretion which the tribunal may review is more akin to the discretion of Ministers in the United Kingdom, especially that exercised after a public inquiry has been held. The specified types of decision subject to this kind of review are steadily being increased as the years go by, and they already cover such important matters as decisions relating to customs tariffs, public service superannuation, deportation orders and air navigation licensing. The tribunal is empowered to exercise any of the powers of the original decision-maker, and must be given access to all documents and other information used by the authority making the original decision. Any person affected by a decision has the right to appeal to the tribunal, and this right extends to interest groups. The impact of the new procedure upon Australia may be measured from the fact that in the first two years of the tribunal's operation it reversed approximately 40 per cent of all original decisions brought before it. An ancillary provision in the Act enables any person affected by an administrative decision which is subject to the review jurisdiction of the tribunal to obtain the reasons for that decision without first having to lodge an appeal. It would therefore seem likely that this provision, somewhat akin to section 12 of the Tribunals and Inquiries Act 1971, and the procedural rules which bind Ministers making decisions after public inquiries, obviates the necessity for further challenge to decisions made in a significant number of cases.

As regards the Australian administrative tribunal system itself the

Kerr Committee recommended that there should be a supervisory body modelled very closely upon the pattern of the Council on Tribunals in Britain, and indeed the Committee stated that this should be the very first step in the process of reform. The only major difference between the suggested Australian body and that in Britain was to be that the Australian Council should consist of five full-time members. This is understandable, for there has never been the same tradition in Australia of voluntary part-time, and often unpaid, public service which has been one of the main features of the English legal system ever since magistrates first emerged between the twelfth and fourteenth centuries. Part V of the Administrative Appeals Tribunal Act 1975 establishes an Administrative Review Council substantially along the lines recommended by the Kerr Committee. But one further development is still awaited. The Review Committee had suggested that there should be an Administrative Procedure Act, making provision for minimum requirements of procedure to be observed by all administrative tribunals,[12] but this has not yet been enacted.

The Australian reforms of recent years are remarkable for their conciseness. It has been possible to learn from the hard grind of trial and error in England, and to establish in two sizeable leaps a system comparable with that which has developed gradually in the headquarters of the common law. The Australian Acts of 1975 and 1977 respectively make provision for the control of tribunal practice and of ministerial decisions which is substantially similar to the achievements to date in England. Yet the control scarcely goes further than English control. Even the Administrative Appeals Tribunal is not as general in its effect as may at first sight appear. It provides a method of redress against ministerial and departmental decisions which is broadly similar to modern English provisions. It is clear that in Australia, as in Britain constant vigilance is now maintained to see how and when the system may be improved, but further developments have yet to be manifested.

---

12 The Committee also recommended that the adversarial system in tribunal procedure should be mixed with an inquisitorial approach. As will have been seen in this chapter, such a mixture of procedures is fairly common in English administrative tribunals.

7 Ombudsmen

> For this is not the liberty which we can hope, that no grievance ever should arise in the Commonwealth, that let no man in this world expect; but when complaints are freely heard, deeply considered, and speedily reformed, then is the utmost bound of civil liberty attained that wise men look for.
>
> John Milton Areopagitica

The most central theme of administrative law is that of judicial control of power, and we have been at pains in this book to stress that theme. It is hoped that the reader will at the very least have been impressed by the devotion of the judges to the constant maintenance of their historic role, and by the myriad ways in which they have where necessary pushed the power of judicial review further forward in keeping with the needs of a population faced by ever more all-embracing executive authority. Yet there have always been some areas of administrative power or executive discretion which have remained immune from the possibility of judicial review. A decision made by an administrative officer which is within his lawful jurisdiction, and which is made neither in breach of natural justice nor in error of law may well therefore be valid, and of course technically reasonable, but nevertheless harsh, or delayed, or inadequately explained. Again, there are whole areas of executive discretion which have always been held to be immune from any type of judicial review. Examples are the discretion of the Crown to grant or refuse so-called political asylum to refugees, or the powers of local education authorities to make discretionary grants to certain types of students. In such cases the traditional remedy available to anyone who considers himself aggrieved has been to approach an MP, with a view to getting him to ask a question in the House of Commons of the responsible Minister, or to approach a local councillor in the hope that he will take the matter up and prevail upon those responsible to change their minds. Any such approach may well be backed up by letters to the press, or by the agitation of some pressure group, but its success is always bound to be problematical, and doubts would always be likely to remain one way or the other as to the justice of the eventual outcome.

It was in response to this haphazard state of affairs that the movement first grew in the United Kingdom for the establishment of some kind of formal extra-judicial channel for the consideration and possible remedy of complaints. Special impetus to the movement was given by the notorious Crichel Down affair. Shortly before the Second World War certain land in Dorset, known as Crichel Down, had been acquired compulsorily on behalf of what was then known as the Air Ministry, a predecessor of part of the present Ministry of Defence. The purpose of the acquisition was to provide the RAF with a range for the training of its bomber crews, and it was legally executed under emergency legislation then in force, but an undertaking was given at the time to the owner from whom it was purchased that he would be given the chance to repurchase it if the Crown should subsequently have no further use for the land. After the war the Air Ministry did indeed have no further use for it, and it was passed to the Ministry of Agriculture, which in its turn let it be known that it was prepared to consider disposing of the land either by sale or by lease. The original pre-war owner was by then dead, but his son-in-law, one Lieutenant-Commander Marten, who with his wife was farming adjoining land which had not been compulsorily acquired, made a bid to purchase the land. This was not accepted, and Crichel Down was sold to the Commissioners of Crown Lands, who then selected another tenant for it. Commander Marten protested and persisted in his protests at his treatment, and eventually the Minister appointed Sir Andrew Clarke QC to conduct an inquiry into the affair. Sir Andrew's Report was published in 1954,[1] and contained serious criticisms of impropriety by several civil servants within the Ministry of Agriculture who had, without any apparent justification, formed an aversion for Commander Marten, and revealed in a series of internal minutes passed within the Ministry a determination to prevent Marten acquiring the land, regardless of the financial or moral merits of his claim. As Sir Andrew wrote in his Report,[2] their attitude 'was engendered solely by a feeling of irritation that any member of the public should have the temerity to oppose or even question the acts or decisions of officials of a Government or State Department'. In the event there was a debate in the House of Commons; the Minister, Sir Thomas Dugdale, resigned; and the civil servants concerned were reprimanded.

1 Report of the Public Inquiry ordered by the Minister of Agriculture into the disposal of land at Crichel Down (Cmd 9176).
2 Cmd 9176, p 31.

But the Crichel Down affair did not rest there, for it was clear from Sir Andrew Clarke's Report that, however improper or undesirable the conduct of the civil servants, it at no stage had been illegal. The undertaking given to the original owner was no more than morally binding, and in any case could be argued as not extending to his son-in-law, even though Marten and his wife were still farming the adjoining land which they had inherited from the original owner of Crichel Down. The Ministry, like any other lessor or vendor, was entitled to dispose of its own property as it thought fit. Thus Marten had no claim in law which he could have prosecuted against the Ministry in any court or tribunal. The affair produced something of an outcry, and the public feeling of disquiet it engendered was one of the powerful causes of the setting up of the Franks Committee on Administrative Tribunals and Enquiries, discussed in the last chapter. Yet it is ironic that the Franks Committee found very soon that, whether by design or otherwise, its terms of reference were restricted to considering procedures connected only with tribunals and statutory inquiries, and that it had no authority to make recommendations concerned with the exercise of the sort of administrative power revealed by the Clarke Report. The Clarke Inquiry was not a statutory inquiry, but was set in motion by an individual Minister acting on his own accord within his own Ministry. So the Franks Report, though performing a valuable service by setting in motion reform over the broad spectrum of administrative tribunals and statutory inquiries, was impotent to deal with the kind of fault revealed by maladministration which does not transgress the law. The first steps in reform within this field had to wait until the next decade.

It was at this stage that the British section of the International Commission of Jurists, JUSTICE, set up an independent committee under the chairmanship of a former Chief Justice of Singapore, Sir John Whyatt, to investigate the Scandinavian institution of the 'Ombudsman', and the Report of this committee, often known as the Whyatt Report, was published in 1961.[3] There is no completely satisfactory English translation of the word ombudsman, but it has been variously rendered as 'commissioner', 'complaints officer' or 'grievance man'. The first ombudsman appeared in Sweden in 1809, though the full powers of the Swedish Ombudsman, which included the right to institute prosecutions, including prosecutions against judges, have not been copied by many of those countries in the present century which have instituted ombudsmen. The first twentieth-century ombudsman, also Scandinavian, was the Danish

---

3 The Citizen and the Administration: The Redress of Grievances.

Ombudsman, created by the Ombudsman Act 1954, and it was this office which particularly influenced the findings of the Whyatt Report.

The Danish Ombudsman is an officer of Parliament whose prime duty is to safeguard citizens against abuse or misuse of administrative power by the executive arm of government. In performance of this task he investigates allegations of maladministration. He inquires fully into the substance of the complaint, and has access to the relevant departmental files, but acts in an informal manner. He then makes a report upon his investigations and findings, and this is published in the national newspapers and, it appears, given wide coverage. He has no power to order anything specific to be done to remedy any maladministration which he may have found, but the Whyatt Committee found that he was often able to achieve positive results 'behind the scenes'. This effect has been assisted by the maintenance of friendly relations between the Ombudsman and the administration, and this state of affairs may well have resulted in part from the fact that a large proportion of the Ombudsman's reports have been favourable to the administration.

The Scandinavian model of ombudsman was copied in Norway and Finland, and the first Commonwealth country (or indeed common law country) to borrow from the Scandinavian experience was New Zealand, which established a Parliamentary Commissioner by an Act passed in 1962.[4] The second non-Scandinavian ombudsman to be created was, however, in Great Britain. The Whyatt Report in 1961 recommended the establishment of a Parliamentary Commissioner, based upon the institution of the Danish Ombudsman. But the Government of the day rejected this, partly because it took the view that it would cut across the time-hallowed doctrine of ministerial responsibility to Parliament, and partly because complaints could be made to MPs, who could either take matters up privately or else use the institution of 'question time' in the House as a means of ventilating grievances. These objections were soon seen to be misconceived. Questions asked in Parliament have always been a valuable means of raising grievances, but there is no means of telling whether the Minister's answer to any question is sound or just – and it is inevitably based upon material provided for him by his civil servants. And the institution of an independent method of testing the quality of the administrative act or behaviour may even assist a Minister to discharge more effectively his responsibility to Parliament. Accordingly a few years later these objections to the Whyatt recommendations were abandoned, and the Parlia-

---

4 Parliamentary Commissioner (Ombudsman) Act 1962.

mentary Commissioner Act 1967 established the first British ombudsman, differing in some details from the institution recommended by the Whyatt Report, but being in substance the office that was suggested in 1961. Although, in contrast to New Zealand, Parliament shied away from the use of such an un-English term as 'ombudsman', we shall see that it was soon to be adopted informally, not just by commentators, but by the British Parliamentary Commissioner himself. As other ombudsman institutions have been created since 1967 both in the United Kingdom and in other countries, it has become clear that this Scandinavian word has now become firmly fixed in the English language, and in the practice of our administrative law.

The Parliamentary Commissioner for Administration

The Parliamentary Commissioner Act 1967 created the office of Parliamentary Commissioner for Administration with a jurisdiction running throughout the whole of Great Britain, though not Northern Ireland. In fact, as we shall see presently, a similar office was created for Northern Ireland two years later. The British Commissioner is appointed by the Crown, and holds office until the age of sixty-five, being otherwise removable only in consequence of an address from both Houses of Parliament, so that his tenure of office is protected in the same way as that of superior judges. Doubtless in the interests of co-operation he is *ex officio* a member of the Council on Tribunals. He may investigate any action taken by or on behalf of a government department or certain other listed authorities, provided that there is no court or tribunal in which such action may reasonably be challenged,[5] though his investigation can only be set in motion as a result of the receipt of a complaint that there has been maladministration. There is, however, a set process prescribed by the Act for the reference of such complaints.

The complaint must be in writing, it must be made by someone resident in the United Kingdom who claims to have sustained injustice in consequence of the maladministration, and it must be made in the first place to an MP within twelve months of the person aggrieved first having notice of the matters alleged in the complaint (though the Commissioner may conduct an investigation pursuant to a complaint not made within that period if he considers there are

---

5 This proviso has been used quite frequently by the Commissioner in respect of tax complaints, for he takes the view that it is unreasonable to expect the complainant to go through the cumbersome and expensive process of litigating against the Inland Revenue.

special circumstances which make it proper to do so). It is then for the MP to refer it to the Commissioner, with the consent of the complainant, and with a request that the Commissioner conduct an investigation into it. This 'filter' of complaints through MPs has always been controversial, but its purpose was closely related to the fear that the Commissioner might be swamped with complaints unless some effort were made to intercept some of the more eccentric or worthless complaints before they should reach him. This fear has probably not been borne out by events, but the architects of the 1967 Act should at least be given credit for trying to deal with a problem which might very well have arisen from the fact that the British Commissioner was to become the world's first ombudsman in a country having a population of more than a few millions. There have so far been five men who have held the office of Parliamentary Commissioner for Administration. The first two, Sir Edmund Compton and Sir Alan Marre, took the view that any complaints made to them direct, ignoring the 'MP filter', were outside their jurisdiction, and thus fell automatically. But the third Commissioner, Sir Idwal Pugh, adopted the practice of sending any such complaint, with the complainant's consent, on to the complainant's constituency MP with a request that he should decide whether or not to refer the complaint formally to the Commissioner, and this latter practice has been followed by his successors, Sir Cecil Clothier QC and the present Commissioner, Mr Anthony Barrowclough QC.

The Commissioner must conduct his investigations in private, and the procedure he adopts is left to his own discretion.[6] But his power to investigate is much strengthened by his right, conferred by section 8 of the Act, to require any Minister, officer or member of a department or authority concerned, or indeed anyone else, to furnish information or produce documents relevant to his investigation. He has the same powers as a court to compel the attendance and examination of witnesses; and the Crown is specifically not entitled to attempt to shelter behind any claim of Crown privilege in respect of the production of documents or the giving of evidence. It is noteworthy that this statutory provision preceded the House of Lords' decision in *Conway v Rimmer*, discussed in chapter 5, by a year. On the other hand information concerning the proceedings of the Cabinet or any of its committees is understandably exempt from the Commissioner's jurisdiction. At the conclusion of any investigation he must send to the MP who requested it a report of the results of his investigation, or a statement of his reasons for deciding not to

6   Sir Cecil Clothier occasionally held hearings, either formal (with the right to legal representation, cross-examination etc) or informal (without representation).

conduct it. A similar report must go to the initial complainant, and to the principal officer of the department or authority concerned. He may make a special report to each House of Parliament, but in any event must make an Annual Report to Parliament upon his work. It has always been the practice of the House of Commons to refer all such reports to a Select Committee for consideration and comment.

The Act, in Schedule 2, lists a large number of departments and other authorities subject to the Commissioner's investigation, but in Schedule 3 it also exempts from investigation quite a lot of subjects within the powers of such departments and authorities. Thus, under these two Schedules, as amended, the Foreign and Commonwealth Office is subject to investigation, and so is the Home Office; but matters listed as not subject to investigation include:

1 Action taken in matters certified by a Secretary of State or other Minister of the Crown to affect relations or dealings between the Government of the United Kingdom and any other Government or any international organisation of States or Governments.

2 Action taken, in any country or territory outside the United Kingdom, by or on behalf of any officer representing or acting under the authority of Her Majesty in respect of the United Kingdom, or any other officer of the Government of the United Kingdom.

3 Action taken in connection with the administration of the Government of any country or territory outside the United Kingdom which forms part of Her Majesty's dominions or in which Her Majesty has jurisdiction.

4 Action taken by the Secretary of State under the Extradition Act 1870 or the Fugitive Offenders Act 1967.

5 Action taken by or with the authority of the Secretary of State for the purposes of investigating crime or of protecting the security of the State, including action so taken with respect to passports.

6 The commencement of civil or criminal proceedings before any court of law in the United Kingdom, of proceedings at any place under the Naval Discipline Act 1957, the Army Act 1955 or the Air Force Act 1955, or of proceedings before any international court or tribunal.

7 Any exercise of the prerogative of mercy or of the power of a Secretary of State to make a reference in respect of any person to the Court of Appeal, the High Court of Justiciary or the Courts-Martial Appeal Court . . .

Thus a fair slice of the whole of the power of these two great departments of state is immune from investigation by the Commissioner. There is, of course, much to be said for leaving the conduct of foreign affairs and such matters as the exercise of the prerogative of mercy outside the scope of investigation by such an officer. But it is encouraging that the nature of these exemptions is kept under constant review by the House of Commons. The present

Select Committee of the Commons consists of eight members, which is a manageable size for the purpose of reaching decisions reasonably quickly, and over the years since 1967 the various Select Committees have made recommendations which have proposed extensions of the Commissioner's jurisdiction, and have brought about improvements in the arrangements for and the efficiency of his work. The result of one recommendation made by the Committee was the Parliamentary Commissioner Order 1979,[7] which narrows the exception to the Commissioner's jurisdiction made by paragraph 2 of Schedule 3 of the 1967 Act, as quoted above, by excluding from it action taken by career consular officials in relation to United Kingdom citizens who have the right of abode in the United Kingdom. The work of the Select Committee is probably facilitated by its practice of meeting the Commissioner himself regularly, and of having him present when they consider specific problems and interview officials.

One patent difficulty provided by the Act is that it nowhere defines 'maladministration', the one quality in an administrator which under the Act should cause an adverse report to be made by the Commissioner. This seems a curious omission by Parliament, but apparently it was an omission by design. The first Commissioner, Sir Edmund Compton, made this plain in an address he gave to the Society of Public Teachers of Law:[8]

> At this point I hear the question: 'But where is maladministration defined?' That was indeed a question that was asked again and again when the Bill was being debated in Parliament. The answer is: 'Nowhere in the Act', which leaves me with the task of recognizing or identifying instances of it in the course of my casework. In this task I am assisted by what I call the 'Crossman Catalogue' – that is, the list of examples of maladministration which Mr Crossman, the then Lord President of the Council, gave in one of the Debates on the Bill in the House of Commons – on October 18, 1966 to be exact[9] – when he said: 'We might have made an attempt in this clause to define, by catalogue, all of the qualities which might count for maladministration by a civil servant – bias, neglect, inattention, delay, incompetence, ineptitude, perversity, turpitude, arbitrariness and so on.'
>
> The significant words are the last ones – 'and so on'. For the Minister was at pains to add that this was not a complete list. He wanted me, assisted by the aggrieved public and Members, to work out the list as I went along.

There was perhaps some merit in avoiding a statutory attempt to

---

7 SI 1979/915 This extension of the Commissioner's jurisdiction was further consolidated by the Parliamentary Commissioner (Consular Complaints) Act 1981.
8 'The Parliamentary Commissioner for Administration' (1968) X JSPTL (NS) 101 at 103.
9 H C Official Report (5th series) col 51.

define or describe the nature of maladministration, for it leaves the door open for an ombudsman to find that all sorts of hitherto unsuspected types of behaviour might amount to maladministration, but the lack of any statutory guidance does also mean that a Commissioner is equally able to adopt an attitude which is so restrictive that comparatively few types of behaviour would ever be interpreted as amounting to maladministration.

This type of restrictive attitude was in fact shown by Sir Edmund Compton, despite his recognition of the power to interpret his powers widely. In particular he linked his view of the meaning of maladministration to his interpretation of a subsection of the 1967 Act which is certainly puzzling. Bearing in mind that section 5(1) empowers the Commissioner to investigate a complaint by a member of the public who claims to have sustained injustice in consequence of maladministration in connection with action taken by or on behalf of a government department or authority in the exercise of administrative functions, the puzzling subsection is the later section 12(3). This declares that 'nothing in this Act authorises or requires the Commissioner to question the merits of a decision taken without maladministration by a government department or other authority in the exercise of a discretion vested in that department or authority'. One might well take the view that this subsection is otiose, because it appears merely to state that whereas the Commissioner has been granted, earlier in the Act, the power to investigate maladministration, he is not empowered to make any adverse report upon any action or decision which does *not* amount to maladministration. But this was not the view of the subsection taken by Sir Edmund. He interpreted it, in several of his early reports, as meaning that his power to investigate maladministration (as granted by section 5(1)) was cut down by section 12(3) in that he was not empowered to question maladministration which may occur as part of a *decision*. Maladministration in the process leading up to a decision was within his jurisdiction, but not the quality of the decision itself.

Whether or not one considers that this interpretation was perverse, it may be commented that the House of Commons Select Committee which received Sir Edmund's reports disagreed with him. In August 1968 they recommended that the Commissioner ought to consider himself able to report on bad decisions as well as any defects in the process leading up to the making of decisions.[10] Sir Edmund accepted this advice, but his reports continued to show that he only found a low incidence of maladministration in the cases he investigated. We

10 Second Report of the Select Committee on the Parliamentary Commissioner for Administration, 1968. See also Sir Cecil Clothier 'Legal Problems of an Ombudsman' [1984] L S Gaz 3108 at 3110.

shall return to this incidence presently, but it may be commented here that the later Commissioners appear to have discovered a progressively higher incidence of maladministration. It seems unlikely that the standard of administration has deteriorated between 1968 and the present day. Indeed one might expect that the integrity among administrators in Britain is even higher today than in most countries. But it may be that the early work of the Parliamentary Commissioner was hampered by a more restricted vision than is to be found today.

Perhaps this earlier restriction in outlook stemmed, in part, and unwittingly, from the fact that the first three Commissioners to be appointed in turn were former civil servants, and it may have been difficult for such men to disengage their approach to the work entirely from their former habits and training. Furthermore, although the Commissioner from the start had a staff of about sixty under him, not one of them initially was a lawyer. The present writer once asked Sir Edmund, after an address he gave, whether he thought he would be helped by having a lawyer or two on his staff. His answer was in the negative, and when I suggested that his work not infrequently might involve the interpretation of powers conferred by statute, and that lawyers might be able to help with such interpretation, he replied that in difficult cases he could always consult the Treasury Solicitor, who is of course a legal adviser to and legal guardian for government departments! Fortunately this climate has changed. During the Commissionership of Sir Idwal Pugh, lawyers were engaged upon his staff, and he himself accepted the view already expressed by the Select Committee[11] that his successor should be chosen from outside the civil service. It is of note that when Sir Idwal retired his successors to date have both been Queen's Counsel. The present incumbent has a staff of over eighty, though apparently the other lawyers engaged during Sir Idwal's period of office have now disappeared! Among other subtle changes, more of climate than of form, is the current preference for being known as the Parliamentary Ombudsman. Today there are other ombudsmen in the United Kingdom, as we shall see, but it is not uncommon for the Parliamentary Ombudsman to be referred to as *the* Ombudsman.[12]

11 Second Report of the Select Committee on the Parliamentary Commissioner for Administration 1975–76.
12 The Parliamentary Ombudsman has inspired a wealth of written comment. Most notable are several books: K C Wheare *Maladministration and its Remedies* (Hamlyn Lectures, 1973); R Gregory and P Hutchesson *The Parliamentary Ombudsman: A Study in the Control of Administrative Action;* F Stacey *The British Ombudsman;* D W Williams *Maladministration: Remedies for Injustice;* and Our Fettered Ombudsman, a Report by JUSTICE.

Similar developments in other countries

So worldwide has been the spread of 'ombudsmania' that it would be impossible here to give anything more than an inkling of the number and varieties of ombudsmen to be found abroad. The variations are great. Although the powers of most ombudsmen are broadly similar to those of the Danish institution, which has been in most respects emulated by the British Parliamentary Ombudsman, with only comparatively minor variations (such as the 'MP filter' in Great Britain), this has not been the universal practice. Nor has it always been the case that ombudsmen elsewhere in the world are individual officers vested with the powers deemed desirable to confer upon them. Thus the powers of the original Ombudsman, that of Sweden, set up in the nineteenth century, to investigate complaints against the judiciary, have been emulated in Finland and Tanzania. And in Tanzania, the first country in Commonwealth Africa to set up an ombudsman institution (in 1966), and Nigeria the form it has taken is that of a collegiate body, which was thought to be more in keeping with African traditions than would have been a single officer.

As has already been stated, the first ombudsman to be appointed outside Scandinavia was in New Zealand, under the Parliamentary Commissioner (Ombudsman) Act 1962. He is appointed by the Governor-General on the recommendation of the House of Representatives, and his powers are to report to the appropriate department or organisation on decisions which are 'unreasonable, unjust, oppressive' and 'wrong'. If proper remedial action is not taken, he may then report to the Prime Minister and to Parliament. The New Zealand experiment is generally regarded as an unqualified success. The bold statutory power to report upon decisions which are wrong might have been a useful feature of the later British Act, for the New Zealand Ombudsman has reported several times that he not only checks administrative abuses, but that he constantly reviews administrative decisions and rights wrongs. It will be noted that there is no 'MP filter', though of course the population of New Zealand is only about one-twentieth the size of that of Great Britain. In many ways the New Zealand Ombudsman has been stronger in his direct effect upon the administration, and even upon the law, than his counterpart in Britain. For example, within about two years of his first starting work, the Government of New Zealand had accepted his assertion that the Government must always act honestly, and thus honour all promises, however bare and unsupported by consideration on the other side. In this way it is now recognised that in New Zealand the full effect of the doctrine of promissory estoppel has been attained.

It is no longer merely the negative position that, as under the English *High Trees House* rule,[13] a government department which promises not to enforce its full contractual rights against another contracting party may be met by a defence of promissory estoppel if it later attempts to enforce those legal rights. In New Zealand, as a result of the Ombudsman's pressures it is also accepted by government departments that a promisee is entitled as a matter of morality to succeed in positively enforcing the full effect of any promise made by a department, regardless of the strict common law position. Thus in practice in New Zealand parties are entitled to rely upon promises and, where appropriate, to base claims against the Crown upon them. The English *High Trees House* principle can now be used in New Zealand as a sword, and not just as a shield.[14]

Ombudsmen of differing kinds can now be found all over the world and in a wide variety of countries, only linked together by their payment of at least lip-service to democracy. Most of the ombudsmen are to be found in Commonwealth or common law countries, including almost all the provinces of Canada and such disparate Commonwealth countries as Guyana, Tanzania and Nigeria. But even in France, where there is a highly developed *droit administratif*, an ombudsman under the name of *Médiateur* was established in 1973.[15] In Australia the Ombudsman Act 1976, typical of many enactments throughout the world in using the title Ombudsman in the official designation of the office created, follows up the recommendation of the Report of the Commonwealth Administrative Review Committee, chaired by Sir John Kerr, that there should be a General Counsel for Grievances, by establishing a Commonwealth Ombudsman; and this office itself was preceded by the establishment of ombudsmen in most of the Australian States.

Sir Guy Powles, who was the first New Zealand Ombudsman, and whose work has been widely respected all over the world, in an article he published in 1978,[16] counted up as many as sixty-four national and local ombudsmen all over the world. But many more have come into existence since then. There would be little point in attempting here to list or trace the development of all these officers and offices. But perhaps it is worthwhile to refer to the provisions he quotes from Sudan, for they establish not only another collegiate-type ombudsman (as in Tanzania and Nigeria), but they also attempt to particularise

13 *Central London Property Trust Ltd v High Trees House Ltd* [1947] KB 130.
14 Cf the English rule, as stated by the Court of Appeal in *Combe v Combe* [1951] 2 KB 215.
15 Loi 73-6
16 'Ombudsmen and Human Rights Commission' Review of the International Commission of Jurists, No 21, December 1978, p 31.

the nature of maladministration. According to Sir Guy Powles, the Sudanese provisions empower the People's Assembly Committee to inquire into any complaint against the administration which indicates that the action taken has been tainted with (a) nepotism, corruption or bias; (b) failure to observe a sound administrative basis; (c) negligence in carrying out a duty; (d) misuse of discretion; (e) incompetence; (f) loss of documents or papers; (g) tardiness and delay; (h) unjust segregation or discrimination; or (i) any similar matters. It may be that the final item on the list resembles Mr Richard Crossman's 'and so on', and that even this Sudanese attempt at defining maladministration cannot be regarded as all-embracing. But there may nevertheless be some merit in trying to list the types of activity which come within the confines of maladministration. At all events the Sudanese provision, as reported by Sir Guy Powles, may be of some help to other ombudsmen in determining whether or not certain alleged actions are undesirable. It strikes an unusual chord to mention 'nepotism' so starkly!

Other United Kingdom ombudsmen

It was early recognised that the creation of the British Parliamentary Commissioner for Administration might be only the first step along the road towards a wider scope for extra-judicial remedies against the administration. The most severely criticised aspect of the 1967 Act, the institution of the 'MP filter'[17] has remained intact. But there has been a whittling away of the matters listed in Schedule 3 as not subject to investigation. We have already referred to the Parliamentary Commissioner Order 1979, which reduced the scope of the exemption of Foreign and Commonwealth Office activity abroad insofar as it directly concerns United Kingdom citizens with a right of abode within the United Kingdom. But one of the most heavily criticised aspects of the Act concerned what at the time was still called the Ministry of Health. This shortly afterwards was merged into the present Department of Health and Social Security, which, like its predecessor is, by Schedule 2, subject to investigation. But under Schedule 3, as originally enacted, the eighth group of matters listed as not subject to investigation was:

> Action taken on behalf of the Minister of Health or the Secretary of State by a Regional Hospital Board, Board of Governors of a Teaching Hospital, Hospital Management Committee or Board of Management, or by the Public Health Laboratory Service Board.

17 See e g Our Fettered Ombudsman, a Report by JUSTICE, published in 1977.

Most of the actual terms and titles used in this paragraph have become outdated as a result of reorganisation of the National Health Service since 1967. But the stark fact was that this paragraph exempted the whole of the hospital service from the jurisdiction of the Ombudsman. Once the ombudsman principle had been accepted and implemented by the 1967 Act it was clear that such a vital lacuna could not last for long. When the Health Service was reorganised a few years later the gap was plugged, for three Health Service Commissioners were appointed, one each for England, Wales and Scotland,[18] with the duty to investigate any alleged failure in a service provided by a health authority, or any other action taken by or on behalf of such an authority, where there is a complaint of injustice in consequence of maladministration. The procedure to be followed by the three Commissioners is similar to that laid down for the Parliamentary Ombudsman, save that a complainant need not channel his complaint through an MP, and may approach a Commissioner direct. The Commissioners' Reports must be made to Parliament, and are in fact received by the same Select Committee of the Commons which receives the Parliamentary Ombudsman's reports. It is, however, somewhat odd, if convenient, that all three posts have since their inception been held by the same man who for the time being is Parliamentary Commissioner for Administration.

The Parliamentary Commissioner Act 1967 was, as has already been stated, limited to Great Britain. But its principle was extended to Northern Ireland two years later, and indeed taken even further. Under the Parliamentary Commissioner Act (Northern Ireland) 1969, a separate Northern Ireland Parliamentary Commissioner for Administration was set up for that province, with the duty to investigate complaints against what was then the Government of Northern Ireland. Since the suspension of devolution to Northern Ireland in 1972, and the imposition of direct rule, the Northern Ireland Commissioner's previous duty to lay his reports before the Northern Ireland House of Commons, and for a brief period thereafter before the ill-fated Assembly, has become a duty to lay them before the two Houses of Parliament at Westminster. His power is now to investigate most areas of central government authority in Northern Ireland. Another statute, the Commissioner for Complaints Act (Northern Ireland) 1969, created the Northern Ireland Commissioner for Complaints to investigate complaints against local authorities and other public bodies, including hospitals and health authorities.

---

18 By the National Health Service Reorganisation Act 1973 (for England and Wales), and the National Health Service (Scotland) Act 1972.

Although complaints to the Northern Ireland Parliamentary Commissioner originally had to be forwarded through a Member of the Stormont Parliament in Belfast, and now must go through Westminster MPs,[19] those to the Commissioner for Complaints were to be sent direct. Initially the office of Northern Ireland Parliamentary Commissioner was held, yet again, by the same person who was for the time being Parliamentary Ombudsman in Great Britain. But since 1973 the two special Northern Ireland offices have usually been held by the same Commissioner, and not by the same person who holds the British office.

As part of the very strong pressure which had been exerted after the 1967 Act for extension and improvement of the ombudsman principle there was a movement for a similar mechanism in the field of local government. It was argued that if there was any maladministration in government departments with their generally high standard of civil service morality, it was even more likely that maladministration would be found in local government, which would be largely unaffected by the strength of the civil service tradition.[20] As it turned out a suitable moment for introducing some form of local ombudsman system was presented by the reorganisation of local government throughout England and Wales (except for London) by the Local Government Act 1972, which was to take full effect in 1974. The main legislation did not in fact make any such provision, but the Local Government Act 1974 did, and its provisions came into force on the same dates as the other Act took full effect, All Fools' Day 1974.

The 1974 Act establishes two Commissions for Local Administration, one for England and one for Wales, and the Local Government (Scotland) Act 1975 establishes a similar Commissioner for Scotland. In this respect, therefore, Great Britain followed the example of Northern Ireland. Although the 1974 Act does not specify the number of Commissioners, there have so far been three Commissioners holding office together for England, who divide the territory between them on a geographical basis, and a single Commissioner for Wales (as in Scotland), though the Parliamentary Ombudsman is an *ex officio* member of each Commission. The Commissioners for Local Administration have the duty to investigate complaints of injustice suffered in consequence of maladministration in connection with the execution of administrative functions performed by a local authority, a police authority, water authority

19   Northern Ireland Act 1974, Sch I, para 4.
20   See e g another Report by JUSTICE (in 1969), The Citizen and his Council.

or any joint board of local authorities. Any complaint must be in writing; it must usually be made within twelve months of the matter complained about; and it must normally be forwarded to a Commissioner by an elected or nominated member of the authority concerned with the consent of the complainant, though this requirement may be dispensed with by the Commissioner if he is satisfied that such a member has been asked to forward a complaint and has refused to do so.

A local Commissioner, in the course of his investigation, has access to documents in the possession of the authority concerned. The investigation will, as in the case of all United Kingdom ombudsmen, be conducted in private, and when concluded the result must be reported to the councillor or other member of the authority who referred the complaint, to the complainant, and to the authority concerned. The authority must then make copies of the report available for public inspection. Where the Commissioner has concluded that injustice has been caused as a result of maladministration, his report must be considered by the authority, which must then notify the Commissioner of the action it proposes to take in consequence. If the Commissioner is not satisfied with the result of his report, he may investigate the matter afresh and issue a further report, but he has no means of insisting upon compliance with his findings. Regrettably it should be noted that, whereas the record of government departments in complying with the recommendations of the Parliamentary Ombudsman is very good, in fact virtually 100 per cent, there have been a number of instances of local authorities failing to accept the criticisms of a Local Ombudsman and refusing to implement his suggestions. Uniquely among United Kingdom ombudsmen a report of the Northern Ireland Commissioner for Complaints may be used as the basis for a claim in the county court for damages or any other suitable remedy. It is the current view of all the other United Kingdom local ombudsmen that, unless local authorities agree that they will in future always implement the recommendations in adverse reports, similar provisions should be introduced in Great Britain.

There are some matters excluded from the jurisdiction of Local Commissioners, such as the investigation of crime, discipline in schools, and matters relating to the pay and conditions of service of local government officers. Jurisdiction is also excluded over any matters in respect of which the complainant has a right of recourse to a tribunal, a Minister or a court, unless the Commissioner considers that it is unreasonable that the complainant should pursue such a remedy. But possibly more controversial is the provision that any matter in which all or most of the inhabitants of an authority's area are affected is outside the Commissioner's jurisdiction.[1] Each Commission must submit an Annual Report to its representative body of members of the various local authority associations and the Water Authorities Association representing authorities under the Commissioner's jurisdiction, such as the Association of Councils and the Association of County Councils.

There is as yet no ombudsman institution charged with the jurisdiction to consider complaints about public corporations, though such an institution has been urged.[2] But the long campaign of disquiet about the methods whereby the police internally investigated complaints against any of their number culminated in the establishment, by the Police Act 1976, of an independent Police Complaints Board, which was then replaced by a new Police Complaints Authority, set up under the Police and Criminal Evidence Act 1984. This Authority consists of at least nine persons appointed by the Prime Minister, none of whom may be, or have ever been, a member of a United Kingdom police force. It supervises the investigation of all the most serious class of complaints, and also has discretion to supervise complaints involving corruption, lesser assaults and action reflecting on the reputation of the police service. The investigation is still carried out by police officers, but the Authority may give directions concerning the conduct and form it may take. A second function of the Authority is the administration of police disciplinary proceedings. It is perhaps a mark of the status of the new Authority, and of the clear intention to ensure that serious complaints against the police are properly and impartially dealt with, that its first Chairman is Sir Cecil Clothier QC who took up office at the beginning of 1985 when he retired as Parliamentary Commissioner for Administration.

There may be no end to the implementation of the ombudsman principle if professional and other organisations choose to adopt it within their own domestic practices.[3] But perhaps it is worth mentioning one such development which has been more formally instituted. Under the Solicitors Act 1974 a Lay Observer is appointed to investigate complaints about the Law Society's handling of complaints against solicitors. His task is to consider the merits of the Law Society's actions, to report to the Society thereon, and to make

1 There are also provisions similar to that in the Parliamentary Commissioner Act 1967, s 12(3), purporting to preclude the Local Commissioners from questioning the merits of decisions taken without maladministration.
2 See e g yet another Report by JUSTICE (published in 1976), The Citizen and the Public Agencies.
3 See e g the Insurance Ombudsman Bureau set up by the insurance industry in 1981, and the Banking Ombudsman set up in 1986.

any recommendations he thinks fit. The Law Society must then inform the Lay Observer of any action taken in consequence. The Lay Observer's reports on individual cases are not made public, but the Lord Chancellor may direct him to report annually upon his work. To date the Lord Chancellor has so directed him, and it is fair to add that the Lay Observer's general reports have revealed on the whole that there is very little basis for the complaints he receives, apart from one very serious case reported in 1984.

The work of ombudsmen in practice

It would scarcely be possible in this book to attempt to give a full picture of the work done by all the various ombudsmen now existing within the United Kingdom. But a few examples may be attempted, mainly for the purpose of illustration. It may be suggested that the most appropriate modern approach to the ombudsmen is to consider their work as a whole, rather than to try to distinguish too finely between the tasks of the different ombudsmen. This is especially so because there is so much room for overlap. Thus, even after the creation of the Northern Ireland Parliamentary Commissioner, the original British Parliamentary Commissioner continued to deal with complaints about action in the province for which a United Kingdom government department was responsible. Again, the British Parliamentary Ombudsman has his finger in so many ombudsman pies, having for some years filled the comparable office in Northern Ireland, being an *ex officio* member of the separate Commissions for Local Administration, and occupying the three technically quite separate offices of Health Service Commissioner for England, Wales and Scotland. Furthermore he is an *ex officio* member of the Council on Tribunals, and although Sir Edmund Compton, in one of the earlier Annual Reports of the Parliamentary Commissioner,[4] opined that overlap between the jurisdictions of the Council and of himself as Parliamentary Commissioner occurred only seldom, there have been more indications in recent years of practical overlap. For example, in the affair already discussed in chapter 3 brought about by the threat of the Home Secretary to revoke television licences which had already been purchased at a lower cost than the increased price which had been announced for the future, and before the expiry of the current licences, many complaints were made to the Parliamentary Commissioner. After full investigation, the Commissioner found the Home Office to be seriously to blame in its

4 Annual Report for 1968.

procedure in that it had not given the public proper warning of its actions, it had been inefficient and had lacked foresight, and it had been insufficiently frank with the public. Yet, as we have already seen in chapter 3, the Court of Appeal, quite independently, held that the Home Secretary's threat was unlawful as an abuse of power.[5] And so the same incident amounted both to maladministration in the process and an ultra vires act in the decision or action pursued. In the result the Home Office repaid the additional licence fees which had been paid under threat of revocation.

The number of complaints received each year by the Parliamentary Ombudsman has remained remarkably constant, ranging from just over 1,000 in each of the years 1967 (which was actually only the first seven months of the Commissioner's work), 1968 and 1980, down to less than 600 in each of the low years 1971 to 1973. An upsurge in complaints received in 1978 may be in part accounted for by the modern practice of the Ombudsman in referring complaints which have been sent to him direct from complainants to MPs asking them whether they will agree to refer them formally for investigation. In 1979 there were only 758 complaints. The number went up to 838 in 1982, but fell back to 751 in 1983 before going up again to 837 in 1984. In each year, however, the Commissioner has found that anything from about a third to three-quarters of all complaints received, even though they have been referred by MPs, are outside his jurisdiction, a factor which may follow in part from the restrictions imposed by the 1967 Act. Even in 1978 the Annual Report of the Commissioner for that year, while recording the record number of 1,259 complaints received through MPs, also reveals that about 70 per cent of them were rejected as outside the Ombudsman's jurisdiction.

But the percentage of cases accepted as within jurisdiction in which the Commissioner has discovered maladministration has steadily increased, rising fairly steadily from a mere 10 per cent in both 1967 and 1968, to 43 per cent in 1976 and a record 55 per cent in 1978. The two departments of state which have shared the doubtful distinction, year and year about, of producing the most cases of maladministration have been the Inland Revenue and the Department of Health and Society Security. In 1978 no less than forty-seven complaints against the latter department were upheld, whilst in another twelve cases departmental action was found to be partly at fault. In the same year forty complaints were upheld against the Inland Revenue, while another twenty-five cases showed some ground for criticism. Yet it is important to keep maladministration

5 *Congreve v Home Office* [1976] QB 629.

within perspective. Over the years there have been few findings by the Commissioner of anything as reprehensible as the administrative misbehaviour in the Crichel Down affair. For the most part maladministration has amounted to such understandable things as delay, failure to explain, rudeness and inflexibility in approach. In 1978, for example, the Commissioner found that the more serious cases discovered usually had deeper roots than administrative malpractice. Often there had been a change in administrative system, arising perhaps from new legislation, which was ill-prepared. Sometimes the system had become so complicated as to baffle not only the public but officials as well. In several Annual Reports the Commissioner has criticised the extraordinary complications of tax law and procedure, and of the social security system. In 1978 the Commissioner gave as his prime example the Land Compensation Act 1973, a complex measure which was passed through Parliament more quickly than its sponsoring department had expected. As a result there was delay in the organisation of full instructions to regional offices about the issuing of formal public notices of opportunity to claim entitlement to retrospective compensation, and in the issuing of explanatory booklets to the public. As a consequence the time limits for retrospective claims under the Act were effectively shortened.

Perhaps the most severe condemnation of departmental maladministration made in recent years was in a special report which received wide press coverage in 1978.[6] There Sir Idwal Pugh severely criticised the behaviour of certain officials in the Department of Health and Social Security who had, over a period of many years, denied to a disabled ex-army officer the correct rate of war disablement pension. Sir Idwal described such action as 'improper behaviour' and 'deplorable deceit'. The Parliamentary Ombudsman is thus quite prepared to hit hard in his reports where this appears to him to be necessary.

On the other hand he will be equally astute to reveal the unreasonableness of some complaints. A case reported on in the period 1978–79 is indicative of this. A man had complained of delay and inefficiency by the Department of Health and Social Security in dealing with his complaints. After carefully investigating some very complex facts, the Commissioner found that the man had made so many claims upon the department, and then so many appeals, at short intervals that the papers were never in the right place at the right time. Thus the complainant's own actions had become a major obstacle to efficiency. In the event, therefore, the Department, at

6   (1978) Times, 25 March.

the instance of the Commissioner, tendered an apology, but no compensation. There are also some cases in which the Commissioner considers that there *may* have been maladministration, but that he cannot be satisfied either way as to the truth of the matter. Such cases include complaints about the rudeness of immigration officers to those they interview on entry to the United Kingdom. In such cases it is obvious that the chances of inability to be certain of precisely what happened are bound to be great, so that actual redress against the administration may only be rarely obtained. Nevertheless the existence of the right to complain to the Parliamentary Ombudsman is likely to act as a powerful deterrent upon those officers in the administration who might otherwise be tempted to abuse their offices by contemptuous or discourteous treatment of other members of the public. It is also clear that among the most common remedies obtained on the recommendation of the Ombudsman is a simple apology. Others include reconsideration of the issue, the payment of out-of-pocket expenses to the complainant, a review of procedures, and the rewriting of leaflets issued by government departments.

The suspicion that there may be more maladministration in local government than at the central government level would seem to be borne out by the reports of the Commissioners for Local Administration. The number of properly referred complaints made averages well over 3,000 each year in England, and about 400 in Scotland and 200 in Wales, though many of them are usually found to be outside the jurisdiction of the Commissions. The Annual Report of the Commission for Local Administration in England for the year ending 31 March 1985 shows 3,389 complaints referred. Of the 292 full investigations completed during the year, maladministration was found in 215, which is 73 per cent of the cases completed, though in 22 of these cases it was concluded that there had been no injustice resulting. It is however very encouraging that there has over the years been a steady build up of the number of cases settled locally after reference to the Local Ombudsman. Such settlements are now achieved in over 15 per cent of all cases referred. Thus in one case mentioned in the Annual Report of the Commission for Local Administration in England for 1983/84 a tenant had complained for some time about damp, only to be told by the local Council that it was condensation. In the event it turned out to be rising damp. She had meanwhile been put to extra trouble and the expense of redecorating on two occasions. The Council looked into the complaint, arranged for the necessary remedial work to be completed, and made a suitable payment to recognise the loss of amenity, expense and trouble.

Complaints concerned matters ranging from the allocation of secondary school places or council houses to leaking roofs and mishaps in the planning process. In one case there was a complaint that the local authority in Walsall had failed to carry out its duty under the Chronically Sick and Disabled Persons Act 1970 to adapt a house for a paraplegic. The Commissioner found maladministration in that the council committee in practice dealt with applications solely in chronological order and without sufficiently taking into account the degree of disability and social or domestic circumstances. This was 'arbitrary and bureaucratic', and it could not be justified on the basis of the 'equal right' of applicants. In the view of the Commissioner the council should judge each case on its merits. The Annual Reports show that the Local Commissioners are prepared to investigate complaints about such matters as the failure to pay compensation promised for damage to property caused by excavations, even though there is a possible legal remedy. But they attempt to limit their investigation to procedural matters, such as delay or the publishing of misleading statements. In one case, however, the Commissioner found that incorrect advice given by a planning officer encouraging the building, without planning permission, of an undesirable extension behind the complainant's property development was maladministration, even though planning permission had then been given retrospectively. But he also found that no injustice had occurred, because it seemed likely that permission would have been granted even if the error had not been made. And in any event a smaller extension could have been built without planning permission. But the failure of a councillor to declare an interest in an issue has also been found to be maladministration.

An interesting case showing judicial support for the role of the Local Commissioners is *R v Local Comr for Administration for the North and East Area of England, ex p Bradford Metropolitan City Council*.[7] The local authority had decided to take a young woman's two children into care, and to place them with different foster parents. Care orders were then made by the juvenile court despite the mother's opposition. The mother complained, outside the usual twelve-month period for complaints, about the local authority's actions to a local councillor, and asked him to forward her complaint to the Local Commissioner, but he decided not to do so. The mother then complained direct to the Commissioner, who decided to investigate the matter. The complaints alleged injustice suffered (1) through a failure by the local authority to use its resources to help the mother to look after her children herself; (2) from hostility shown towards her by a senior

7 [1979] QB 287.

social worker of the authority; (3) from the separation of the children against her wishes; and (4) by reason of a statement by the social worker that she could and would have the children adopted without the complainant's consent. The local authority applied for an order of prohibition to stop the Local Commissioner from investigating the complaints. The Court of Appeal held that the Commissioner was entitled to investigate the case since none of the four complaints would entitle the mother to a legal remedy. Furthermore the Commissioner had properly disregarded the limitation period for complaints in view of the mother's mental capacity and helplessness which constituted special circumstances.

The Annual Reports of the Commissions for Local Administration do, however, reveal that since the English Local Commissioners began work in April 1974 they have not been satisfied with remedial action taken by the authority concerned in an average of 8 cases each year. The reasons given by the authorities for acting or failing to act have been various, sometimes amounting to allegations that the Local Commissioner had got the facts wrong, and sometimes asserting simply that what the authority had done did not amount to maladministration – in other words, plainly rejecting the Commissioner's report. This contrasts badly with the general practice of government departments in accepting and attempting to implement the findings and recommendations of the Parliamentary Commissioner, however bitter a pill any such finding may seem to be; and it reflects poorly upon those local authorities who have not been prepared to eat humble pie after an objective review of their behaviour.

Examples of cases in which further reports were deemed necessary by the Local Commissioners for England are not earth-shaking, but then the great majority of the work and jurisdiction of local government is on a much more minor scale than is that of the central government. Yet each such case is important to the individual who feels aggrieved, and who may later be found by the Local Commissioner to have had a reasonable grievance. In a case from Birmingham, the City Council, which as a metropolitan district council is an education authority, had delayed payment of a student grant with the result that the student incurred overdraft charges. As a result of the initial report upon the case in 1977, the bank later waived these charges. But in a further report in 1979 the Commissioner believed this to be an unsatisfactory outcome, and he urged the Council to reimburse the bank. In a case from Bristol the council had given inadequate advice as to the rateable value of property, and as a result the complainant had received only a minimum grant. Despite an adverse report from the Commissioner the council decided not to make any *ex gratia* payment to the complainant, and the Commissioner then felt obliged to make a further report expressing dissatisfaction with the council's decision. Again, despite the strong adverse report of the Commissioner upon the Walsall Council's failure to take adequate steps to house a paraplegic, referred to above, the Council refused to make any changes in its practice. In a further report in 1979 the Commissioner records his total dissatisfaction with the Council's behaviour.

Sometimes the point of difference between the Council and the Local Ombudsman is small, and indicates the not uncommon position that the main thrust of the ombudsman's report has been accepted, though not all its details. Thus in one case the London Borough of Wandsworth had unreasonably delayed by several months the processing of the application by a private tenant for a rent allowance. The Commissioner was satisfied that the delay had caused him considerable worry and distress, and that had it not been for a private loan from a friend he would during the period concerned have been destitute. The Council accepted the finding, and offered an apology together with a sum of £13.62 as compensation calculated on the basis of the interest the complainant may have had to pay on his private loan. The ombudsman accepted that the calculation was fair, but also considered that the sum arrived at took not adequate account of the distress caused to the complainant, and he asked for it to be rounded up on that account to £30. Despite considerable correspondence and the issue of a further report on this point, the Council persisted in refusing to increase the sum offered.

It is perhaps inevitable that the Local Commissioners should become involved in the party political disputes of local government, though it is less than satisfactory when the Commission's umpiring function is then rejected. In 1979 the Commissioner found maladministration where the Watford Council had excluded from the press bench reporters who were not members of the National Union of Journalists. The Council noted the report but took no further action, and the Commissioner had to issue a further report stating that the Council should at least have sent letters of apology to the journalists who had been excluded. Another case investigated in the same year involved Haringey London Borough Council. There the Commissioner found that the Council had maladministered in replacing a school governor without prior warning. This had been done in connection with the caretakers' strike which has already been mentioned in chapter 3, and was apparently because of the governor's failure to support the policy of the majority (Labour) party on the council concerning the strike. She had learned of her replacement indirectly, through a letter from the headmistress. Even though the

Minister of State in the Department of Education and Science had considered the new appointment valid, the Commissioner roundly condemned the way in which the replacement had been effected in the following words: 'it cannot be good administration let alone fair to the individuals concerned to appoint new governors before those they are to replace have been removed from office or even told that they are about to be removed'. Thus the Commissioner did not deny the right of a council to replace school governors, even on political grounds (as is so commonly done by local education authorities), but she was in effect urging that such replacement must only be accomplished by a fair procedure.

The Reports of the Health Service Commissioners have so far contained less evidence that there is widespread maladministration in the Health Service, though the Report for England covering cases investigated during April–September 1980 found some justification for complaint in 34 out of the 53 cases examined. But there has, perhaps not surprisingly, been a rash of complaints about the police which have found their way to the Police Complaints Board, which has recently been replaced by the Police Complaints Authority, as noted above. The Annual Report of the Board for 1978 shows that, out of 11,940 complaints, the internal police inquiry had resulted in disciplinary charges being preferred in 59 instances; and that the Board then recommended disciplinary proceedings in a further 15 cases. The test applied by the Board was whether 'disciplinary action would seem reasonable to the man in the street'.[8] On the whole the Board has found that internal police investigations have been effectively conducted, and that there is no evidence of lack of diligence in carrying these out. But in 1978 it did note occasional 'signs of undue emphasis being given to points favourable to the police and unfavourable to the complainant'.[9]

Just as one may expect a fair number of complaints about the police, whether or not they turn out to be justified, so it is not surprising that people complain from time to time about solicitors: hence, in the modern climate, the creation of the Lay Observer. His Annual Reports do not, however, indicate that he has found much malpractice in the Law Society's handling of such complaints. In his Annual Report for 1978[10] he records 254 new complaints, of which only 112 were within his jurisdiction. Out of the 90 cases in which he had completed his investigation he was critical of the Law Society's treatment of the complaint in only three, though in none of them did

---

8   HC 4 (1978–79), p 4.
9   Ibid, p 10.
10 HC 16.

he disagree with the actual action eventually taken. In a further three cases he recommended the Society to reconsider some aspect of the complaint. But his reports are not quite as negative as would appear at first sight. For example, in 1978 again, the Lay Observer specifically suggested that, following any complaint, the Law Society should inform the individual firm of solicitors concerned, and the profession generally if appropriate, of any elements where, in the Society's opinion, a better service could have been given. He also suggested that there should be an extension of his powers to include a direction that he should inform the Law Society where any practice by the profession seems to him to be against the general interests of clients, and to make recommendations accordingly.

Conclusions

In the course of this book we have given some consideration to the nature and strength of judicial review of administrative action. But in this chapter we have discussed the ways in which such judicial review has been supplemented in recent years by extra-judicial methods of dealing with complaints of maladministration. There is no suggestion, either here or in any other written work, that the ombudsman method is perfect or fool-proof. Far from it: it has built into it a kind of self-denying ordinance, for none of the different types of ombudsmen which have now been implanted into our system has the power to order anything to be done. Yet, despite much academic scepticism recorded in the professional journals at the time of the Parliamentary Commissioner Act 1967, it is now generally conceded not only that ombudsmen do no harm, but that they do some positive good, and provide a useful adjunct to judicial review. The statistics of complaints registered and of findings of some degree of maladministration bear out this view. There *is* some maladministration to be ferreted out, and government departments in particular do try to accept findings of their errors, and to learn from them. There is as yet some intransigence shown by local authorities, but this does not in itself invalidate the new system, and it may be hoped that with time the practice of accepting criticism and attempting to expunge error will grow.

In several Reports the Parliamentary Ombudsman has complimented MPs on the way in which they have dealt with complaints and assisted complainants. It may not be too far-fetched to suggest that there is a new spirit of partnership between the traditional Parliamentary representatives and the new Commissioner in carrying out the age-old task of investigating constituents' worries. The courts too have held that the Parliamentary Commissioner's discretion in deciding whether or not to hold or pursue an investigation is complete. He cannot lawfully be prevented from carrying out his statutory function, and conversely, in *Re Fletcher's Application*,[11] leave to apply for mandamus was refused where the applicant had sought an order to compel the Commissioner to investigate a complaint. This total independence must clearly apply to the other various ombudsmen, and is a valuable feature of their standing within our legal system.

Those who scoff at the ombudsmen tend to stress the fairly high proportion of cases in which they find that complaints are outside their jurisdiction, or else unjustified or even plainly misconceived. But that does not mean that all complaints are judged to be of this character. In a country in which the standard of public morality is generally high, and where most people try to the best of their ability to do an honest job honestly, it is not surprising that most complaints are wrong or ill-founded. The ombudsmen's reports show that *some* complaints are either wholly or partly unjustified. Most of such cases are humdrum, and often minor. But perhaps the very occasional *cause célèbre* helps to point to the value of the system. Such a rare case was the Sachsenhausen affair, a case which the Parliamentary Commissioner dealt with in his very first year of work.[12]

During the Second World War many people who were United Kingdom citizens, or who were resident in the United Kingdom, suffered loss of liberty, damage to their health, or death as a result of Nazi persecution in concentration camps. Several years after the war the West German Government paid a sum of £1,000,000 to the United Kingdom Government as compensation to such people or their dependants. The Foreign Office administered the scheme for paying out this compensation, and laid down rules of eligibility by which applicants had to show either that they had been detained in a concentration camp or, if their place of detention was not a concentration camp, that the conditions they had experienced were comparable to those in a concentration camp.

Some of the men and women who had been captured or detained by the Germans during the war had been engaged in special operations for the Allies, and among their survivors after the war were a small group who had been detained in buildings abutting on the Sachsenhausen concentration camp. Those buildings were outside the main compound of the camp, and the prisoners had suffered long periods of solitary confinement in degrading conditions. Nevertheless those who applied for a share of the fund provided for compensation

11 [1970] 2 All ER 527n.
12 Reported in the 3rd Report of the Commissioner, HC 54 of 1967–68.

were told by the Foreign Office that they did not qualify because they had been held in adjoining areas which were not part of the camp proper, and that they had not endured conditions comparable in severity to those experienced in concentration camps. The decision was contested by the applicants, but despite pressure from many quarters during the years 1965 to 1967 the Foreign Office refused to alter its decision, and even took the view that the sum of money was already exhausted anyway by other more legitimate claims.

Eventually, after the Parliamentary Commissioner had started work in 1967, a complaint about the Foreign Office decision was forwarded by Mr Airey Neave MP, himself a former prisoner of war in Germany, and the first British officer to escape from Colditz Castle and get back to Britain. (It is tragic and ironic that Mr Neave, in 1979, was assassinated in the precincts of the Palace of Westminster by Irish republican extremists.) The Commissioner, rightly determining that there were special circumstances rendering it desirable that he should investigate the case despite the lapse of more than a year since the complainants became aware of their grievance, for he had only just embarked upon the work within his jurisdiction, considered the matter with great care. He concluded (1) that the process by which the Foreign Office decided that the applicants had not been in the concentration camp proper was based upon partial and largely irrelevant information; (2) that the rule under which the Foreign Office was working meant that a claimant who had not been in such a camp might have to pass a more severe test of eligibility than a camp claimant; and (3) that the claimants had suffered injustice in that the rejection of their claim, and the terms in which the rejection had been defended by the Foreign Office, had done harm to their standing and reputation.

The Foreign Secretary of the day, Mr George Brown, made a most interesting statement thereafter in the House of Commons.[13] While accepting full ministerial responsibility for what had happened, he stated that he still did not accept the finding of the Commissioner that what had been done amounted to maladministration by the Foreign Office. But he went on to affirm that 'having established the office of Parliamentary Commissioner, whether I think his judgment is right or wrong, I am certain that I would be wrong to reject his views'. Accordingly he was prepared to reverse the previous decision, and to pay compensation to the claimants.

As Sir Kenneth Wheare has said,[14] this was an impressive demonstration of the value of the Parliamentary Commissioner and

13 758 H C Official Report (5th series) cols 112–116.
14 *Maladministration and its Remedies* p 126.

it established the reputation of the office at the outset. The impetus to the development and furthering of the ombudsman experiment has been continuous ever since. The Review Committee of Administrative Law in the United Kingdom, which has been referred to in several chapters of this book, has among its terms of reference the consideration of whether the administrative agencies should be required to observe a code of administrative practice, and if so whether any, and what, remedy or redress should be provided for a breach of such code. It is also to consider the desirability of including the right to damages or compensation as a means of redressing grievances. It therefore remains to be seen how much progress this committee can make with its examination. There may be some scope for further judicialisation of some areas of the administration; and there may be a place in the future for a code of administrative practice. But for the present the gradually ever-increasing respect for ombudsmen is a significant means of obtaining justice in circumstances where judicial review is not possible. Perhaps the 'MP filter' may one day be removed, or at least widened so that complaints to the Parliamentary Ombudsman may go through peers or other officers and agencies. Again perhaps there will one day be an ombudsman whose jurisdiction covers Quangos[15] and public corporations.[16] It has even been suggested that all existing United Kingdom statutory ombudsmen should be combined to form three Commissions for Public Administration, one for England and Wales, one for Scotland and one for Northern Ireland,[17] though the gains from such a reorganisation have not been very clearly spelt out. Many improvements in detail are possible of fulfilment in course of time. But for the present a good start has at least been made.

15   Some recommendations on this were made by the Select Committee on the Parliamentary Commissioner in 1984: Fourth Report, Session 1983/84.
16   A possible pattern might be the French *Médiateur*, who has a wide jurisdiction covering complaints about central and local government, and also about nationalised industries – indeed all the various organisations responsible for *le service public*. Like the New Zealand Ombudsman he may criticise an administrative decision as being simply wrong.
17   *Controlling the State: Towards Fairer Administration*, SDP Open Forum Paper 3, 1983.

Index

Administrative agencies—
  Crown, the, *see* CROWN, THE
  local government authorities, *see* LOCAL GOVERNMENT AUTHORITIES
  police, the, *see* POLICE
  public corporations, *see* PUBLIC CORPORATIONS
Administrative law—
  definition of, 15–16
  droit administrif, and, 1, 47, 48, 62
  efficiency, and, 16–17
  existence of, 1, 48
  judicial decisions,
    quasi-judicial decisions and administrative decisions distinguished, 93
  judicial and non-judicial powers and duties distinguished, 92–93, 94–95, 98–99, 100, 104–105
  quasi-judicial decisions,
    judicial decision and administrative decision distinguished, 93
    proceedings involving, 93–94, *see also* INQUIRIES
  Remedies in Administrative Law, Report on, 127, 128, 129, 130
  Working Paper No 40, 128, 129
  remedies of,
    certiorari, *see* CERTIORARI
    damages, actions for, 118, 125
    declarations, 118, 123, 125
    injunctions, 118, 122, 125
    locus standi, 124–125, 139–140
    mandamus, *see* MANDAMUS
    Order 53 Rules of the Supreme Court, 130–134, 140–142
    prohibition, *see* PROHIBITION
    reform of, 126–134, 139–143, *see also* Remedies in Administrative Law *above*
  statutory source of, 15
  study of, 18
Appeal—
  certiorari and, 120–121, 126

Appeal—*continued*
  review distinguished, 42–43, 46–47
  Tribunals and Inquiries Act 1971, under, 204–207
Attorney-General, *see* RELATOR PROCEEDINGS
Board of Visitors—
  disciplinary proceedings by, 105
Case stated—
  appeal by way of, 204
Certiorari—
  appeal and, 120–121, 126
  exemption from, 82
  instances of, 78, 87, 95, 99, 100, 104, 105, 107
  nature of, 80, 118–119, 120
  remission of case for reconsideration, and, 133
Commissioners for Local Administration—
  Annual Report of, 229, 233, 234, 235
  appointment of, 227
  complaints to, 227–228, 233
  judicial support for, 234
  jurisdiction of, 228–229
  powers of, 228
Common law—
  Crown Privilege, rules as to, 156–168
  natural justice as presumption of, 15
  statute, and, 15, 17
Complaints, Commissioner for, 226–227
Compulsory purchase orders, 29, 55, 89–90, 102, 103
Constable—
  control of, 7–9
  responsibility of, 7–9
  torts committed by, 9
County councils—
  powers of, 6–7
Courts—
  inferior, 17
  superior, 16

243

244 *Index*

Crown, The—
  contracts, with enforceability of,
    commercial contracts, 151, 152
    contracts dependent on future grant of money from Parliament, 150, 152
    contracts fettering future executive action, 150–152
    contracts of service of military or civil service personnel, 150, 153–154
  decline in powers of, 2–4
  monarch in powers of, 2–4
  monarch distinguished, 4–5
  other administrative authorities, 5, *see also* LOCAL GOVERNMENT AUTHORITIES, POLICE, PUBLIC CORPORATIONS
  prerogative power of, 5, 66, 115
  privilege, *see* CROWN PRIVILEGE
  proceedings, *see* CROWN PROCEEDINGS
  remedies against,
    declaration, 123–124
    injunction, 124
    mandamus, 121
  tortious liability of, 154–156

Crown privilege—
  argument as to, 159–161
  Australia, in, 168–169
  class claims, 160–161, 165
  common law rules as to, 156–165
    Conway v Rimmer, 161–165, 167, 168
    Duncan case, 157–159, 160, 161, 163
    Glasgow Corporation case, 158
  disclosure against public interest, 165–168
  inspection by judge, 159–160
  Reynolds case, 160
  statutory provision, 156

Crown proceedings—
  Act 1947,
    contractual liability, 149, 153–154
    Crown privilege, *see* CROWN PRIVILEGE
    tortious liability, 154–156
  Amphitrite case, 150–151
  history of, 148, 149
  petition of right and, 149

Delegated legislation—
  compulsory purchase orders, 29, 55, 89–90, 102, 103
  enabling statutes, 25, 26, 28, 29, 30, 31

Delegated legislation—*continued*
  enabling statutes—*continued*
    earliest, 38
    scrutiny of, 39
  generally, 21
  judicial review of,
    basis of, *see* ULTRA VIRES DOCTRINE
    occasions for, 30
  ministerial regulations as, 22–23, *see also* STATUTORY INSTRUMENTS
  necessity of, 39–40
  Parliamentary scrutiny of, *see also* STATUTORY INSTRUMENTS
    Select Committee on European Secondary Legislation, 25
    Select Committee on the European Communities, 25
  prior publicity for, 29–30
  provisional orders, 26
  reason for, 21
  safeguards,
    formal Parliamentary, 23–29
    political, 29–30
    procedural conditions as, 29
  special procedure orders, 26
  types of, 22
  universities, 21–22

Discretion—
  judicial review of, 73–74
  restriction on, after inquiries, 198–199
  unfettered, 59–61, 98, *see also* ULTRA VIRES PRINCIPLE

District councils—
  non-metropolitan, powers of, 6–7

Error of law—
  Anisminic case, the, 81–86, 87, 88
  cases on, 77–79, 80
  decisions founded on, void or voidable, 80–81, 86–89
  effect of, 80–81, 86, 89
  judicial review, as ground for, 77–79
  jurisdiction, going to, 83–86, 87, 88, 89
  types of, 80–81

Franks Committee Report—
  appeals from tribunals, 205
  chairmen, legal qualifications of, 209
  effect of, 37, 127, 172, 199, 207–208, 209
  Lands Tribunals, 186
  legal aid, extension of, to tribunals, 208

Index 245

Franks Committee Report—
continued
openness, fairness and impartiality, 200–201, 207
reception of, 200
rent tribunals, 183
reporting of decisions, 208
separate administrative courts, 200, 201

Governmental intervention—
origin and growth of, 2–4, 17–18
dramatis personae of, 4–5

Health Service Commissioners, 225–226, 237
House of Commons—
growth in power of, 3

Inner London Boroughs, 6
Inquiries—
appeals, *see* APPEALS
criticism of, 199–200
meaning of, 172–173
nature of, 94
procedure, 194–195, 196–199
tribunals distinguished, 172–173, 194

Judicial review—
administrative action, of, *see* JUDICIAL REVIEW OF ADMINISTRATIVE ACTION
'application for', 128
areas immune to, 213
deport, Home Secretary's powers to, of, 108
discretion of, 73–74
executive action, of, 1
non-statutory inferior bodies, of, 100–101
tribunals, of, 16
Judicial review of administrative action—
criminal proceedings, in, 122
France, in, 46–48, 117, 118
grounds for, *see* ERROR OF LAW, ULTRA VIRES PRINCIPLE
prerogative orders, *see* PREROGATIVE ORDERS
rent regulation, tribunals concerned with, of, 184
reform of,
Administrative Division of High Court, 147–148, 201, 206

Judicial review of administrative action—*continued*
reform of—*continued*
Australia, in, 143–145, 146
generally, 143
grounds for review, 143–147
Review Committee on Administrative Law in the UK, 40, 145–146, 210
separate courts, 147–148
UK, in, *see* ULTRA VIRES PRINCIPLE
Judiciary—
independence of, 16, 64–65

Lay Observer, 229, 237–238
Local government authorities—
London, in, 6
organisation of, 6–7
provincial, 6–7, 68
London—
local government powers, in, 6

Mandamus—
Crown, against the, 121
exemption from, 82
instances of, 56, 71
nature of, 119
Ministerial powers—
Donoughmore-Scott Report on, 24, 37–40, 93, 127, 146, 172, 200, 209
judicial review of, 94
Review Committee on Administrative Law in UK, 40–41, 146, 210
Ministerial responsibility—
generally, 12
origin of, 3
public corporations, for, 12, 13–14

Natural justice—
audi alteram partem,
authority for, 96–98
Board of Visitors, disciplinary proceedings, 105
dismissal cases, 97, 99, 105–106
judicial review, denial of, 9
licensing cases, 94–95, 103–104
meaning of, 92
satisfying requirements of, 101–103
statutory exclusion of, 99
common law presumptions, as, 15
fair procedure, and,
generally, 111, 114–115
occupational licences, 112–114
oral hearing, request for, 113, 114

Natural justice—*continued*
  fair procedure, and—*continued*
    planning enquiries, 111–112
    reason for decisions, 114
    substantive decisions, and, 111, 116
  importance of, 92
  nemo judex in causa sua,
    licensing cases, 103–104
    meaning of, 92
    rent assessment committees, 106
    test for, 107
  rules of, *see also* audi alteram partem; nemo judex in causa sua
    application of, 109, 111
    DoT inspectors, appointment of, and, 108
    exclusion of, 107
    national security cases, in, 107–108
    primacy of, 115
    student cases, 110–111
    suspension from political party pending inquiries, and, 109–110
Northern Ireland Parliamentary Commissioner, 226–227

Ombudsman—
  Crichel Down affair, 214–215
  damages, award of, by, 145–146
  Denmark, in, 215–216
  elsewhere, 223, 224–225
  generally, 215–217, 238–241
  Great Britain, in 216–217, *see also* PARLIAMENTARY COMMISSIONER FOR ADMINISTRATION
  maladministration,
    causes of, 231–232
    local government, in, 227–229, 233
    meaning of, 220–222
    prevalence of, 231
    redress where, 233, 234–235
  necessity of, 213–214
  New Zealand, in, 216, 223–224
  other UK,
    Complaints, Commissioner for, 226–227
    Health Service Commissioners, 225–226
    Law Society's Lay Observer, 229–230, 237–238
    Local Administration, Commission for, *see* COMMISSIONERS FOR LOCAL ADMINISTRATION

Ombudsman—*continued*
  other UK—*continued*
    Northern Ireland Parliamentary Commissioner, 226–227, 228
    Police Complaints Authority, 229, 237
    Police Complaints Board, 229, 237
    public corporations, 229, 241
  Sweden, in, 215
  UK, in,
    other ombudsmen, *see* other UK ombudsmen *above*
    the Ombudsman, *see* PARLIAMENTARY COMMISSIONER FOR ADMINISTRATION
    work of, *see* work of, in UK *below*
  Whyatt Report, 215–216
  work of, in UK,
    Health Service Commissioners, 237
    Law Society's Lay Observer, 237–238
    number of complaints, 231
    Local Administration, Commissioners for, 233–237
    overlapping jurisdictions, 230
    Police Complaints Board, 237
Order 53 Rules of Supreme Court—
  generally, 130, 132, 134, 140–141, 142
  locus standi under, 141–142

Parish councils—
  powers of, 7
Parliament. *See also* HOUSE OF COMMONS
  growth in power of, 2–4
Parliamentary Commissioner for Administration. *See also* OMBUDSMEN
  complaints to, 217–218
  independence of, 238–239
  investigation,
    areas, exempt from, 219–220
    powers of, 218
  reports of,
    Annual, 219
    individual cases, on, 218–219
  status and jurisdiction of, 64, 217, 219–220
Police. *See also* CONSTABLE
  Complaints Authority, 229, 237
  Complaints Board, 229, 237
  control of, 7
  Royal Commission on the, 9

Prerogative orders,
  certiorari, *see* CERTIORARI
  locus standi, 124–125, 132
  mandamus, *see* MANDAMUS
  prohibition, *see* PROHIBITION
  procedural disadvantages of, 119–120,
    130–131
  theory behind, 119
  time limits, 119, 133
Private rent regulation—
  development of, 17–18
Procedure—
  historical importance of, 117
  prerogative orders, for, 119–120
  reform of, 117–118
Prohibition—
  nature of, 119
Public interest immunity. *See also*
    CROWN PRIVILEGE
  disclosure against public interest, 166–
    168

Relator proceedings—
  Attorney-General's role in, 138–139
  injunction, action for, by,
    Gouriet case, 135–140
    locus standi, 125, 139–140
    McWhirter case, 134–135
  nature of, 138
  Order 53 Rules of the Supreme Court,
    effect of, 140–141
Rent regulation—
  history of, 173–174
  types of tenancy, 174–175, 177–178
Royal Prerogative—
  generally, 3, 5

Statutory instruments—
  generally, 22–23
  Joint Committee, 24–25, 32
  laying before Parliament,
    generally, 23, 24
    mandatory or directory, 26–28
  Parliamentary scrutiny of,
    Select Committee, 24, 28
    Standing Committee, 25
  publication of, 35–36

Tribunals—
  appeals, 204–207
  Committee on Administrative
    Tribunals and Enquiries, Report
    of, *see* FRANKS COMMITTEE REPORT

Tribunals—*continued*
  Council on, 182–183
    Annual Report of, 182, 203
    composition and constitution of,
      202–203, 204
    function of, 202
    generally, 182–183, 196–197
    successes of, 203
  criticism of, 199–200
  growth in, 170
  inquiries distinguished, 172–173, 194
  Lands Tribunal,
    composition of, 185
    decision of, 186
    jurisdiction of, 185
    procedure, 185–186
    purpose of, 184–185
  Mental Health Review,
    decisions of, 188
    jurisdiction, 187–188
    procedure, 187–188
  necessity of, 170–172
  reform of, *see also* FRANKS COMMITTEE
    REPORT
  Australia, in, 210–212
  rent regulation, concerned with,
    appeals, 183–184, 205–206
    consolidation of, 176–177
    decisions of, 182
    informality of, 181
    judicial review, 184
    jurisdiction of, 177–180
    procedures for, 180–182
    rent assessment committees, 174,
      175–176, 177
    rent officers, 177
    rent tribunals, 174–175, 176
  Social Security Appeal
    appeals to, 190
    application for benefit, 189–190
    benefits, types of, 189
    composition of, 191
    decisions of, 193
    jurisdiction of, 190, 194
    procedure, 192–194
    welfare state, history of, 188–189
  standardisation of procedure before
    Tribunals, 201

Ultra vires doctrine—
  appeal and review distinguished, 42–
    43, 47
  application of, 32

248 *Index*

Ultra vires doctrine—*continued*
  cases on, 32–36
  grounds for challenge under, 34–35
  nature of, 31
  publication of statutory instruments and, 35–36
Ultra vires principle—
  classification of, 43–44
  practical application of,
    détournement de pouvoir (abuse of power) contrasted, 47
    generally, 44–46
  substantial evidence rule, 89–91, 116, 145
  unreasonable exercise of power,
    act outside ambit of conferred power, 48–49
    Board of Education, by, 49–51
    closure of schools during industrial action, 76–77

Ultra vires principle—*continued*
  unreasonable exercise of power—*continued*
    comprehensive schools, 68–73
    election promises, in carrying out, 74–75
    inadvertent overstepping of ambit of conferred power, 49
    invalidity of, under, 45–46, 49
    local authorities, by, 51–55
    London Transport, as to, 74–75
    Padfield case, the, 55–62
    planning authorities by, 54–55
    punishment for unrelated act, as, 67–68
    Skytrain, 65–67
    television licences, 62, 64
    types of, 48–49